Parlor Ladies

and
Ebony Drudges

Parlor Ladies
and
Ebony Drudges

African American Women,
Class, and Work in a
South Carolina Community

Kibibi Voloria C. Mack

With a Foreword by
Elizabeth Fox-Genovese

The University of Tennessee Press • Knoxville

Ͷ

Copyright © 1999 by The University of Tennessee Press / Knoxville.
All Rights Reserved. Manufactured in the United States of America.
Cloth: 1st printing, 1999.
Paper: 1st printing, 2011.

Library of Congress Cataloging-in-Publication Data

Mack, Kibibi Voloria C.
    Parlor ladies and ebony drudges : African American women, class,
and work in a South Carolina community / Kibibi Voloria C. Mack;
with a foreword by Elizabeth Fox-Genovese. —1st ed.
        p.   cm.
Includes bibliographical references and index.
ISBN 10: 1-57233-843-1
ISBN 13: 978-1-57233-843-2

1. Afro-America women—South Carolina—Orangeburg—Social
    conditions.
2. Social classes—South Carolina—Orangeburg—History.
3. Orangeburg (S.C.)—Social conditions.
I. Title.
F279.O6 M33 1998   305.48'896'075779—ddc21
                                          98-25345

To my loving daughters,
Nabulungi, Yakini,
Sibongile, and Abikanile,
and my loving nephew and nieces,
Kafele, Kanika, and Melissa,
with undying love forever.

Contents

Illustrations

Tables

Foreword

Throughout history, the everyday lives of ordinary women have provided the glue that holds families, communities, and societies together. Until recently, however, most historians virtually ignored these lives, presumably on the grounds that they have been so unremarkable as to defy sustained attention or comment. It is as if historians, focusing upon the drama of war, politics, and social struggles, simply did not "see" the women who always and everywhere have formed the bedrock of social life. During the past few decades, social historians and women's historians have done much to rectify this neglect. Indeed, much recent historical scholarship has tended to reverse former priorities and to privilege the experience of such previously marginalized groups as women, blacks, and working people. The proliferation of women's and African American history has directed our attention to a wealth of new information, experiences, and questions. This work establishes a context for Kibibi Voloria Mack's engaging exploration of the working lives of the black women of Orangeburg, South Carolina. But *Parlor Ladies and Ebony Drudges* does not simply fill in another piece of the mosaic that women's historians have been assembling. Raising new questions, it offers a fresh perspective on the history of African American women and invites us to follow new paths of inquiry.

In these pages, we meet an arresting group of southern black women who fashioned lives, nurtured families, and built communities within the frequently draconian constraints of the Jim Crow South. On Mack's showing, work—hard work—runs like a unifying thread through many black women's lives, for work most of them did labor. But, as she unflinchingly insists, not all. In the wake of the Civil War and Reconstruction, an

African American elite emerged in Orangeburg, as in other cities, and its women did not share the fate of their less-privileged sisters. Not only did they not work themselves, but they had servants to relieve them of the household labor that figured so prominently in most women's lives. Labor, Mack nonetheless insists, defined most black women's lives, and it ranked high among their—and other African Americans'—contributions to the development of their city, their region, and the country as a whole. From the earliest slave ship landings in the seventeenth century until the present, black people have labored in the service of their own people and others, virtually in every occupation and at every conceivable task. Until the end of the Civil War, the vast majority lived in legal bondage and labored under coercion. Even after emancipation, the majority continued to labor under coercion—or as much coercion as the laws of the market, tenancy, share-cropping, and segregation could impose upon them. The command, coercion, and extortion of black labor has cast a long shadow over African American history, and historians have, perforce, regularly paid black labor its due. Dr. W. E. B. Du Bois himself established the model and set the tone, organizing and directing a series of pathbreaking monographs on southern black labor, which culminated in his own monumental Black Reconstruction in America.

Du Bois especially, if somewhat romantically, underscored the centrality of black women's labor to the life of their people. Most memorably, in *Darkwater: Voices from Within the Veil*, he wrote, "As I look about me today in this veiled world of mine, despite the nosier and more spectacular advance of my brothers, I instinctively feel and know that it is the five million women of my race who really count. . . . If we have today, as seems likely, over a billion dollars of accumulated goods, who shall say how much of it has been wrung from the hearts of servant girls and washerwomen and women toilers in the fields? As makers of two million homes these women are today seeking in marvelous ways to show forth our strength and beauty and our conception of the truth." Labor, Du Bois insisted time and again, constituted the very fabric of black women's lives; labor underwrote their irreplaceable contributions to their families, communities, and people. These "black women toil and toil hard," and in proportionately larger numbers than their white "sisters"—"over half of the colored female population as against a fifth in the case of white women." They "are a group of workers, fighting for their daily bread like men; independent and approaching economic freedom!" Although the emergence of women's history focused new attention upon women's work in general, the work of African American women in particular remained largely in shadow, not least because of the apparent paucity of sources. Studies published since the 1980s have gradually brought black women's work into sharper relief, but much of this scholarship has primarily attended to their work in the rural South, during and after slavery. That women's work was unremitting and hard cannot be doubted. Much of it, especially work in the fields of others, tore black women from the work for their own families, which both they and their husbands and children strongly preferred. Following the tone set by Du Bois, these studies have gradually brought a picture of rural black women's lives and labor into focus. But the lives of urban black women, especially those whose class position freed them from obligatory work, has largely remained in shadow. Only slowly and intermittently have a few historians begun to illuminate the lives and work of women in cities and towns, including those of nurses, teachers, librarians, and social workers. Here, Darlene Clark Hine and Stephanie Shaw have opened promising new lines of inquiry even as they have broadened our understanding of the intricate tapestry of black women's work.

In *Parlor Ladies and Ebony Drudges,* Mack clarifies and impressively deepens this understanding by exploring the work and working lives of black women in a New South Carolina city between 1880 and 1940. Above all, she locates the black women of a small southern city within an intricate social network that not merely distinguished between blacks and whites, but among blacks themselves according to the complex calculus of class. Mack divides the black women of Orangeburg into three main social classes: working class, middle class, and upper class. Not surprisingly, the vast majority of Orangeburg's African American women belonged to the working class, and work dominated and structured their lives, primarily in agricultural and domestic employment. Middle-class women, in contrast, had more opportunity to work in their own homes even when they were working for wages, and the women of the small upper-class elite did not typically have to work at all. In evoking women's experience and perceptions of their work, Mack draws heavily upon interviews with women from the Orangeburg African American community, and her use of the women's voices and perceptions endows her account with a compelling immediacy. These oral histories and interviews also illuminate the women's own perceptions of the social stratification of the black community, even as they help to explain the women's goals for themselves and their children.

Mack explicitly disclaims any intention of providing a full socioeconomic analysis of Orangeburg's African American community, insisting that her primary commitment is to bring the experience of individuals to life. Yet, in so doing, she simultaneously brings to life the dynamics of class relations and the cultural norms that informed and structured them. Color, she frequently reminds us, played a decisive role in the articulation of class position. For, in the absence of evidence to the contrary, it was widely assumed that the lighter a person's skin and the straighter their hair, the more likely they were to belong to the elite. Indeed, in the interest of consolidating the external representation of social status, elite men as well as women were known to pursue products and treatments that would "improve" both the texture of their hair and the color of their skin. A woman's ability to pass the fabled "brown bag test" (to have a complexion no darker than a brown paper bag) did not alone guarantee her access to the upper class, but an inability to pass that test would seriously cripple her prospects of making the "best" possible marriage and might even result in some loss in social status. Most women's status did primarily depend upon family connection: the status of the woman's family of origin and of the husband with whom she started her own family. In the world of Orangeburg, an upper-class woman might never marry, but most who did not continued to live with one or another family member rather than on their own. Unmarried women's tendency to reside with family implicitly underscores the importance of family relations and community sensibilities in defining a woman's status, for many—perhaps most—of the women who remained single were capable of supporting themselves. Thus the decision to live within the web of the family apparently had more to do with social and cultural than economic considerations.

The social and cultural dimensions of class figure prominently in the lives of all of Orangeburg's African American women. Mack skillfully draws out the threads of these social and cultural sensibilities, weaving them into an arresting, if sometimes disconcerting, picture of women's role in the formation and perpetuation of the black community. In the case of religion, for example, she shows that while the mass of working women belonged to Baptist and Pentecostal churches, the women of the upper class strongly favored the Episcopalian, AME, or Presbyterian churches. Indeed, she reports one unkind speculation that the women of the African American elite would have preferred to endure segregated seating in an acceptably fashionable church rather than rub shoulders with their less-affluent brothers and sisters among the Baptists.

Social distinctions in church membership and religious observance are assuredly not unique to the African American community: white folks have cultivated them since time immemorial. But Mack's forthright evocation of them, like her forthright evocation of the preoccupation with color as a social marker, serves an important purpose. For if Mack occasionally betrays a hint of impatience with the pretensions of the elite, she also displays a nuanced understanding of their motivations. This was an elite that overwhelmingly depended for its status upon the income of the male head of the household and, in almost all instances, that income depended upon the man's earnings from an occupation or profession. Or, to put the matter differently, this was not an elite that enjoyed the security of substantial inherited wealth. Elite status was not given but had to be recreated continually and sustained by work. Under these conditions, it was understandable—if not admirable—that those who had worked their way to the top would use all of the resources at their command to sustain their position.

Among those resources, none seems to have ranked higher than education. Orangeburg's African American elite placed a high value upon education, which it not merely viewed as a mark of distinction, but exploited as an important buttress of its own position. Mack illuminates the ways in which Claflin University served as a reservoir of opportunity for elite African Americans, who increasingly monopolized the opportunities it afforded. For if Claflin provided affluent African Americans with an advanced education, it also provided them with professional employment (and attendant salaries) and, over time, with private primary and secondary education for their children. Not until 1937 did Orangeburg provide a public high school that black people could attend, which meant that the large majority of Orangeburg's blacks, who could not dream of private school for their children, had to forgo all prospect of secondary education. This situation further strengthened the elite's grip on its privileged status and enhanced its ability to deflect aspiring members from its ranks.

These conditions may help to explain why a majority of working-class African American women tended to discourage educational aspirations in their own children. But their lack of interest in pushing their children toward educational attainments also reflected severe economic constraints. Like many working people throughout the country, especially recent immigrants, they knew that their family could not give up the economic contribution of any one of its members. In their eyes, paid work trumped education every time, and as soon as a child was old enough to earn a wage, he or she should do so. The prospects and priorities of middle-class African Americans predictably fell between these two extremes and varied according to a myriad of accidents and external circumstances. Members of the middle class could reasonably aspire to more education and greater stability and respectability than their working-class brothers and sisters, but in the essential respect of women's work, their experience more closely resembled that of the working class than of the elite. The women of Orangeburg's African American middle class worked out of necessity, and without their work their families would have had no hope of sustaining their middle-class status. But unlike their working-class sisters, middle-class women did not typically work in the fields or in the homes of other people. And although some remained close to domestic labor, working in their own homes as seamstresses or laundresses, others moved into a variety of white- and pink-collar occupations. Mack brings us the voices of women from all of these groups as well as those of many of their descendants. Their accounts of their working lives evoke the rich texture of their experience, including hardships and disappointments, and readers will come away from this book with a new appreciation of African American women's humor, vitality, and courage. The book as a whole, however, does not invite complacent romanticization. For, as Mack firmly reminds us, the relations among African American women of different classes do not suggest an all-encompassing sisterhood. Women played an important part in the differentiation among social classes and in the defense of social stratification. Perhaps more than anything, Mack demonstrates that the ultimate respect for African American women requires us to view their history with the same combination of admiration and criticism with which we view the history of any other group of women. If women indeed provide the glue of families, communities, and societies, they deserve their fair share of credit for the bad as well as the good that those groups have wrought. This thoughtful and illuminating book ushers us into a world and a dimension of women's experience that has too long remained shrouded and even unsuspected. It introduces us to the texture of African American women's lives in a small southern city and to the values and allegiances that endowed those lives with purpose and meaning. Kibibi Voloria Mack's evocation of these lives decisively broadens our understanding of African American women's history to which it makes a valuable and welcome contribution. More, it gently challenges us to expand and deepen our understanding of American women's history.

Elizabeth Fox-Genovese

Acknowledgments

The transformation of this study from doctoral dissertation to book would have been very difficult without the financial assistance of various institutions and the encouragement and support of various individuals. I want to thank the History Department at the State University of New York–Binghamton for its initial financial support of my dissertation research and Linda Forcey of Women Studies, who served on my dissertation defense committee and gave me insightful comments and zealous encouragement to revise the manuscript for publication. I also want to thank both the College of the Holy Cross and the University of Massachusetts at Boston (UMASS–Boston) for providing me with the financial support to continue research on this project. Specifically, I appreciated the support and educated comments I received from peers at UMASS–Boston while trying to balance a challenging teaching load and serve as interim Chairperson of the Africana Studies Department. A special thank-you goes to Woodruff Smith, Richard Lyons, Lou Ferleger, Lois Rudnick, and Robert Johnson for all their support. Most of all, I want to thank my "sister-peers," Jean Humez, Judi Smith, Julie Winch, and Susan Swan, for their excellent critiques.

It was a Henry C. Welcome Fellowship from the Maryland Higher Education Council that allowed me to finish revising this book. For this, I owe my biggest thank-you to President Freeman Hrabowski and Acklyn Lynch, chair of Africana Studies, at the University of Maryland Baltimore County, for recognizing merit in my project and nominating me for this prestigious award. I also want to give a special warm thank-you to Elizabeth Fox-Genovese and Hayward Farrar, who have been fans of this project and my best critics. You both have continually been a great inspiration to me!

One of my most difficult tasks was pulling together, for the first time, "bits 'n' pieces" of information in to provide a historical overview of African American lives in Orangeburg before 1940. Several individuals, including the late T. K. Bythewood and Clarence Tobin, Hugo Ackerman, Dorothy Scott Mack, Eloise Tyler Williams, Geraldine P. Zimmerman, and my own granny, the late Celia Perry Tilley, saved me from experiencing further frustrations and headaches as they unselfishly poured forth enormous amounts of verbal and documented information, enabling me to compose the first systematic historical account of African Americans' early presence in Orangeburg.

The friendly and supportive staff members at the local public library—Orangeburg County Public Library—and the libraries of Claflin College and South Carolina State University provided me with valuable archival manuscripts and primary data that further answered what seemed to be impossible questions at times. A special thank-you to helpful librarian Capers Bull of the Orangeburg County Public Library, Larry Mitchell of Mitchell Photography, and the many wonderful senior citizens I interviewed for the study.

Lastly, I owe a huge debt to my personal loved ones for all the times that I could not spend "unlimited" or "relaxed" family moments with them because "I had work to do." This is especially for my four loving daughters, Nabulungi, Yakini, Sibongile, Abikanile; my supportive friends, Ronald Craig Shelton and John David Rickenbacker; my patient mom, Dorothy Scott Rivers Mack; my supportive sister and best friend, Caroletta Mack Richardson, and loving brothers, C. J. Mack Jr., and Charles Hubbard Jr.; my aunts, Lucille Zeigler and Eloise Williams; my surrogate sisters, Barbara and Sheila Rivers; my late father, C. J. Mack Sr.; and my late grandma/babysitter, Celia Perry Tilley. Each of you have been very patient with me and extremely supportive of me summer after summer in Orangeburg and day after day at home, while I worked madly to finish this project along with teaching, moving, decorating, nagging, and parenting. You all have witnessed firsthand a contemporary "hard workin' woman." Thanks for "putting up with my butt." I love you all so much.

Introduction

One of the African American people's greatest contributions to the Western world was their labor. Intellectual giant W. E. B. Du Bois cogently argued that African American labor in the United States "revolutionized modern commerce and modern life," and that African American women, in particular, were pioneers in this regard.[1] According to Du Bois, the African American woman, "more than the woman of any other group in America, [was] the protagonist in the fight for an economically, independent womanhood in modern countries. Her fight [had] not been willing or, for the most part, conscious, but it [had], nonetheless, been curiously effective in its influence on the working world."[2] He noted that she "toil[ed] and toil[ed] hard," and that her contributions were not only in labor, for she also influenced white families through her personal contact as a servant. Lastly, Du Bois recognized that there was also a minority of African American women who worked sincerely toward a general social uplift of African American people.[3]

Asa Gordon, another African American intellectual of the early twentieth century, furthered the notion of African American women's labor contributions by reflecting specifically on women from South Carolina. He explained how both their endless work in rice swamps and cotton fields and their dedicated female club work led to "constructive work towards the building of civilization." In turn, their low wages lucidly demonstrated how their labor was brutally exploited. Gordon lamented that "it [was] the too familiar demonstration of [African American] womanhood literally giving labor, an overflowing measure of it, to build up the economic prosperity of [a] society in which she . . . scarcely hoped to share decently, not to say justly."[4]

During slavery, the labor of female slaves was just as important as that of male slaves, but it manifested itself in different ways. After slavery, women's labor remained important as former slaves adapted to their long overdue and welcome life without "massa." The period between 1880 and 1940 was one of adjustments, both to their new free status and to constant social changes. Social deterrents continued to hamper the upward mobility of most, reinforcing their inferior status. For others, however, as new opportunities opened, they benefited immensely, eventually forming the early African American middle and upper classes.

The Study

In this study, I examine and compare African American women's work history in Orangeburg, South Carolina, between 1880 and 1940 according to the women's specific socioeconomic classes. I challenge the traditional thesis that all African American women toiled and toiled hard, arguing instead that this was true only for those who belonged to certain socioeconomic classes. There was, in fact, a significant minority who did not have to work and even had a staff of domestics to do their housework. Contrary to findings in other research, I discovered that most African American parents did not go out of their way to educate their sons or daughters, as before 1940 educating children tended not to be a priority. Furthermore, I dispel the image of a sine qua non African American sisterhood or solidarity resulting from a common racial and gender discrimination.

This book does not focus on class development but on describing, according to social class, the variety of life-styles and the types of work performed by African American women in Orangeburg. In order to paint a fuller picture, I briefly discuss how class distinctions came to be and how they affected African American women in Orangeburg, but this book is not an attempt to document in detail the historical emergence and development of class, class divisions, and class relations within the African American community. Nor is it an attempt to give a full account of the historical development of class consciousness. To construct a complete, systematic study of class development and consciousness in the African American community of Orangeburg would warrant a separate investigation. To date, there is no cohesive work on this topic.

This study offers a brief historical description of obvious class differences as they existed in Orangeburg's African American community for the purpose of better understanding the history of the women of that community. Thus, I consciously chose not to survey how class categories have been arrived at within the various Marxist, feminist, or other sociological schools of thought in relation to race and gender. Instead, I decided to rely on research that has focused specifically on examining class stratification within the African American community and use the same terms employed in that research—*upper class, middle class,* and *working class*—throughout this book, as these major economic groups also existed in Orangeburg.[5]

Socioeconomic class stratification was not unique to this southern African American community. Stratification occurred in both white and nonwhite communities all over the United States. It is difficult to devise a model or formulate the exact criteria needed to define what constitutes a particular socioeconomic class. The ethnic and cultural diversity in the United States interferes greatly with creating such a model, in part because in different ethnic communities people's perceptions of what is upper, middle, or lower class varies according to their own criteria or restrictions, which are in turn based on their specific cultural and material reality. This is not to deny that there does exist certain objective, definitive characteristics that define and identify a certain class. However, in defining class in a particular community, people's perceptions are just as important as objective material realities.

I chose to use the term *working class* to refer to most African Americans in Orangeburg, who were constantly employed, earned low wages, and normally worked in menial agricultural and domestic jobs. Their race prohibited them from working in Orangeburg's mills and factories, since these jobs were reserved only for Orangeburg's white working class. Though small in number, there were African Americans who did not work for various reasons. Some were vagabonds or beggars, some fell prey to drunkenness or were merely idle, and some, including "prostitutes, gamblers, outlaws, renegades," and others involved in worthless or unscrupulous deeds as defined by society, were engaged in profitable criminal activity.[6] I purposely excluded women solely engaged in these illegal activities because they did not fall within the scope of this study. My focus is solely on Orangeburg's African American females who were actively engaged in some form of legitimate paid and/or voluntary work.

As I prepared to begin research, it was obvious that the majority of women I studied worked in either domestic or agricultural capacities in the early twentieth century. Yet it was also clear that a significant number worked in skilled, professional capacities, a fact generally overlooked when discussing the work history of African American women. Class, race, gender, and, sometimes, age or marital status discriminated more harshly against African American women as compared to other women. All of these factors shaped why, how, and where these women worked and lived, both inside and outside of their homes.

Most African American women in Orangeburg belonged to one of three major classes: the upper-class "elite," the growing middle class, and the large working class. The criteria used for categorizing the members of this community are based on first, information gathered from various sources, including primary and secondary literature in which scholars attempted to provide a class analysis of the African American community before 1940;[7] second, oral interviews in which all the informants were asked the same set of questions, which provided significant and insightful information on how a combination of factors—property ownership, educational attainment, occupations that resulted from special training, family heritage, place of residence, church membership, places where one shopped, incomes, and schools attended by the children—contributed to defining social status; and third, my personal experience of growing up in Orangeburg.

Most of the women examined or interviewed in this study were married. Most females listed as being single in the various Orangeburg census reports lived with their families or were still connected to the household in some way. In fact, the overall social status of the family of origin played a key role in determining the class positions of the women in this study. However, for single females over age eighteen, final class position was determined by either their personal achievements or their families, whichever was higher. A few single women over age eighteen lived alone and, in most instances, were professional women connected to the colleges or schools. These women most likely relocated to Orangeburg because of schooling or employment and had no local family ties. However, their class positions, too, were determined by their personal achievements.

Whether upper-, middle-, or working-class, the women worked to maintain and improve their financial and social positions. It has been argued that all African American women struggled to uphold their families as they worked hard, both inside and outside their homes. Nonetheless, these women did not exist in a vacuum, uninfluenced by their environment. There were differences in the kind of work they performed as well as in their social life-styles as a result of their class status. Regardless of class differences, however, it was race that linked these women as a social group, in that they all experienced and shared the common problem of racial hostility and racism in Jim Crow Orangeburg.

Conventional research models have tended to overlook conflict and diversity within the African American female community, focusing instead on shared racial oppression, and have therefore concluded that the community was united regardless of class. My research, however, has not borne this out. Most studies have rightfully argued that there was little or no cohesion between white and African American women because of racial differences, but little attention has been paid to the African American female community, showing how there was little or no cohesion among these women due to their interclass differences. Major research on African American women continues to downplay the impact that education, occupation, skin color, and family history might have had on stratifying this group to the point of disunity.

The Research

Orangeburg is an appropriate setting for analysis of African American women's work for various reasons. First, it is a small city with both rural and urban characteristics, with a population ranging from approximately twenty-five hundred in 1880 to nine thousand by 1940. (Past research, for the most part, has concentrated on women living in large urban cities.) Orangeburg is situated between two larger cities: the capital city, Columbia, and the historic former slave seaport, Charleston.

Second, Orangeburg has a sizable African American population. From the mid-nineteenth century to the early twentieth century, African Americans composed more than half of the overall population (see table 1), largely due to the large numbers of former slaves living in Orangeburg County. Third, Orangeburg is the home of two coed African American colleges, established in 1869 and 1896, respectively, which produced a new educated elite group of male and female African Americans. The presence of these schools are important, since historically, education in Orangeburg has played a major role in shaping the African American community.[8]

I used a wide range of sources in this study, including the United States census, local college catalogues and newspapers published prior to 1940, archival materials, and both primary and secondary books and articles. The most significant source was the oral history data collected from senior citizens in Orangeburg, largely female and African American from varied backgrounds. This useful information provided data for periods during the 1920s and 1930s that otherwise was not available. It was through this source that I discovered some of the best kept secrets about southern African American female relations, secrets that have been ignored or overlooked in other studies.

Table 1

Population of Orangeburg County, 1880–1940

Year	White	African American	Other	Total
1880	12,942	28,453	—	41,395
1900	18,220	41,442	—	59,663
1920	22,163	42,718	—	64,907
1930	23,087	40,640	—	63,864
1940	23,791	39,908	8	63,707

Source: David Duncan Wallace, *South Carolina: A Short History, 1520–1948* (Columbia: University of South Carolina Press, 1961), 710.

Because I grew up in Orangeburg between the 1950s and the 1970s, I am familiar with the economic and social history of many of the families in the city, enabling me to select women from the various economic backgrounds to be interviewed. Also, because of the more intimate and friendly nature of small southern cities, I was fortunate to be given other names to consult for interviews by my informants, providing me with numerous other names to add to the list I had already compiled from consulting with ministers, family members and friends, business people, and archivists in the city.

Each of the informants was asked the same set of questions, which elicited meticulous details surrounding both their parents and grandparents lives as well as their own lives. All of the informants were cooperative and friendly, particularly once they were able to somehow place me in their world, which they usually did by inquiring who my parents were, what my grandmother's name was, where my mother worked, or even what church my mother attended. I found that if they were successful in discovering some piece of information that could create a level of familiarity between us, they usually volunteered a bit more information than asked for or spoke more candidly on a "hush hush" topic. The average informant was in her early seventies and tended to recall a considerable amount of information, dating back to her grandparents and, sometimes, even to her great-grandparents. There were, however, a few informants who were unable to provide sufficient answers to my questions either because they could not recall or because they never knew the information.

While some scholars challenge the veracity of oral testimonies, others praise and encourage their use because they retain the authentic voices of the subjects. Understanding the limitations of oral data, careful scrutiny and historical corroboration is made so as not to record or validate distorted interpretations of history. Writing this short history of African American women's work is a task made more difficult by the fact that there is no written history of African Americans in Orangeburg. Because of this major absence and the limited resources, which usually focused on very narrow themes, many times the oral testimonies were successful in filling voids or answering puzzling questions.

There continues to be a dearth of social and intellectual scholarship on African American women in South Carolina. In fact, there is no major publication examining African American women's history or, in particular, their work in the state after 1880. Earlier studies by Asa Gordon and I. A. Newby both acknowledge the arduous work and indispensability of African American women's work in South Carolina,[9] but neither present an in-depth analysis of their work, life, or contributions to the state.

While there are a few other studies that have examined specialists, including basket weavers and educators, overall there has been very little research on postbellum African American women in South Carolina.[10] As for Orangeburg, a comprehensive history of the city has not yet been written. Research on the city has been limited to examining white genealogical histories, its white slaveholding community, or general sketches of early white Orangeburg.[11] With the exception of a few works on education and African Americans in Orangeburg,[12] there has been no major research on African American people nor its women until now. Hopefully, this study will encourage further research on the history of both the city and its women.

I entered this study with many questions in mind: Did all African American women in Orangeburg work inside or outside their homes as generally believed of African American southern women? Did their men's labor mainly determine their families' class positions? Were domestic positions or housewifery the only occupations available to these women and, if not, what role did class play in determining their work or social activities? How did race and gender shape their work culture? Did it vary according to class? What role did education play in determining their class or self-perceptions? Was there a sisterhood based on race and gender between these African American women in Orangeburg, regardless of class? The following chapters will examine and compare Orangeburg's African American women's work and social culture from 1880 to 1940.

Part I.
Pseudo-Aristocratic
Women of Ebony:
The Elite

1.

Upper-Class African Americans

Charles Johnson pointed out that members of the African American upper class were generally "respected by [their] community, . . . had a comfortable income, . . . stability of residence, superior cultural standards, and . . . influential connections."[1] More important, they were conscious of their own upper-class status in the larger African American community. In turn, they were recognized as being a separate, superior class by other African Americans in the community.

Several in-depth studies of African American upper-class families have provided much insight into the lives, activities, and consciousness of this relatively privileged group. These families had their roots in the antebellum era and were found in both the North and the South.[2] Known as the old upper class or "old families," they drew "largely from the ranks of free [African Americans], . . . house slaves, . . . privileged bondsmen, and even certain West Indian immigrants." They differed from the African American masses in "wealth, education, values, and [in many instances] complexion." The postbellum elite thus emerged from antebellum free and enslaved African Americans who were dark-, brown-, and light-skinned. However, most of the well-to-do African Americans with light-skinned complexions quickly distanced themselves from other African Americans once slavery ended.[3]

While "the center of the black aristocracy in the United States" might have been Washington, D.C., from the end of the Reconstruction era to World War I, this elite was present throughout the United States, especially in the major cities. Initially they were highly skilled, as many worked as "prosperous head waiters, real estate speculators, politicians, cooks, [and] professionals." Others were "caterers, barbers, [and] other types of entrepreneurs" who earned enough money to live comfortably, imitating "the aristocratic white people with whom they came in contact."[4]

These African American "aristocrats," dark-, brown-, or light-skinned, were not really aristocrats but merely "pseudo-aristocrats," as they could not boast of inherited "landed estates or ancestral county seats," compared to the white aristocracy. Willard Gatewood asserts that "the distance between the colored aristocracy and the white upper class was as great or greater than the gulf that separated the [upper-class elite] from most [African Americans]."[5]

In South Carolina in 1880, according to Alrutheus Taylor, African American "proprietors of stores constituted the most affluent of their class in South Carolina. . . . Approximately fifteen percent of the population engaged in that occupation. . . . These stores were the chief trading centers of their communities, carrying general merchandise, miscellaneous foods, dry goods, hardware, and liquors." The precise wealth of these African Americans is unknown, but we do know that they invested their money in farm stock, deposited it in banks, or reinvested it in their homes or in new businesses.[6]

The African American shopping district on Railroad Avenue, 1997. Today it is called Boulevard Street.

In 1880, Orangeburg's African American upper class was small and not necessarily a professional one. Economically, it resembled a financially secure white middle class more than a white upper class. This African American elite, however, was the most economically stable group in its community, whose skills in carpentry, in the barbershop, in blacksmithing, and in dressmaking made them indispensable to both African Americans and whites. Unlike other African Americans, they owned significant assets, including land, sizable homes, and, usually, a successful business.

Jim Crow segregation and racial discrimination in Orangeburg forced African Americans to rely on their own resources as much as possible. Thus, a relatively self-sufficient community emerged within the larger white one. It had its own shopping district on Railroad Avenue, where the "entire business block . . . across from the college, was . . . brick in construction and owned by [African Americans]."[7]

Orangeburg's African American community of "traders and laborers" had by the twentieth century become a well-established group of skilled artisans and professionals. They established their own businesses and companies, including a volunteer fire-fighting company called the Comet Company, which was founded as early as 1869. There were successful moneymaking businesses, including a few that served

By 1997 stores in the African American shopping district on the lower end of Russell Street have closed except for the barber shop on far left.

both African American and white clients. Some of these business owners became a part of Orangeburg's early African American elite in the late nineteenth and early twentieth centuries.[8]

One prominent African American, A. D. Dantzler, opened the first African American bank in 1904, the Zion Savings Bank. Businesses in the 1920s, such as the J. J. Sulton and Sons Lumber Company, Maxwell's Grocery Store, Dash's Taxi Company, Daniel's Taylor Shop, and the Bythewood Funeral Home in the Bythewood Building were a few of the successful commercial examples. In fact, the Bythewood Funeral Home had emerged to become "one of the largest undertaking establishments in the South." The increased number of lucrative businesses further led to the widening of the economic gap among African Americans. These few proprietors accumulated wealth that greatly surpassed that of the town's average African American.[9]

Between 1920 and 1940, Orangeburg's most affluent African Americans still largely belonged to the proprietary or professional group. Seamstresses, tailors, carpenters, blacksmiths, and barbers constituted a part of Orangeburg's well-to-do elite. They worked hard, putting in long hours to

A Sulton Lumber Company Truck hauling lumber manufactured in Orangeburg and sent to various parts of the world, 1931. This elite family were the first to own a truck in Orangeburg County. Courtesy of the Sulton Family.

The Bythewood Building still houses Bythewood Funeral Home, which, before 1940, was reputed to be one of the largest funeral homes in the South.

serve not only their community but also the well-to-do white professionals, merchants, and families of leisure. Usually, the wealthier African American artisans were those with the largest white clientele. For example, African American contractors and other artisans built many homes and buildings for the white community. Their work roles remained indispensable to the city, long after slavery had ended. In fact, general bricklaying and plastering came to a stop when unionized African American workers successfully struck over an argument for a set wage of eighty-five cents an hour for a nine-hour work day.[10]

In 1940, Orangeburg's African American elite was still a small, financially secure, propertied one, owning their businesses and homes. Because of Jim Crow regulations that prevented interracial fraternizing on any level, some profitable African American businesses requiring more intimate contact between the owner and clients chose to serve only white customers, as did the Pendarvis Barber Shop. In this barber shop, white customers never had to worry about coming in contact with African American customers. In turn, the barber shop was able to charge somewhat higher prices, making far greater wages than those barbers catering only to African Americans. Other businesses, including Maxwell's Grocery Store, J. J. Sulton and Sons Lumber Company, or Daniel's Taylor Shop, served both African American and white customers. Each, however, followed the usual Jim Crow customs of catering to their white customers before their African American ones. These businesses were respected in both communities.[11]

Those African Americans working at Orangeburg's colleges, Claflin University and State Agricultural and Mechanical College of South Carolina (State A&M) enjoyed a respectable position in their community. College-educated professionals held a more prestigious social status, becoming a significant, influential part of Orangeburg's African American elite. This was particularly true for those working as faculty, staff, and administrators.

Many of the early instructors at Claflin University were white females from New England. While Mamie Garvin Fields concurs that she was taught at Claflin by white teachers from New England, she adds that there were also African American instructors. According to Horace Fitchett, among Claflin's earliest teachers and trustees were African Americans "who had been free, fairly well educated, and relatively economically secure in antebellum South Carolina," with some even "completing courses of study at the [white] University of South Carolina." Earnest Lander Jr. pointed out that in the "sub-collegiate department, . . . quite commonly instructors . . . held no college degrees, while holders of master's degrees from reputable institutions were rare" up to 1940. He added that at "Claflin in 1913, only one of fourteen instructors in the 'Manual Training' department held a bachelor's degree."[12] Despite these academic shortcomings, these educators were still held in high esteem in the African American community.

As these two colleges helped to increased the literacy level and promote self-improvement activities in the African American community, they simultaneously played a key role in enhancing class differences and developing skin-color caste divisions among African Americans. Horace Fitchett argued that "Claflin had its inception in Charleston," in that since "1774 certain classes of [African Americans] had been given the advantage of some education." When Claflin opened in 1869, "it had identified with it men of prestige and appreciation of the importance of education. The children, relatives, and friends of these pioneers in education registered in the school. Thus, it was refuted to be an institution for the [African American] aristocrat in those early days." Subsequently, the first person to graduate from the Normal Department in 1879 was Eugenia Middleton. She was the daughter of both a trustee at Claflin and a native from Charleston's well-to-do African American community. She later received her bachelor's degree from Claflin in 1884.[13]

Like other elite African Americans in the South, the members of upper-class Orangeburg were closely affiliated with both Claflin and State A&M as either students or employees. It was not uncommon for such colleges to serve as beacons promoting the material and cultural values of upper- and middle-class whites in the United States. The curriculums emphasized white American culture, largely ignoring African cultural heritage. The subtle pressure to identify with and accept white culture and history as proper generally resulted in those at the colleges feeling somewhat superior to and further alienated from other African Americans in the community.[14]

Horace Fitchett argued that there developed a kind of "in-group" structure among college people: "The common association which the institutional life of the school provided gave the proper atmosphere for those intimacies and interests" to develop, eventually ending in courtship and marriage among those attending and graduating from the college. Some of Orangeburg's early African American elite families included the Sasportas, Middletons, Millers, Minuses, Sultons, Dangerfields, and Moorers. They relocated to Orangeburg from Charleston, Beaufort, and other cities as students from well-established families who were often of mixed racial heritage. Upon graduation, they usually married their colleagues and accepted employment at Claflin and, later, South Carolina State A&M.[15]

The role education played in promoting class and color-caste divisions in the African American community was not unique to Orangeburg. Edmund L. Drago's important study of Avery Normal Institute in Charleston reveals that the school reflected "a city rife with divisions." His examination illustrates the social divisions that existed within Avery. There were not only social class divisions but also an "intra-racial" segregation based on skin color. This color-bar segregation allowed a small sector of African American students of mixed ancestry, especially "the blue-eyed, fair-skinned children," certain advantages and privileges not available to the average student at the school. Lewis K. McMillan pointed out that this in-group socializing or a similar intra-segregational relationship also existed at State A&M since its inception in 1896. The first two presidents of the college, Thomas E. Miller of Beaufort and Robert Shaw Wilkinson of Charleston, were mulattos who came from prominent Reconstruction families of free antebellum background in South Carolina. McMillan argued that an "educational inbreeding" completely permeated A&M's early history, along with "the deadly malady of favoritism." Students and graduates of well-to-do or prominent mulatto families, including those who were inadequately trained, were appointed to faculty positions and top administrative positions based on "intimate personal friendship" with those already in power, regardless of their qualifications.[16]

Carter G. Woodson spoke critically of the emerging attitude of the "highly educated [African Americans]" between 1880 and 1940 that was rapidly widening "the gap between the masses and the 'talented tenth,'" a term coined by W. E. B. Du Bois to describe the most-educated sector of the African American community. Woodson criticized the educated elite for merely going "to school to memorize certain facts to pass examinations for jobs." He posited that they were forsaking the duties of their forerunners, who in 1880, "went off to school to prepare themselves for the uplift of a downtrodden people." Woodson saw education as a tool to improve self in order to help others. He viewed the emerging attitudes of the elite in the early twentieth century as reflecting a "trend . . . towards selfishness" and cliquishness, resulting in disaster for the African American masses. While they were involved in racial uplift work, according to Benjamin Davis, editor of an Atlanta newspaper, African American college administrators and faculty were still "stand-offish" and tried to uplift the masses "by standing off trying to lift [them] up with a forty-foot pole."[17]

Orangeburg's own educated elite did consciously distance themselves from the downtrodden African American majority, even though they were involved with social uplift work to help the masses. It is reasonable to question how many of these upper-class African Americans were sincere missionaries in their work or only performed uplift work because it was expected of them. Were some upper-class members merely paternalistic individuals possessing superior attitudes toward the downtrodden? Were they consciously alienating themselves socially from this downtrodden, inferior group so that white society would be able to differentiate them from inferior African Americans? While these unanswered questions are important, it is clear that despite sharp class cleavages, there were many upper-class African Americans in Orangeburg who sincerely committed themselves to helping the majority poor and this significant group worked diligently to improve the lives of the poor in both Orangeburg and throughout South Carolina.

Along with the respectability associated with working at the Orangeburg colleges, the salaries of the African American administrators and faculty provided a comfortable living. Some college salaries were probably less than the incomes of the more successful store proprietors or skilled professionals in Orangeburg's upper class, including barbers, carpenters, seamstresses, or tailors, who all had sizable white clientele, but academic work endowed a respectable social status and sufficient income to live on a par with the wealthier members of the upper class.[18]

MacMillan's valuable study of State A&M's salary distribution showed that in 1907, President Thomas Miller earned $1,800 annually. His top five administrators and faculty members earned $900 each, while the average faculty member earned between $400 and $500. Other instructors, probably associated with the primary and secondary schools, earned around $350. By 1918, the new president, Robert Shaw Wilkinson, was earning around $2,130 and was provided with housing accommodations. His highest paid administrator, Nelson Nix, earned $1,980, while the other higher paid administrators and faculty members earned between $1,170 and $1,465 annually. At that time, the average faculty salary ranged between $600 and $900. These incomes were much higher than that of the average African American in Orangeburg. The elite could afford better housing, diets, health care, dress, and many of the other amenities associated with an upper-class life-style. For example, when President Wilkinson became ill in 1925, he left the inadequate Jim Crow health care services in South Carolina and traveled to New York City to seek the best medical services available. This was a privilege not accessible to the less fortunate, who were forced to either nurse themselves back to health or use the inferior Jim Crow facilities.[19]

The life-style of Orangeburg's African American elite in the early twentieth century was not too far removed from that of the larger United States. They, too, were "working aristocrats," employed as business owners, successful artisans, educators, lawyers, physicians, and ministers. Orangeburg's African American elite included such families as the Wilkinsons, Maxwells, Pierces, Fordhams, Daniels, Nixs, Greens, and Rowes. Their wealth did not compare to that of the white upper class in the United States, including that of Orangeburg's white elite families, such as the Dukes, Salleys, Albergottis, Jennings, Wannamakers, Sims, Glovers, and Cornelsons.[20] These African American aristocrats, like their peers throughout the United States, could not boast of inherited landed estates or ancestral county seats, as found among Orangeburg's white aristocracy. Yet they were sharply distinguished from the rest of the African American majority as they enjoyed a more privileged and comfortable life-style.

They were the first in the African American community to own the attractive horse and buggy in the nineteenth century and, later, the automobile, which provided their families with convenient, modern transportation for shopping, working, or visiting. Owning their own homes, these upper-class families resided in the more reputable areas in their community, such as the Russell Street Extension, the Goff Avenue Extension, and Treadwell Street, which was almost in the center of the African American commercial district, located along Railway Avenue.[21]

Families such as the Pierces, Maxwells, Greens, and Daniels lived in attractive, sizable homes located in the affluent sections of Treadwell Street and Railway Avenue. A few of these families, like the Wilkinsons and the Sultons, lived outside the traditional upper-class community and elected to live either near or within select white areas.[22] For example, the Sulton brothers, McDuffy and John J. Jr., built twin, mansionlike homes next to each other in the sparsely populated area of widely spaced homes on the Russell Street Extension. Living among whites, this old mulatto family not only was well respected but also lived free of racial incidents. According to Marion Salley, well-to-do African Americans had lived in the well-kept, isolated neighborhoods since the early nineteenth century: "Goff Avenue, yet not within the city limits, [was] a suburban village known as 'New Brooklyn'" and was previously the old confederate and, later, federal war camp field. There "one [found] attractive homes, showing that the owners [were], or [had] been prosperous [African Americans]."[23]

Geraldine Pierce Zimmerman still occupies this spacious column home built and occupied earlier by her parents, Hazel and James Pierce, on Treadwell Street.

   The homes of the elite tended to be spacious brick or neatly painted white frame houses that were usually two-story models. The rooms were large and included a living room, a sitting room, a dining room, kitchen, and several bedrooms, of which one was reserved for guests. They were adequately furnished and, by the 1930s, contained relatively modern appliances. Just as white upper- and middle-class homes in Orangeburg were serviced with the luxuries of electricity and indoor plumbing before the working-class whites were able to attain such amenities, the African American upper-class homes were also the first in their communities to have such services, including bathrooms replete with tubs. Their yards, sometimes used for entertaining and social events, were arranged to complement the beauty of their homes. They had attractive, manicured lawns with year-round trimmed, beautiful shrubbery that produced brightly colored Azaleas and other flowers in the spring and summer.[24]

   Jim Crow segregation prevented southern African Americans from integrating and assimilating into the larger white society. Hence, according to Willard Gatewood, the "commodious, tastefully furnished" homes of the African American elite became the center of their social life and the "scenes

A present-day view of the parlor room in the Pierce home. Pianos were common in the homes of the African American elite.

of numerous social affairs." The African American elite in South Carolina occasionally held "lavish and always tasteful entertainment," including dinner parties, formal and semiformal parties, and literary gatherings. In Columbia, for example, a local African American newspaper reported the lavish affair given by a Dr. J. G. Stuart in 1925 in its society column. It was a successful "stag party" held at Stuart's "palatial residence on Pine Street" and "was enjoyed by a host of friends in and out of the city, . . . including Dr. Green [from] Orangeburg." It was not uncommon for the elite of Orangeburg, Charleston, Columbia, and other nearby towns to attend each other's functions.[25]

Aside from possessing secure incomes, comfortable homes, and perhaps some other property, education was probably the most important determinant of class position in the African American community in Orangeburg before 1940. As a factor, it further divided this community into a "haves" and "have nots" and played a major role in enhancing an upper-class consciousness among the elite, who gradually became even more socially alienated from the uneducated majority. Earning an education, especially higher education, was a coveted privilege, and thus most African Americans interested in schooling could only dream of

Today Marilyn Green Epps resides in the home of her parents, Cora Ransom Green and Dr. Seibels Green, on Treadwell Street.

Marian Birnie Wilkinson and her family lived in this home on Russell Street Extension near the Sultons long after the death in 1932 of her husband, Robert Shaw Wilkinson, president of State A&M.

completing primary school or attending college. Those underprivileged few who did attend school entered with hopes of graduating from college to join, one day, the class of the respected "haves."

In Orangeburg, African American upper-class children attended the two best primary and secondary schools in town, both a part of Claflin and State A&M. A few were even sent away to attend white preparatory schools in the North. Afterward, these upper-class students either attended one of the colleges in Orangeburg or went away to study at one of the other well-established institutions in the country, such as Fisk University in Tennessee, Oberlin College in Ohio, Hampton Institute in Virginia, or Spelman and Morehouse Colleges in Georgia. Some pursued degrees in teaching, chemistry, law, medicine, and mathematics.[26]

Ancestral heritage—descent from a family with a respectable history, an ancestral connection to white aristocratic families, or a relation to those involved in Reconstruction politics or those who had accumulated great wealth or property—further enhanced upper-class status in Orangeburg. Some families boasted of little or no slavery in their backgrounds, as with the Sultons, Wilkinsons, or Millers. For example, Thomas E. Miller, State A&M's first president, descended from a family of free antebellum African Americans in Beaufort who also owned slaves. The Millers became one of South Carolina's most prominent African American Reconstruction families, and their son, Thomas Miller, served as both a lawyer and congressman before becoming president of State A&M. Another family, the Fordhams, was also a prominent Reconstruction family involved in politics. Its patriarch, John Hammond Fordham, was not only a lawyer and politician but also a coroner, tax collector, postal clerk, and drugstore owner.[27]

The social distinctions that determined upper-class standing in the African American community were not unique to Orangeburg. Studies by E. Franklin Frazier, Gunnar Myrdal, and Willard Gatewood presented striking similarities to the stratification present in Orangeburg. They argued that the African American upper class usually descended from an old, propertied family and most likely had some outstanding personal achievement, possibly descending from a background of little or no slavery. They usually had "greater literacy," exposure to higher education, or, perhaps, "considerable mechanical skills."[28] Frazier's, Myrdal's, and Gatewood's findings also showed that respectable occupations and high incomes were important factors but did not

Today Sulton family members continue to reside on Russell Street in the two stately homes built by brothers McDuffie and John J. Jr. *Left* the home of Bessie George Sulton, and *right* the home of Daisy Hume Sulton.

The patriarch and matriarch of the Sulton family, Emma and James Sulton, c. early 1900s. Emma was a Cherokee Indian. Courtesy of the Sulton Family.

necessarily take social precedence over the importance of family history or a college education.

Ira Berlin, Michael P. Johnson, and James L. Roark demonstrated that skin color and mixed ancestry was not new to the postbellum South. They showed how this played a key role in stratifying the early antebellum free African American elite in Charleston, New Orleans, Mobile, Pensacola, and other antebellum southern cities. Their studies show how complexion was used to signify "economic distance from slavery."[29] E. Franklin Frazier and Gunnar Myrdal studied the larger African American community, while Hortense Powdermaker narrowly focused on a single, small southern community. They all found, however, that despite the "constellation of factors" that determined upper-class status, such as property, income, and education, "skin color, white blood, or mixed ancestry" still were seen as significant in enhancing status. Frazier's research further revealed a continuation of the antebellum color prejudices found among upper-class African Americans toward darker-skinned African Americans in early-twentieth-century Charleston.[30]

The skin color of Orangeburg's upper-class African Americans ranged from dark, such as among the Rowes, Fordhams, Nixs, and Pierces, to brown and light brown, such as the Wilkinsons, Sultons, or Daniels, to the very light brown or "white-looking," including the Moorers, Carsons, Sasportases, Cullers, Bythewoods, or Maxwells. These same color prejudices were found among Orangeburg's elite.[31] Skin-color consciousness, or "colorphobia," was a significant phenomenon among Orangeburg's early African American upper class. Whether this colorphobia was imported to Orangeburg by individuals belonging to the old, snobbish, colorphobic elite mulatto families relocating to Orangeburg from Charleston, Beaufort, or other cities is not clear. However, by the early twentieth century, this color-bar discrimination was a reality in Orangeburg's African American community. While light-skinned complexion alone did not determine class status, it created certain advantages that sometimes allowed lighter-skinned African Americans more opportunities for advancement in their community, both socially and economically.[32]

The notion of having white, Indian, or a mixture of both ancestries appeared to have created a strong sense of family pride among some African Americans. Such pride led to the emergence of attitudes of superiority over those lacking such non-African bloodlines. Thus, African Americans of mixed ancestry consciously married those of similar heritage, a practice common in antebellum and postbellum Charleston. In Orangeburg, light-skinned African Americans married other light-

McDuffie and Bessie Sulton with seven of their grandchildren in the 1950s. Courtesy of the Sulton Family.

(left) McDuffie Sulton's son, James, at age twenty-four. Courtesy of the Sulton Family. *(right)* James McDuffie's future wife, Ruby Clowers, at age twenty-two, c. mid-1940s. Courtesy of the Sulton Family.

skinned African Americans, while the those with brown skin generally married other brown-skinned African Americans.[33]

At times, these upper-class African Americans, who were light- or brown-skinned with naturally curly or straight hair (that is, "good hair"), had certain advantages over darker-hued African Americans. Non-African phenotypical characteristics were seen as superior, regardless of class position. Some whites displayed favoritism toward lighter-skinned African Americans in certain situations. For example, Bessie Delaney from Raleigh recalled that when she and her sister, Julia, both college students, sought factory jobs in New York City during the summer, the factory only wanted "to hire Julia because she was lighter."[34]

Jim Crow Orangeburg also allowed various privileges to lighter-skinned, elite African Americans. For example, white-operated stores would let them be served first once they waited on their white customers, even if other darker-skinned or poorer African American customers had been waiting longer. In the African American community, light-skinned elite females were usually selected for the beauty queens, while darker-skinned females were overlooked. Upper- or middle-class light-skinned

James and Ruby Sulton, shown here in 1997, still reside on the family's property on
Russell Street.

students were elected for class representatives or club officers in school, even if others were better qualified. The light-skinned elites were generally offered the more prestigious or respectable jobs on the college campuses when they were students and after they graduated. This reverse color-bar discrimination, or color intra-segregation, strongly prevailed throughout Orangeburg between 1880 and 1940.[35]

Upper-class African Americans such as the Wilkinsons, Sultons, or Daniels may not have been as light-skinned as others in their class, but their medium- to light-brown skin, naturally straight or curly hair, and non-African American phenotypical features strongly displayed mixed ancestral heritage. In Orangeburg, regardless of whether some or all of the mixed-heritage upper class looked disdainfully at their darker-skinned elite counterparts, their sentiments tended to be expressed less explicitly than in Charleston. However, there were some among Orangeburg's African American elite who, unmistakably, displayed attitudes of superiority, snootiness, and blatant color prejudices toward the less-educated, darker, or poorer African Americans living in the wretched areas of town.[36]

It was not uncommon for some African Americans in Orangeburg, who were born with darker complexions or with African-textured hair, to seek spouses with lighter skin complexions or straighter hair. To them, this allowed them an opportunity to further enhance their social status through association with lighter-skinned people. It also enabled them to produce offspring with lighter complexions than themselves, so that they might possibly have the desired "good hair." African Americans from different class backgrounds who desired such features themselves reverted to using various measures to lighten their own skins or change their hair textures. Various advertisements in African American newspapers, magazines, beauty salons, or barber shops promoted such products, including Dr. Fred Palmer's Skin Whitener Ointment or Nadinola Bleaching Cream. According to Palmer's Skin Whitener's advertisement,[37] "No matter how dark your complexion, you can make it fascinating with Dr. Fred Palmer's Skin Whitener Ointment. This preparation . . . softens and lightens the darker skin, clears up pimples, blotches, and tan marks, and does away with that oily, shiny look."[38]

Another Palmer advertisement described the woman who used its product as "bewitching because she has light, smooth, soft skin." Positioned next to the advertisement was a picture of a sophisticated-looking African American woman with very light skin. The Nadinola Bleaching Cream advertisement stated that it would let you "have light-toned lovely skin," while its supplementary "Nadine Face Powder" would create a more "light-toned lovely skin for you," adding that the powder came in "many shades lighter than the natural skin."[39]

Besides lightening their skin, African Americans also explored ways to change their natural hair texture. According to Mamie Garvin Fields, before these hair straightening products, African American women "didn't straighten their hair. [They] just used to wash it, brush it out, and arrange it according to the type of hair [they] had . . . [which] could be any, from African to European and everything in between. . . . The people with the European type of hair dressed it like the white women around. The people with the African hair wore African styles . . . [such as] a lot of little plaits, . . . cornrows, . . . or else they divided the hair in sections and wrapped them with thread." However, for those African American women who wanted "good hair," similar to those who were naturally born with straight or curly hair, they used the "Poro System."[40]

Once Madame C. J. Walker invented a method to straighten African American hair, others who took her courses in New York City began to devise their own creams and methods to straighten hair. It was Annie M. Turnbo Malone, one of Walker's students, who invented the Poro System, which eventually became popular among South Carolina's African American women.[41] One of the system's advertisements asserted that "the glory of a woman lies in her hair; long, soft, and fluffy with silken sheen and why not?" It called for women to not only use the Poro Hair Preparation but also the Poro Hair Grower to promote growth in order to have long hair.[42]

Besides straightening their hair, others opted to color their hair to match the hair colors found among white women and some light-skinned African American women born with nonblack hair. As one advertisement read, "To win the heart and hand of that certain man, don't let ugly hair come between you and the man you want! Use 'Godefray's Larieuse.' It will make your hair a rich, even shade of jet black, black, dark, medium, or light brown or blonde—giving it the silky-softness and lustrous sheen that men can't resist."[43] These advertisements obviously reflected the preferences many African American men held for women with lighter skin and straighter hair.

Women, however, were not alone in changing the texture of their hair. Men in Orangeburg desiring good hair were grateful for the young Marion Evans creation of Evans and Beauty Preparation. Sold in select drugstores and barber shops, barbers used this product to straighten men's hair. While the actual factory was in Columbia, Evans successfully created a mail-order service that "extended over several states."[44]

Not all African Americans succumbed to distorting their natural skin complexions or hair texture. Nannie Helen Burroughs was most critical and outspoken in denouncing those who marveled over such looks: "There are men right in our own race . . . who would rather marry a woman for her color than her character. . . . The White man who crosses the line and leaves an heir is doing a favor for some black men who would marry the most debased women, whose only stock in trade is her color, in preference to the most royal queen in ebony." Burroughs also criticized women for using "skin lighteners and hair straighteners." She said "what ever woman who bleaches and straightens her hair out needs, [was] not her appearance changed, but her mind [changed]." She added that if they expended the same amount of time trying "to get white to trying to improve the conditions of their people, then the race could make great strides."[45]

Upper-class African Americans were already socially divorced from the masses due to the differences in their wealth, education, life-styles, and pride in family heritage. Yet they consciously distanced themselves socially, while some displayed obvious attitudes of snobbery and superiority. They had their separate social lives and private social clubs that further excluded the majority and reinforced the class consciousness of this close-knit group.[46]

Upper-class African Americans were criticized by other African Americans. For example, Willard Gatewood mentions that the elites were seen as being "self-centered, snobbish, and hypocritical 'exclusives,' . . . playing the race racket only when personal gain or preferment was in the offering; otherwise, they were unwilling to identify with [African Americans]." Others saw them as promoting a segregation very similar to the social life-style that whites promoted through Jim Crowism.[47]

One person, the Jamaican-born Harlem activist, Marcus Garvey, founder of the Universal Negro Improvement Association (UNIA) in 1919, was an outspoken critic of elite organizations. He denounced such organizations as the "Blue Vein Society," which was composed of "near-white [African Americans]" and the "Colonial Club, a West Indian group which erected the same standards for admission." At their "annual balls, monthly soirees, and pink teas, . . . no less than a quadroon was admitted." At times, Garvey "denounced mulattos even more sharply than he did whites." Fictitious short stories—including Charles Waddell Chestnutt's "The Wife of His Youth" and Nella Larsen's "Passing"—accurately reflect the color prejudices and exclusivity of the light-skinned elite in the early twentieth century, revealing the high value the elite placed on having light-skinned complexions and being financially successful in an unwelcoming white society.[48]

However, Orangeburg's African American "upper crust or pseudo-aristocrats" did not have the "independence, power, or economic resources" of the white Orangeburg elite.[49] They strove for respectability as they emulated white Orangeburg's genteel culture. Simultaneously, they asserted a consciousness and pride in their own class standing and accomplishments as best they could, being a people living in a racially hostile white society.

While the African American majority attended the more "grass-roots" or Holiness churches, the upper class, who viewed themselves as being more culturally refined, consciously selected membership in the more "high-toned" Episcopal, Methodist, Presbyterian, and Catholic churches. In Columbia, South Carolina, for example, there were eight Baptist churches, three African Methodist Episcopal (AME) churches, and one Episcopal, Congregational, and Presbyterian church each, illustrating that the majority of African Americans were interested in attending the more grass-roots Baptist churches or the "upscale" grass-roots AME churches. Carter G. Woodson critically argued that if the elite were still permitted to attend mixed congregation churches, they would compromise their pride and sit in the segregated seating rather than attend the grass-roots churches with the majority. [50] They "perceived themselves as being of the social 'upper crust' and were also seen by other [African Americans] as occupying a lofty status." Thus, it was mainly elite African Americans who worshipped at the Episcopal churches, including "St. Phillip's in New York City, St. Thomas in Philadelphia, St. Luke in Washington, D.C., All Saints in St. Louis, . . . St. Mark's in Charleston," and St. Paul's in Orangeburg.[51]

According to Edmund L. Drago in his examination of the African American elite in Charleston, this upper-class community broke from the overcrowded, historically white "Grace Parish" in 1865 to form their own church called St. Mark's Episcopal. One of its founding members, Richard Birnie, was a well-to-do "cotton shipper" of mixed ancestry who became "a prominent lay reader" in the new church. St. Mark's was considered snobbish and elitist and drew a color line within their own community that excluded darker-skinned African Americans from their services. In the course of Drago's research, various anecdotal remarks emerged suggesting that the church's congregation had criteria for how its members should look: light-skinned, naturally straight or curly hair, and non-African phenotypical characteristics. While this church's membership consisted largely persons of mixed ancestry who, outside of church, consciously identified with each other as a group, Drago finds no historical evidence to support these anecdotal claims regarding St. Mark's deliberately practicing an intragroup color bar.[52]

Drago recounts the history of Marian Raven Birnie, the daughter of Richard Birnie of St. Mark's Church. She "graduated with high honors from Avery [Normal Institute in Charleston] in 1888, [and] taught at her alma mater until she married Robert Shaw Wilkinson." Wilkinson, also a Charlestonian and a descendant of mixed ancestry, graduated from Avery and went on to become one of the first African Americans to integrate West Point Military Academy in 1884. He received his undergraduate degree at Oberlin College and his doctorate at Columbia University. Afterward, Wilkinson taught first in the Physics and Chemistry Department at Kentucky State University in Louisville and then at Orangeburg's State A&M. In 1911, he was named the second president of State A&M. It was with the initial arrival of the Wilkinsons that the first and only African American Episcopal church in Orangeburg was established.[53]

The services held at St. Paul's Episcopal Church were respectable and high-cultured, appealing specifically to the higher socioeconomic classes in the African American community. From the onset, St. Paul's congregation consisted of those from "preferred backgrounds" whose complexions tended to range from extremely light to brown. Others in the upper-class attended either the Presbyterian or Methodist church. To the elite, the more grass-roots Baptist and Holiness churches were a part of the working-class religious bastion and were thus culturally and socially inferior.[54]

Before the establishment of St. Paul's Episcopal Church, however, there already existed a high-culture church for Orangeburg's African American upper class—St. Luke's Presbyterian Church. When State A&M was founded in 1896, Thomas E. Miller, an African American member of the House of Representatives, was invited to become its first president. Miller "agreed to come to Orangeburg, rather than to offer for re-election to the House of Representatives, on the condition that he could work toward the establishment of a new Presbyterian Church." Hence, he founded the Railroad Avenue Presbyterian Church in 1897, the name of which was later changed to St. Luke. Besides being president of the college, he also served as the church's first minister and presided until 1900. At this time, the respectable Reverend Uggams, the grandfather of future entertainer Leslie Uggams, took over the church's ministry. From 1909 to 1924, Reverend Simon H. Scott became the minister and also "operated a parochial school" for African Americans. Even though the school's tenure was brief, Orangeburg's African American community could boast of having another option for schooling its youth, outside of the overcrowded Sterling and the private schools at the colleges. In summary, the African American elite generally attended Trinity Methodist Episcopal, St. Luke's Presbyterian, and St. Paul's Episcopal Churches.[55]

Carter G. Woodson scolded the "educated" African American elite for leaving the traditional churches to be run by "exploiters, grifters, and libertines." He asserted that the church in the African American community was the only institution solely controlled by them. Thus, he criticized this skillful elite community for deserting these institutions and practicing "Jim Crowism" by having their own color-caste, class-segmented churches. Woodson argued that this elite should have continued the tradition of developing the greatest asset of their race—the traditional church. However, by the 1930s increasing numbers of highly educated African Americans sought the more intellectual and ritualistic atmospheres found in both the Episcopal and Catholic churches.[56]

Despite their wealth, Loren Schweninger points out that even the most prosperous African Americans recognized that their futures were inextricably linked to that of the African American masses. This frustrated upper class, too, "felt the injustices of racial oppression, violence, or intimidation in the South." Despite the elite's wealth, intelligence, and status in their own communities, whites in Orangeburg still saw them as equally inferior to the less fortunate African American masses. Edmund L. Drago

St. Paul's Episcopal Church was seen as a high-cultured church that largely appealed to the African American elite. It remains the only African American Episcopal church in Orangeburg.

Trinity Methodist Church, later called Trinity AME, was built on Railroad Avenue, across the railroad tracks from both Claflin and State A&M colleges.

correctly states that "[African American] ancestry, no matter what the legal definition states, was enough to force even the lightest-skinned and wealthiest black person to the back of the bus."[57]

The *Plessy v. Ferguson* "separate but equal" ruling in 1896 applied to all African Americans, regardless of class, skin color, age, and gender. Booker T. Washington, president of Tuskegee Institute and a respected leader among many African Americans and some whites, advocated that African Americans be patient and tolerant of segregation. He posited that they should, instead, place emphasis on "economic initiative and self-help, rather than civil rights." While some upper-class African Americans concurred, others disagreed vehemently, including leader-activists W. E. B. Du Bois and Monroe Trotter.[58] The elite experienced the brunt of racism and segregation, as they had more to lose. They possessed the skills, wealth, education, and confidence to assimilate fully into the larger society, but were legally prohibited because of their skin color. This deprivation was frustrating and demeaning to them. They attempted to live comfortably, according to their means, but were still disrespected and threatened by whites. According to Roi Ottley and William J. Weatherby,

The *New York Sun* newspaper reported that there were more than three hundred families who could afford to buy houses from forty thousand to one hundred thousand in value, live on the scale of white people who spend from ten to twenty-five thousand dollars a year. The [paper's] survey was made after whites had stoned the homes of [African Americans] living in Brooklyn, following the appearance of the first large automobile owned by [an African American] family. That this family had also brought property in the best residential section was perhaps cause for resentment.[59]

Racial discrimination prevented upper-class African Americans from freely indulging in the public realm at their whim. In New York City, they were "barred from fashionable [white] restaurants like Delmonico's and Sherry's" and "unwelcome[d] in reputable places of amusement conducted by whites." In Charleston, they were not allowed to frequent the historical seaport park area called "the Battery," except for "one day each year, the Fourth of July." On this occasion, whites "stayed home and . . . [African American] people 'took over' the Battery for a day." In Orangeburg, they were not permitted to frequent the white-owned restaurants, hotels, the library, or parks. The beautiful flower park, Edisto Gardens, was totally off limits to African Americans. However, the city did permit a remote, undeveloped area near Edisto Gardens to be used for African American gatherings on designated days and times.[60]

Willard Gatewood argues that it was these African American aristocrats in the early twentieth century who "provided much of the inspiration and leadership for organized efforts on behalf of civil rights," as they were "the best educated, most articulate" members of the race. Edmund L. Drago adds that the eventual "racial radicalism and the economic forces of World War I accelerated the fading of the color line" and moved this light-skinned aristocracy "towards a more solid alliance with the darker-skinned elite and the rest of the community." Part of the reason for this new alliance was due to a growing, educated middle class who challenged the elite's leadership monopoly.[61] In Orangeburg, a superficial alliance emerged between upper-class and middle-class African Americans when it came to improving conditions in the community; however, the greater alliance and intimacy actually occurred between upper-class and upper-middle-class African Americans in Orangeburg because they shared more cultural and economic characteristics.

The African American elite's criticisms of racism, discrimination, and violence were also heard through their newspapers. One Columbia paper in particular, the *Palmetto Leader*, carried news of events in Columbia and Orangeburg regarding educational matters and the activities of the elite. Up until the late 1930s, many of its articles focused heavily on race issues, including those related to Marcus Garvey, the National Association for the Advancement of Colored People, the Ku Klux Klan, and violence directed at African Americans all over the United States.[62]

The Upper-Class Female

In the late nineteenth and early twentieth centuries, the ideology of the "cult of domesticity," which declared that women's true sphere was the home, was still embraced by the majority of people in the United States, regardless of race, gender, and class. In actuality, only a small sector of the population was able to practice this Victorian life-style: the upper-class elite. Sarah Hale, who published the popular and influential magazine *Godey's Lady's Book*, taught that a true lady was "delicate and timid, . . . required protection, . . . possessed a sweet dependency, . . . [was] modest, . . . and had charming and insinuating manners." Her major tasks were housekeeping and supervising her hired servants. True womanhood emphasized grace, charm, "innocence, modesty, piety, purity, submissiveness, and domesticity."[63]

During the antebellum and postbellum eras, upper-class white girls were raised as "nice little girls should be raised." They were taught everything from the proper time young ladies should retire to bed to how they should eat or enter a room. As little girls, they received their informal training by emulating their mothers; once they were older, they were sent to select boarding schools for formal training. In Orangeburg, for example, white genteel girls attended the Legare Academy. Coming "from South Carolina's aristocratic families, [they] were taught subjects suitable for their station in life." They studied "a smattering of English, a speaking acquaintance of French, a splash of philosophy, some mathematics and as firm a grounding in music and the arts as each young woman was capable of absorbing."[64]

Though some have argued that African Americans have been excluded from the benefits of capitalism during the nineteenth and early twentieth century,[65] class distinctions did exist. A small sector of elite African American women experienced a different social reality. They took full advantage of and enjoyed the amenities available to African Americans living in a racially discriminating society. They emulated the proper, prescribed mannerisms and social life-styles associated with white middle- and upper-class society. However, they still were not considered members of the cult of true womanhood by whites. They were girls and women, but never genteel ladies. Instead, they were "immoral scourges." Paula Giddings asserts that even with their accomplishments, white society did not see them as worthy women. Assumed naturally to have "low and animalistic urges" that casted "them outside the pale of the movement for moral reform, [African American] women were seen as having all the inferior qualities of white women without any virtues."[66]

Although African American women of all classes embodied this idea of domestic femininity and true womanhood, these ideals were manifested in ways that reflected their social reality, which was plagued with discrimination, segregation, racism, and, for most, poverty.[67] The concepts of true womanhood within the elite African American community had its roots in the antebellum era. The free, well-to-do elite made certain that their sons and daughters received the formal and informal training appropriate to their social position. Adele Logan Alexander discusses the upbringing of the mulatto offspring of the well-to-do white Hunt family in rural Sparta, Georgia. The young Hunt girls lived in the mansion with their unmarried parents, their upper-class white father, Nathan Sayre, and their mulatto mother, Susan Hunt. These girls "did not work outside the family [but] were diligently trained in household duties and responsibilities." Like any other genteel girl, Lula Hunt, for example, "was taught to do fine needlework, enjoyed music, and 'prize[d] old and beautiful things.' She loved flowers and gardening but never chopped or picked cotton. As a girl, she learned how to drive a horse and buggy but not how to steer a plow."[68]

Postbellum elite African American girls were taught that "repose of manner and a soft voice" were "two of the greatest claims that a girl may possess." They, too, were "encouraged to affect modesty and purity," learning that "talkativeness, especially in a loud voice and in public, was a sign of lost control . . . and ill-breeding and bad taste." Such teachings of feminine etiquette continued long after the antebellum era within the elite African American community. Louisa Smith Robinson of Orangeburg recalled how in the early 1900s her mother emphasized the "unladylike" things girls should not do, adding that they "were a conservative family who knew the proper thing to do" and "were always concerned with the family's reputation."[69]

They, like elite whites, also had the "coming out" of their daughters as seen with the various fashionable semiformals or formals Willard Gatewood describes in various cities. These African American debutantes were presented to the larger well-to-do or financially secure community. In Orangeburg, the Marian Birnie Wilkinson Club for young African American females had their special functions for young ladies from preferred background. Even the informal gatherings for elite young daughters received attention in the African American newspapers, as was the case when the *Palmetto Leader* described the lovely affair of "Miss Flora Julia Fordham" in Orangeburg in 1928 "in honor of her sixteenth birthday."[70]

The main purpose of celebrating "coming of age" was to notify the community that a daughter was approaching adulthood. Like the white upper class, the African American elite also groomed their daughters to select mates from the same background and, in some instances, with the same skin color. In Orangeburg, Geraldine Pierce Zimmerman insisted in an oral interview that usually the light skins married the light skins, but "the color bar was crossed with 'white Negroes'—whom we called the very light-skinned—when they married into 'brown' families. However, this happened only if they had similar economic backgrounds."[71]

Often once an African American suitor's economic worth was confirmed, her parents approved accordingly. The father of Daisy Gathers Williams of Orangeburg initially refused to approve his daughter's engagement until her suitor, Willie Williams, "had a cage to put his little bird in. So, once Williams . . . built a four room house for them to live in, the proposal was accepted."[72]

Throughout the nation, elite African Americans established "a variety of clubs, societies, and associations." Charleston had its exclusive parlor societies for elite women and the Brown Fellowship Society for men and women, which, according to Mamie Garvin Fields, was defined by its name as a club for "brown, not black, [African Americans] to belong to." Orangeburg, too, had its exclusive card clubs, the Friday Nighters or the Saturday Nighters. The children of these women had their own social clubs, such as the Red Ribbon Club or the Pollyanna Club, which recruited female youth from "preferred backgrounds."[73]

Class snobbishness reigned among Orangeburg's elite. They resided in select communities "across the railroad tracks" from the African American masses and socialized with their peers in their own social clubs. It was common for these elite women to wear clothes purchased from exclusive fashionable specialty shops. Even though they could not try on the clothing, shoes, or hats in the stores, they still shopped at white-owned, exclusive dress shops in Orangeburg, such as Kohn's, Alice Glover's, or Gossard's; at exclusive department stores, including Mirmow's, Mosely's, and McNamara's; or at high-quality shoe stores such as Glover's or Stroman's. Others frequented exclusive stores such as Maxwell's in the larger city of Columbia to shop for "fine spring dresses" or "high-class dresses" sold at prices the African American majority could not afford. They made appointments at African American–owned beauty shops to have their hair styled, faces massaged, or nails manicured to maintain their sophisticated appearances.[74]

Formal education for upper-class African American females was a sine qua non for belonging to this elite group by the twentieth century. Even during the antebellum and Reconstruction periods, literacy and some sort of formal education was still important. Even though schools for African American children were illegal in the antebellum South, elite African Americans found ways to educate their children. In Charleston, for example, Anna Berry was a slave taught to read by her young masters; in turn, she would slip away and teach other African Americans in her secret school in "her family's house on George Street, back in an alley."[75]

After the war, Charleston children attended the free Shaw School and had mostly single, white "rebel" teachers, who taught them to respect the old confederate culture of the South. There were also two African American teachers, an "Essie Alston and a Sally Cruikshank," who was an upper-class female and active member of the Brown Fellowship Society. After attending Shaw, some children entered Charleston's only African American high school, Avery. Avery, a private school, charged a fee and supposedly had a sizable enrollment of "mulatto children, light-skinned half-sisters and brothers, grands and great-grands of white people."[76]

In Orangeburg, young upper-class African American females were initially tutored in private homes by college students or faculty members since there were no African American preschools before 1940. Afterward, most of the elite girls attended the private primary school and high school at Claflin or State A&M colleges. For example, Geraldine Pierce Zimmerman recalls that in 1917 she entered Claflin's grammar school and went on to complete first through eighth grade. At that time, her father had accepted a teaching position in the Industrial Arts program at State A&M. Since the children of faculty members were allowed to attend the college's private primary and secondary schools free of charge, young Geraldine enrolled in State A&M's high school, where she graduated in 1929.[77] Others sent their children up North to attend highly selective high schools. For example, Lula Love Wilkinson, the daughter of President Wilkinson of State A&M, attended Drew Seminary in Carmel, New York, in the early 1920s, graduating valedictorian from a class of fifty girls in 1926.[78]

Upon graduation from Claflin or State A&M high school in Orangeburg, many upper-class women attended Claflin University or State A&M College, while others chose to attend African American colleges outside of the city. Flora Ella Fordham, the first registered nurse (RN) in Orangeburg, graduated from Hampton Institute in 1903. Others included Geraldine Pierce Zimmerman, who graduated from Fisk University in

1932, and Marilyn Green Epps, who graduated from Spelman College in 1938. Lula Wilkinson, who opted to attend her father's alma mater, and Florence Sulton both graduated from Oberlin College in the early 1930s.[79]

More men than women went on to higher education. In 1890, there were three hundred African American males who received baccalaureate degrees as compared to thirty females. Most females, after receiving their licentiate instructione (L.I.) degree from the normal training school, pursued their careers as teachers, seamstresses, or homemakers. However, female enrollments at Claflin and State A&M continued to increase between 1900 and 1920. In 1911, the majority of African American women still studied the required female subjects at both colleges, although a few students at A&M took courses that were required for males, such as mechanical drawing and arts, agriculture, and typewriting. Most, however, were still enrolled in the teaching program at the colleges.[80]

Orangeburg's African American women in this pseudo-aristocratic class were expected to follow certain social behaviors to reflect their elite social status. Their social manners, their dress or hair, their education, where they lived, who they married, how they socialized, and who they associated with were all significant factors in their everyday lives that were not to be compromised. They were very conscious of their elevated social positions in the African American Orangeburg community and emulated the white ideals of the cult of true womanhood.

2.

Upper-Class Women's Work outside the Home

Orangeburg's African American upper class was small but influential. To become a member of this elite group was not easy, since family heritage and background played a significant role in determining class status. Not all upper-class African American women were born into this class. A few came from working- or middle-class families and their status rose due to their educational achievements and subsequent respectable jobs. Others attained elite status by marrying upper-class men. Jacqueline Jones, in her study of black women, work, and the family, ignores the existence of an upper-class African American elite and refers to middle-class African American women as the elite. In Orangeburg, however, there were upper-class elite women whose origins were in the upper-class and who brought skills and money to the marriage.[1]

Paid Work

When upper-class men and women married each other, they further enhanced their social status and wealth. With higher education playing such a significant role in determining social class in Orangeburg, elite members employed at the colleges placed their families in an even higher social position. According to Geraldine Pierce Zimmerman, in 1908 her mother, Hazel Tatnall Pierce, had a college education in both business and typewriting from Alabama A&M and brought a sizable inherited income to her marriage when she married James Arthur

Pierce. Nonetheless, Zimmerman insisted that it was her father's occupation at State A&M as an industrial arts professor that "determined the upper-class status of her family. His job in the early 1900s placed [their] family in a certain status quo. His job placed [them] in the upper echelon in Orangeburg."[2]

The husband's occupation or income was not necessarily the determining factor in maintaining an upper-class position or enhancing status. A woman's occupation or respectable background could also bring greater prestige or prosperity to the family. This was true especially for females who had lucrative incomes before or during marriage. For example, Marilyn Green Epps states that while growing up, her family's upper-class status stemmed from the social and economic positions of both parents. Her father, Dr. Seibels Remington Green, a graduate of Meharry Medical School in 1917, was a physician who also sold real estate in Orangeburg. This was not an uncommon practice, as "a large proportion of the [African American] physicians [were] engaged in business in addition to their professional activities." Despite his respectable profession, his income was not necessarily higher than that of his wife, Cora Ransom Green, who worked as a successful seamstress in her home. Some of Dr. Green's patients paid him cash; others gave him "chickens, vegetables, and other foodstuff" in lieu of money. Cora Green, on the other hand, earned a lucrative income which many times exceeded her husband's.[3]

Because of their education, elite African American women were usually well trained in some profession or skill. Those going on to professional schools were, most likely, from upper-class backgrounds, and their families had the resources to support their endeavors. The National Business League reported that by 1900, African American women could be found as doctors, lawyers, journalists, artists, and teachers.[4]

But, as Willard Gatewood argues, most elite African American women were "parlor ladies." The upper-class African American community's wealth resembled that of the white upper-middle class in the United States as opposed to that of the white upper-class community. Thus, while their women did not have to work to maintain their status, some still chose to work. Trained formally through their education for teaching or entrepreneurial careers in domestic science, they earned "pin money" to spend as they pleased. Even when these women attended school, they did not have to work as students, since their parents supported them financially. The few who opted to work while in college to earn extra spending money were given the more desirable campus jobs in the offices, library, or labs as student assistants.[5]

In 1880, the majority of married African American and white women were listed in the Orangeburg census as being "at home." Upper-class African American women were listed in the census as "keeping house," except for two who worked as teachers. Even though the census of 1880 shows that they were "keeping house," it was possible they were also engaged in some form of gainful employment related to their educational training. The census does not indicate this, but they easily could have worked at home, sewing or even teaching private lessons in music or education to children. Two husbands were teachers, probably either working at Claflin University or teaching in one of the rural, makeshift schools in Orangeburg County. Most were successful carpenters, either self-taught or perhaps professionally trained in the vocational curriculum at Claflin.[6]

Like curriculums at other African American colleges, Claflin's curriculum also promoted Booker T. Washington's industrial education to master a trade. Males were required to take vocational classes and females domestic science classes, such as crocheting, sewing, dressmaking, needlecraft, and cooking. Aside from other courses in literature, foreign language, theology, and so forth, some women also studied music and teacher's class/pedagogy, while a smaller number studied mechanical drawing. Generally, the required courses prepared these women for domestic ladyhood and, simultaneously, taught them trades that enabled them to earn a living. By 1890 Claflin's curriculum included sewing and dressmaking, which further broadened the student's skills and prepared them for career work before and, probably, after marriage.[7]

Most female students before the turn of the century still graduated from the two-year normal training school; only a few continued and finished college. Since most women aspired to teach, a college baccalaureate degree was not a necessity, as the terminal degree to teach was the licentiate instructione granted by the Normal Training School. Educated upper-class females, like most females, graduated largely from the Normal Training School with either teaching certificates or vocations in dressmaking, millinery, and other trades traditionally studied by females.[8]

By the turn of the century, State A&M College was now complementing Claflin in educating and serving the African American community. While Claflin always had a predominantly white administration and faculty, A&M had an African American administration, including South Carolina's first African American college president (in 1896), Thomas Miller. These well-educated, financially secure administrators were, perhaps, the most influential members of Orangeburg's African American elite and played a key role, consciously and unconsciously, in further widening the social gap that existed within the African American community.[9]

Upper-class African Americans affiliated with the two colleges consciously intensified their efforts to create a close-knit community with the haves, separating themselves socially from the have-nots. They entered into the early twentieth century, continuing to live in their own neighborhoods, to attend certain churches and schools, and to socialize among themselves. Even when the elite women were engaged in volunteer "uplift" work, which is discussed in the next section, they continued to isolate themselves from the same people in the African American community whom they sought to help. This class separatism was not unique to Orangeburg's African Americans affiliated with the colleges but was evident among the African American elite affiliated with historically African American colleges throughout the South.[10]

A more professional and educated African American upper class emerged by 1900 as more men and women gained degrees in higher education. As a result, a more constricting class evolved, rising above those artisans who did not have advanced educational degrees in their crafts. The carpenters, shoemakers, butchers, house painters, and others who previously represented Orangeburg's well-to-do community in the late nineteenth century were replaced by an educated elite.

The majority of both white and African American women from all classes were still listed as being "at home" in the Orangeburg census of

Senior girls enrolled at Claflin University, 1898. Most of the girls went on to teach or become seamstresses. From *Annual Catalogue of Claflin University and College of A&M, 1898.*

1900 and most of the African American women worked as domestics and farm laborers. The 1900 census shows upper-class women, too, were listed as being "at home." While they did not work outside the home, two were listed as being dressmakers. This indicates that others might have also been employed in their homes, even though the census still did not reflect this. Their educated husbands worked in relatively lucrative and respectable businesses as barbers, tailors, brickmasons, contractors, and merchants, or as professionals, including lawyers, physicians, and college instructors. Those businesses that served mostly or all white clientele were paid more for their services and thus enjoyed greater financial success. Most upper-class single females of varying ages were listed as being "in school" or "at home" in the census of 1900. Two females were listed as dressmakers, probably also working in the home, while two others were teachers. All, however, were employed in jobs suitable for genteel ladies.[11]

In the Orangeburg census of 1910, the number of women engaged in dressmaking or teaching, including on the college level, increased in 1910. Within the African American upper class, these jobs were considered respectable and appropriate employment for elite women. The few single upper-class females listed in the 1910 census as being employed worked as a dressmaker, registered nurse, stenographer, and teachers at both the college and preparatory school level. While other upper-class females were listed as living in these households, information as to whether they were at home, school, or somewhere else was not available.[12]

Between 1911 and 1920, upper-class female students, along with other females, continued to study courses in domestic economy at Claflin and State A&M, particularly those related to preparing them for a career. They continued to take the required women's courses in dressmaking, sewing, millinery, and fancy work. Mamie Garvin Fields attended Claflin University, graduating in 1908. She says that most females "were still learning the crafts [her] mother had learned—crocheting, tatting, and embroidery." They studied millinery, where "they learned to make straw . . . and soft [material] hats," making their own decorations of "rosettes, . . . flowers, . . . flower buds, . . . leaves, . . . fruits, . . . [and] grosgrain ribbon." In dressmaking, they learned "to draft their . . . own patterns" to make "suits, . . . dresses, . . . skirts, . . . shirtwaists, evening clothes, day clothes, and even underwear." Fields points out that it was dressmaking that "made it possible for [her] to earn money while staying at home."[13]

A small number of women between 1911 and 1940 took courses that had predominantly male enrollments, such as tailoring, agriculture, and typewriting. Margery Davies describes how the expansion of record keeping, correspondence, and office work in general led to a "demand for an expanded clerical labor force . . . and to fill the need for clerical workers, employers [now] turned to the large pool of educated female labor." While this shift from male to female low-level clerical workers excluded African Americans because of racial discrimination, Claflin and State A&M did not begin to offer clerical courses until 1907 and 1911, respectively. However, female enrollments in these courses remained lower than male enrollment, probably due to the few job opportunities available to African American females despite the feminization of clerical jobs by 1900.[14]

Both Claflin and State A&M eventually established business departments by 1928 to offer accounting, secretarial, and clerical courses. This curriculum still prepared their students for the expanding job market in business, despite the social restrictions Jim Crow segregation and racial discrimination placed on their hiring. However, by the mid-1930s at State A&M, there were more females than males enrolled in the Business Administration Department, and the increasing number of female graduates who studied clerical courses resulted in greater numbers being employed in administrative positions at African American–owned businesses and schools. State A&M's administration hired more and more women as clerks, bookkeepers, secretaries, and stenographers. Others, including the nurse, dietitian, librarian, assistant librarian, and the acting dean of home economics, worked in nonclerical administrative positions in the college in 1930.[15]

It was common for females to graduate from the teaching program at Claflin or State A&M. The early college catalogues of both schools recorded its student graduates' occupations. Whether females chose to major in business administration, education, home economics, or the sciences, they all appeared to elect teaching as their career. State A&M also specified in its catalogue the number of teachers who were also married while teaching. A few other students were listed as clerical workers, principals, and nurses. Besides teaching, the second largest group of female graduates was listed as being "married"; however, neither college indicated whether these married graduates might also have been gainfully employed while at home.[16]

Unfortunately, after 1920 no information that continually recorded female postgraduate activities is available. Some of the earlier catalogues tended to include the names along with the occupations of the graduates; however, there was no information regarding their familial backgrounds. Such data would have provided insight as to whether these female graduates came from upper-, middle-, or working-class families.

Hence, it is difficult to ascertain exactly what type of jobs upper-class women or women from any other class held once they graduated from Claflin or State A&M prior to 1940.[17]

South Carolina state law prohibited married women from teaching in the city schools, but they were permitted to teach in the county schools. In Orangeburg, when teacher Daisy Gathers married Willie White Williams, who was both a mechanical arts teacher at State A&M and owner of a blacksmith shop in the community, she gave up teaching to become a housewife until her last child was born. When she returned to teaching in the 1920s, she could not teach in the public schools—Dunton, Riverside, or Wilkinson in the city of Orangeburg. Thus, she had to travel several miles to teach in Orangeburg County. Numerous other upper-class African American women in Orangeburg, including Marian Birnie Wilkinson, Sadie Smith, Hazel Pierce, Bessie George Sulton, and Daisy Hume Sulton, graduated from college, worked a few years in outside professions, married, and then retired from their outside paid work to raise their children and run their households. These "parlor ladies" had leisure time that allowed them to venture into another form of outside work—volunteer work.[18]

A few others continued to work from within their homes as teach-

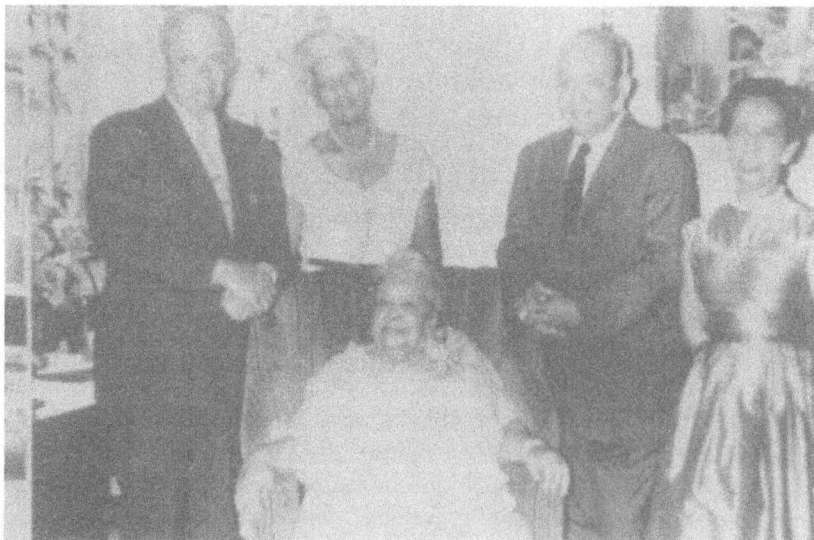

Marian Birnie Wilkinson *(seated)*, called "Mother Wilkinson," with her four grown children *(left to right):* Robert Jr., Helen, Frost, and Lula, c. mid-1960s. Courtesy of Geraldine Pierce Zimmerman.

Marian Birnie Wilkinson *(center)* continued to be involved at State A&M long after her husband, President Robert Shaw Wilkinson, died. To her left are Dr. Benjamin Mays (president of Morehouse College) and his wife, Marian Wilkinson, and to her right are her son Dr. Robert Shaw Wilkinson Jr. and his wife. Photo taken in the 1940s. Courtesy of Geraldine Pierce Zimmerman.

ers or seamstresses. For example, Hazel Pierce's daughter, Geraldine Pierce Zimmerman, taught at State A&M's primary school. She later married her college sweetheart in 1935, Dudley Malone Zimmerman, who was a school principal in another city. The childless couple eventually returned to Orangeburg in 1938 after Dudley accepted a teaching position at State A&M. As for Geraldine, once she married she wanted to continue teaching; however, she became a housewife and taught piano lessons at home, since State A&M was not in the practice of hiring married couples.[19]

Some educated, married upper-class women took on new outside employment as a direct consequence of their husbands' jobs. Elite women who commonly worked in such jobs were the wives of African American college presidents. It was these women who enjoyed, perhaps, the most elevated and prestigious social status within the community of elite African American women. Jacqueline Rouse describes the role of Lugenia Burns Hope, the wife of President John Hope at Morehouse. A "first lady" was "to be . . . a role model and mother figure for the student body of the college, . . . mother to her [own children], and a promoter and official hostess for the school as she stood by her husband in all . . . endeavors. She was to care for her home, [children], his quests, the live-in students, and the female faculty and . . . she was expected to continue and expand her social activism—though the college would be her first loyalty."[20]

It was not uncommon for these college president wives to teach at the college or its grammar school or to direct one of its programs. Mary McCrorey, the wife of President H. L. McCrorey of Johnson C. Smith in Charlotte, taught psychology, education, English, and secretarial work. Margaret Washington, wife of President Booker T. Washington of Tuskegee in Tuskegee, was the director of girl's industries and dean of women. In Orangeburg, Marian Birnie Wilkinson, wife of President Robert Shaw Wilkinson at State A&M and the mother of four children, presided over the boardinghouse for women at the college. Since her family lived on the campus, it was convenient for her to both oversee the activities of the boardinghouse and supervise her own household.[21]

Other elite African American women employed at Claflin and State A&M were given first choice for jobs at the colleges. They usually held the traditional jobs designated as women's work. At the beginning, neither college hired female administrators and faculty. By 1924, however, both had gradually hired a sizable number of females to work in low-level administrative positions as secretaries, clerks, matrons, and office assistants. As for teaching, women were usually hired to teach in the teacher training school, the preparatory school, or the grade school.[22]

At Claflin in 1919, there were six female faculty members teaching the domestic courses, one instructor in the music department, and eight teachers in the grammar school. Of the four instructors in the manual training school, none were women. By 1931, the women mainly worked in the Practice School, which trained teachers; in the Vocational Department; with the administration as nurses, matrons, clerks, and a dean of women; in the Music Department; and in the Accounting, Secretarial, and Clerical Department, later called the Business Department. By 1940, females made up half the faculty at Claflin, while at State A&M, they constituted almost one-third.[23]

At State A&M in 1918, most women worked in the Home Economics and Preparatory Departments and in the administration as clerical workers. Few were in the History, Science, and English Departments. In 1930, five out of seventeen faculty members in the Liberal Arts, Business Administration, and Music Departments were women. Only women taught in the high school and teacher training schools. There were no women instructors in the Agricultural and Mechanical Arts Departments.

By 1939, as table 2 shows, there were twenty female faculty members out of fifty-nine, most of them associate professors and instructors. Other women worked in administrative jobs, mostly lower-level positions.[24]

John Hope Franklin points out that the Depression began in the early twentieth century for southern African Americans as soil erosion, the boll weevil, and other problems created havoc in farming. By the 1920s, some elite African Americans were compelled to reenter the labor force. A few upper-class African American women in Orangeburg returned to work in order to earn supplementary income to maintain their standard of living. For example, Louisa Smith Robinson of Orangeburg recalled how her mother, Sadie Smith, superintended Claflin's cafeteria for a few years and worked briefly one summer supervising the staff responsible for feeding students enrolled in Claflin's Minister School. Maxine Sulton Crawford described how the recession in the 1920s dreadfully affected her father's successful lumber business. According to Crawford, "Mother stopped teaching around 1906, when [at age twenty-two], she married . . . father. Later, however, when the recession affected the lumber company by decreasing the demand for the labor and building [around her early forties], she returned to work around the late 1920s." Crawford pointed out that her mother "began teaching in Orangeburg County for thirty dollars a month. In 1932 [at age forty-eight], she stopped, but by 1937 [at age fifty-three], she taught again," and, finally "in 1941 [at age fifty-seven], she stopped permanently."[25]

A few upper-class married women who opted to continue to work outside the home taught in the private schools at Claflin and State A&M at the primary and secondary levels. These jobs compensated the teachers with top salaries, paying $100 a month. In the 1930s Orangeburg's public schools not only did not allow married women to teach but also paid its African American teachers around $37.50 a month, less than their white counterparts. A few upper-class women taught on the college level at either the local colleges or colleges in other cities or states. Maxine Sulton Crawford told how her older sister, Florence Sulton, taught music at Claflin University after graduating from Oberlin College. After one year, she left to teach at Tuskegee Institute in Alabama.[26]

A small number of African American women in the South decided against majors in typically female subjects, such as domestic economy, and entered the traditionally male fields of natural science and medicine. For example, Helen Wilkinson Sheffield of Orangeburg, the oldest daughter of President Wilkinson of State A&M, studied chemistry like her father. Afterward, she joined State A&M's faculty, and by 1911 was teaching chemistry in the Science Department. This was most

Table 2

State A&M Faculty Positions by Gender, 1931–40

Faculty Position	1931–32 F	1931–32 M	1932–33 F	1932–33 M	1933–34 F	1933–34 M	1936–37 F	1936–37 M	1937–38 F	1937–38 M	1938–39 F	1938–39 M	1939–40 F	1939–40 M
Professor	5	19	6	20	6	19	4	18	5	17	5	17	5	19
Associate professor	5	3	5	3	5	2	5	3	5	6	5	7	6	7
Assistant professor	0	0	1	1	1	2	2	3	2	3	5	12	3	3
Instructor	6	15	4	13	1	10	3	10	4	11	3	10	6	10

Source: Catalogue of State Agricultural and Mechanical College of South Carolina, 1931–34 and 1936–40.

Note: Data on faculty positions were not available in the catalogues of Claflin University. The 1935–36 *Catalogue of State Agricultural and Mechanical College of South Carolina* was missing from the collection.

unusual, since before 1940 most female college instructors taught in the Domestic Economy, Music, or Education Departments or in the grade schools. Perhaps her father's position as college president enabled her to join the science faculty as the only female without incident.[27]

Geraldine Pierce Zimmerman graduated from Nashville's Fisk University in 1932 with a major in mathematics. Upon her father's request, she returned home to Orangeburg to work. Unfortunately, there were no job openings to teach math on the College level at State A&M, where her father taught, and thus she accepted a teaching position at its grammar school, Felton, where she taught first grade full time and math part time to seventh and eighth graders.[28] Another student in Orangeburg, Flora Ella Fordham, received her degree from Claflin in 1900. Fordham decided not to teach, sew for a living, or become a homemaker like most of her peers. Instead, she wanted to become a nurse. She aspired to follow the footsteps of Anna deCosta Banks, who in 1893 was the first trained RN in South Carolina. Initially, Fordham's mother strongly objected to her daughter studying nursing. She "did not want her daughter alone in the room with a man," as this would be "quite unladylike." Hers was an archaic view more commonly held in the early nineteenth century, when nursing was criticized as being an improper profession for ladies because "delicate refined women" did not have the "strong arms" or "the physical strength necessary" for assisting men "to the close-stool, or supplying him with a bed pan, or adjusting the knots on a T-Bandage." The conventional view of nursing gradually changed, however, as women successfully performed nursing duties during wartime.[29]

For elite African American females who decided to enter nursing before the twentieth century, Darlene Clark Hine points out that they had no choice but to attend segregated training schools. White nursing schools did not accept African American students, so it was at Hampton Institute in 1890 that the first African American nursing school was established. Even after they earned their degrees, according to Hine, they still "encountered obstacles" because of their race, "ranging from . . . employment discrimination, . . . salary inequities, . . . and a denial of membership in major professional organizations."[30]

When Flora Fordham eventually enrolled in the Hampton Training School for Nurses in 1903 and earned her RN degree, she became "the first trained nurse to practice in Orangeburg." For years, she "was the only one doctors would call to assist [them] in home maternity cases," particularly since "there was not even a hospital in Orangeburg" until one was built on Glover Street in 1919. Fordham, dedicated to her career, "sacrificed and gave up social activities that interfered with her

(left) Hazel Tatnall Pierce, 1939. When Hazel married, she brought a sizable inheritance income to her marriage. Courtesy of Geraldine Pierce Zimmerman. (right) Geraldine Pierce Zimmerman at age twenty, 1931. Courtesy of Geraldine Pierce Zimmerman.

work. She even denied herself the normal life of marriage and children." Despite her degree in nursing and her indispensable services to physicians, racial discrimination and segregated health-care practices limited her opportunities to practice to her capacity. According to Joyce Anne Elmore, these trained nurses were unfairly limited to working in the community in private care, setting up training schools, or working in the early makeshift African American hospitals.[31]

Some married upper-class African American women in Orangeburg remained financially productive after they stopped work outside of home. Married to an instructor at State A&M, Hazel Pierce had a sizable inherited income that allowed her to help her family. In addition, she would sometimes type papers for students for a few dollars, and she eventually started a little private school of seven to eight students in her home, teaching the upper-class and upper-middle-class children of college administrators and faculty members or other African American professionals. In the early twentieth century, Orangeburg had no preschool or kindergarten that prepared African American children for Claflin's or State A&M's private schools. Thus, Pierce charged five dollars a month for each child, earning her a suitable income. Sadie Smith,

Geraldine Pierce Zimmerman in 1997, in front of the family home. She received her degree in math from Fisk University in 1932 and taught primary school at State A&M before marrying and becoming a housewife. Courtesy of Geraldine Pierce Zimmerman.

on the other hand, took in college student boarders who provided her with a consistent income while at home.[32]

Other upper-class African American women in Orangeburg continued to pursue their careers at home after marriage. When Sally Daniels married, she decided not to complete her home economics degree at State A&M; instead, she worked at home as a seamstress, sewing for wealthy white families and thereby earning substantial sums that contributed to her family's income. She also sewed for African American families, charging them less money.[33]

Cora Ransom Green, who received her normal school teacher training degree from Claflin in domestic science, worked for one year after graduation as a seamstress, visiting the homes of white upper-class women. Once married, she stopped working outside the home but still pursued a career as a first-rate seamstress in the 1920s and 1930s. Her services were actively sought by upper- and middle-class white families in Orangeburg, who usually came to her residence for fittings. She even employed an upper-class African American high school student, Maxine Sulton, whom she paid four to five dollars a week to assist her after school in tasks such as hemming, bounding button holes, and inserting zippers. Green used her money to educate her children in music and dance and to maintain the household's upper-class life-style.[34]

Even with their degrees and talents, African American upper-class women had limited employment opportunities outside the home. Racial discrimination and Jim Crow segregation continued to restrict them to certain jobs and denied them the privilege of pursuing the same jobs that white educated women held, even during the Great Depression.[35] The New Deal programs implemented in Jim Crow Orangeburg were racially segregated, as they were throughout South Carolina. Any money, provisions, or jobs given to African Americans and whites were distributed unequally, with whites beneficiaries. To fill this void in employment and further assist African Americans during the Depression, other programs were eventually set up by philanthropists and private organizations.[36]

Anna T. Jeanes, a northern philanthropist, donated money to develop the "Jeanes Program," which was "designed to change ideals, attitudes, and conducts of individuals so that the rural people will achieve a better life." The Jeanes Program hired educated women from the city to travel to homes in the county to teach rural women modern techniques to improve their childrearing and homemaking skills, such as proper disciplinary measures for children, healthier food preservation, or preventative medical care. Jeanes teachers also helped service and improve the various African American schools in rural Orangeburg. When Cora Green's children were of school age, she worked as the first Jeanes teacher in South Carolina, and during the summer months, she ambitiously pursued a master of arts degree in home economics at Fisk University.[37]

Upper-class African American families in the early twentieth century usually had between two and four children. While a majority of upper-class mothers did not work outside the home, those who did held jobs considered appropriate for genteel women, never working as domestics, cooks, or farmhands. Except for the Depression years, when some elite women sought outside work to help sustain their households, these women did not work outside the home. On the other hand, they were usually financially secure and had the choice of working or not working. Between 1880 and 1940, those who worked were often instructors or administrators, initially at one of the two colleges and later in the public schools. Others worked as dressmakers, milliners, or private teachers. Their earnings were basically their private money, which they used to improve their homes, provide their children with music and dance lessons, and pay for other leisure activities for the family.

Unpaid Work

African American women had been involved in some form of volunteer "racial uplift" work since slavery. They had formed mutual-aid societies, aided fugitive slaves, or worked to enhance the inferior social conditions of free African Americans living in both the South and North. Linda Perkins argues that these early charitable organizations were primarily organized for survival and self-improvement, not for self-serving purposes, as with some of the organizations founded by white women. Even when upper-class African Americans in the early twentieth century were criticized as being "a self-serving elite," on the whole, they were still more "socially and racially conscious of their obligations to the masses" as compared to the white upper class and their obligations to the white masses. The church was also the center of many activities and the magnet that pulled African American women together to improve conditions in their communities. Aside from benevolent societies and the church, education played a major role in racial uplift work. Linda Perkins, Paula Giddings, and Cynthia Neverdon-Morton all show how African American women's education was not merely for self-improvement and self-gratification. Even though this sentiment did exist among upper-class African Americans, it was more a tool used to fix the terrible conditions their people experienced.[38]

In the late nineteenth century, upper-class African American women in Orangeburg did volunteer work outside their homes, usually raising money to furnish clothing and food for the needy through their churches or through various events organized by Claflin or State A&M. Before the emergence of organized club work, they worked actively in the church through their various missionary societies. Through Trinity Methodist Episcopal Church in particular, which was affiliated with Claflin University, the elite women helped form various missionary societies between 1866 and 1900, reaching out into the community. Little information can be found today that recounts the full extent of these societies' activities, but bits and pieces of information describe the Women's Foreign Missionary Society as financing missionary work in Africa, the Women's Home Missionary Society as making certain the gospel was spread in Orangeburg County among African Americans, and the various ladies' aid societies as providing assistance to those in need.[39]

Upper-class African American women in the early twentieth century also continued their work in Trinity Methodist Episcopal Church in Orangeburg, but their work was now complemented by other elite women's work from St. Paul's Episcopal and St. Luke's Presbyterian Churches. Not all their church work was directed toward social uplift, however, for they also busied themselves with improving the church itself, especially in rebuilding.[40]

Emilie Sasportas Bythewood was active in raising money to build a church building for St. Paul's Episcopal Church. The early church was housed in State A&M's Young Men's Christian Association (YMCA) building, constructed on State A&M's campus shortly after 1896, when the college first opened. Daisy Hume Sulton was an active member of one of the ladies' aid societies at Trinity Methodist Episcopal Church, the Women's Society of Christian Service. She hosted numerous "oyster suppers" between September and January in her stately home on Russell Street to raise money to build a new church building. She "basically did all the cooking with the help of her cook, Miss Alma McPherson. Church members would come and enjoy oyster suppers at [her] home. All the money raised would go to the church." Sulton "just viewed . . . the oyster and other food goods . . . used as a donation to the church."[41]

Like Daisy Sulton and other upper-class women at Trinity Methodist Episcopal Church, Sadie Smith was busy constantly, baking goods and cooking chickens to sell so the church could raise money. According to Louisa Smith Robinson, women raised the money and were the "financial backbone" of Trinity, while the men's contribution came through the actual physical building of the church. Daisy Gathers Williams broke with the upper-class tradition of belonging to the Methodist, Episcopal, or Presbyterian church and instead was an active member of the Treadwell Street Church of God and the president of the women's missionary society. She frequently visited the sick, made aprons, baked bread from yeast, and made quilts to help raise money for the church. Elite church women held programs, raised money to help the church, and continued to do missionary work through their various church societies in Orangeburg. They were instrumental in feeding the homeless and making the church more sensitive to the needs of African American people.[42]

According to Paula Giddings, by the early 1890s there were already many African American women's clubs throughout the United States concerned with race and gender issues. Cynthia Neverdon-Morton points out that these self-help clubs, societies, and organizations formed by African American women were created "to improve the general condition of [their] homes, schools, and communities." The organizations operated in a nonsupportive, racist society that showed little or no concern for the survival of the African American community. By 1896, these various clubs had united under the National Association of Colored Women (NACW), which "concentrated on reformatories, old folk's homes, social settlements, nurseries, working girls' homes, study of civics, needlecrafts and domestic science, [and] development of social uplift work." Because African Americans were denied the benefits of the various government- or privately owned white social organizations set up to help local citizens, the NACW functioned as a surrogate social welfare system. It "focused on community development, established orphanages, homes for the elderly, schools, [and] supported religious programs."[43]

Some elite, educated activists formed the National Association of College Women, which "sought to improve higher educational opportunities for [African American] women and thus prepare them for leadership." They decided to "focus on improving the facilities, faculties, and curricula of [African American] colleges." The organization had 122 members, with "3 Ph.Ds, scores of women with master's degrees and numerous Phi Beta Kappa's." It challenged African American colleges to evaluate the status of females to that of men on their campuses, sending a questionnaire in 1924 to the schools to see if female "students, faculty, and administrators" had the same "opportunities for promotion [or growth] . . . as . . . men."[44]

The National Association of College Women also expressed concern about the restrictions placed on female students at these schools. In discussing the early development of African American colleges in South Carolina, Earnest Lander Jr. described how "the rules of conduct in the

[African American] colleges were similar to those imposed upon students in white institutions." Claflin and State A&M also had rules regarding gender relations, mobility on and off campus, and dress codes.[45]

Claflin University stated in its 1872 catalogues that "ladies and gentlemen . . . will not be permitted to visit or walk together without special permission." It also prohibited nonresident students from living off campus in 1885, and in 1888 its rules stated strongly that "girls will not be allowed to room in town, under any circumstances, unless they are in the care of their parents, guardians, or immediate relatives." There also was to be "no socializing between the sexes; no dancing; no dance parties, nor card playing." Regarding dress in 1922, the regulations stated that "to dress in silks, [or] loud colors is not to be well dressed. Simplicity, neatness, and proprietary in dress are encouraged." On the other hand, "slovenliness, carelessness, and a lack of taste [were] as objectionable as loud, gaudy, and expensive dressing. Both extremes [were] to be avoided." The school further declared that "an overdressed child may become selfish and snobbish."[46]

Claflin, in fact, had established "a clothing committee . . . made up of the Art teacher, the Domestic Arts teacher, . . . the Preceptress, and two senior girls," who were to assist girls in making "decisions concerning dress and to help them with their clothing problems." Students were advised "to consult with this committee before purchasing their clothing." In general, to be "dressed beyond one's means" or to wear "loud colors" was not considered "well-dressed." Upon request, specific information was sent to entering females "regarding the wardrobe."[47]

State A&M's rules regarding females were also detailed and restrictive. In 1911, "no young woman [was] permitted to leave the grounds of the College unless accompanied by the matron or a lady teacher." Even when attending church, they were to be accompanied "by a professor or instructor of the college." As for "communication in any form with the opposite sex," it was "prohibited." By 1918, restrictions were also placed on visiting habits: "Girls who come from places near Orangeburg, but who board in the dormitory, will not be permitted to go home continually. Parents of such students will please not make request in violation of the rule. Girls boarding in the dormitory, having relatives and friends residing in Orangeburg, will not be permitted to visit them often."[48] In 1931, the college's catalogue informed its students that "girls in all departments residing beyond the limits of Orangeburg County [were] required, at the discretion of the President, to live in the college dormitories and board on the campus."[49]

At State A&M in 1911, both males and females had to wear uniforms. In 1918, the girls' uniform consisted "of a middy blouse suit of navy blue serge or of some white material, such as poplin or canvas." The school advised that it "need not be of an expensive nature, for it [was] intended to encourage economy, . . . and take the place of the usual varied wardrobe." State A&M's rules for women's outer wear in 1926 stated, "The coats of the young women shall be suited to the individual taste of the wearer with the regulation that they be not of bright and conspicuous hue, but of conservative color. The 'sport' coats of flashing color are disapproved; the more conservative browns, blues, grays, and blacks are suggested instead. The hat shall be conservative in keeping with the coat or suit, and filled to the appearance of the wearer."[50]

Perhaps these clothing rules were a serious attempt to downplay the class differences of the entering female students, particularly since State A&M began focusing only on the dress of first- and second-year students. However, the college was actually shaping the ideas of both the students and their parents on how to dress according to conservative middle-class standards. Stating that its purpose was "to promote economy and avoid distinction and embarrassments that [arose] from different conditions," the college required female students, excluding juniors and seniors, "to wear a uniform dress, consisting of a navy blue skirt and white middy, dimity or natural color pongee blouse, or blue coat suit." It further stated that "only white or navy blue sweaters" were permitted, as "slip covers [were] not . . . allowed." The students were required to wear uniforms during class hours, even while off campus. On campus, they were "permitted to do laundry or dormitory work in wash dresses," but afterward had to "appear at all meals and on the campus in uniform." The uniform in 1931 was a "tailored skirt (blue), tie (black or blue) a tailored blouse (white), low heel, black or brown shoes." They were to wear it "when traveling to and from home" as well. By 1937, there was no mention of a dress code in the State A&M catalog, as the college now distributed a "copy of regulations . . . to each student's room to inform both parents and students."[51]

Concerning such rules and regulations at African American colleges, the National Association of College Women's leader, Lucy Diggs Slowe, dean of women at Howard University, was quite outspoken and most critical, arguing that the rules were "archaic, degrading, and insulting." Colleges should prepare women to be leaders, she declared, but "when a college woman cannot be trusted to go shopping without a chaperon, she [was] not likely to develop powers of leadership."[52]

There is no record as to whether any elite women of Orangeburg were members of the National Association of College Women. Nor was there evidence of this organization's impact, major or minor, on African American women's roles at Claflin or State A&M. However, Slowe continued "her crusade to win [African American] women equality and respect on [African American] campuses." She posited that African American colleges, "created [a] delayed infancy among women students. She found that [African American] women received little in courses, activities, or role models that prepared them for leadership and noted that most women were almost pushed into the field of education, . . . were absent from the policymaking bodies of these colleges, despite the existence of a small yet growing cadre of well-trained [African American] women who were willing to make a contribution to [African American] higher education." Despite the odds against these Orangeburg female students, they became active and formed their own exclusive clubs on campus, such as the Alpha Kappa Alpha Sorority in 1908 and the Delta Sigma Theta Sorority in 1913, through which elite African American female students were able to contribute to their community.[53]

Margaret Washington of Tuskegee Institute, Lizzie Jenkins of Hampton Institute, Lugenia Hope of Morehouse College, and other elite African American women saw educated females as having "special responsibilities to the race." Lucy Laney urged women to carry their skills to the community to help "develop better hygiene habits, . . . aid those who were imprisoned, . . . help rid prejudice," and teach young children. She encouraged these graduates to become "public lecturers" and "give advice and directions for others" by teaching Sunday school or developing "neighborhood classes for the purpose of instructing others on how to sew and cook."[54]

Elite African American women in South Carolina also "found time to render services to those less fortunate than they, . . . giving freely of their incomes to further the causes they supported." In 1909, a chapter of the National Association of Colored Women was formed in Columbia, South Carolina, at the Sidney Park Church and was called the South Carolina Federation of Colored Women's Clubs (SCFCWC). It was under the leadership of Orangeburg's Marian Birnie Wilkinson, along with a few other chartered members from Orangeburg, including Celia D. Saxon and Lizella A. Jenkins Moorer. Its objectives concentrated on "culture, education, good character, and the improvement of human relationships." Members saw themselves as "lifting up the fallen." Their main purpose was to help others, following the NACW's motto, "Lifting as We Climb." Throughout the state, branches of the NACW sprang up, addressing the unique needs and interests of each specific locality.[55]

Jacqueline Rouse points out that "legal segregation and Jim Crowism" partly forced these women "to begin building their own socioeconomic foundations," usually via "churches, benevolent and fraternal societies, schools and universities, and neighborhood businesses." In South Carolina, for example, due to the absence of husbands and sons during World War I, many African American families' economic conditions worsened, particularly since the salaries and benefits received by African American soldiers were low and unequal to those received by white soldiers. Through fund raising and donations, the clubs developed a social welfare system that provided food, clothing, and other basics to help the financially less fortunate.[56]

Upper-class African American women, especially those "in prestigious positions, often did not merely enjoy the perquisites of their positions but instead sought to use them to influence change in their communities." The wives of presidents at the early African American colleges were, in particular, very active clubwomen and dedicated their free time to improving the African American community. In Orangeburg, Marian Birnie Wilkinson, State A&M's first lady, was not only a chartered member and first president of the SCFCWC but also the "third president of the National Federation," the NACW. According to Edmund L. Drago, Wilkinson "had a productive history of helping the less fortunate, beginning from her younger days in Charleston." She was an active member of the Red Cross and "during World War I, she organized recreation centers for [African American] soldiers at Fort Jackson, South Carolina." Furthermore, "the Hoover administration sought her counsel on a child welfare program."[57]

In Orangeburg, she continued her social uplift work, including dedicating a substantial amount of time to improving the conditions of children, especially females. Under her leadership the state's branch of the NACW decided to help the growing numbers of young orphan girls who were becoming more exposed to World War I military personnel in South Carolina by establishing a home for them called the Fairwold School near the capital city of Columbia. Etta Butler Rowe, the second president of the SCFCWC and a "much-beloved teacher" at State A&M recalled the history of funding for the Fairwold School. She stated that the SCFCWC

> raised $30,000 with which to begin its work. An old farm house located near . . . Fairwold, S.C., was secured, and . . . the protection of colored girls in [the] state [began]. . . . As the war moved on . . . the organization [needed] . . . funds, appealed to the Legislature for help. The sum of $2000 was given annually [and] the women work[ed] hard to provide the large supplement. . . . Delinquency among [the] girls ran high—[they were] grabbed on all occasions for small and great offenses, lodged in jails, etc. Then the terrible thing happened—The powers that be, . . .

so losing faith in the [African American] girl, the appropriation was
withdrawn in 1929, the excuse being that no [African American] girl
was worth saving. . . . [Now], the support and maintenance of the Home
[fell] directly on the shoulders of the [Federation].[58]

During the Great Depression, the funding and maintaining of social
institutions specifically designed for African Americans was not a major priority for state and local governments, reflecting the racial prejudices of the era. It was not unusual for funding for such facilities to be
eliminated first, so money was raised by the federated clubs, "interested
persons, churches, and organizations" in order to maintain the home.
On one occasion, "while on his bed of affliction, a few weeks before [his
death]," Dr. R. S. Wilkinson, Marian Wilkinson's husband, "ordered
that [the food and coal for Fairwold] be sent . . . immediately from his
personal funds." When the home was destroyed by fire and the girls left
homeless, the initiative and hard work of Marian Wilkinson resulted in
the Episcopal Parish House in Columbia housing the girls temporarily
and then offering them the use of some church property near Cayce,
South Carolina, on which to build a new home. Under the heroic leadership of Wilkinson, the state's clubwomen busied themselves with rais-

Members of the Sunlight Club in Orangeburg, c. mid-1960s. From *Fiftieth Anniversary. South Carolina Federation of Colored Women's Clubs.*

The Sunlight Club Community Center. The club, which successfully served the African American community in Orangeburg, was the first of its kind in the state to have its own center. From *Fiftieth Anniversary. South Carolina Federation of Colored Women's Clubs.*

ing money by appealing to the South Carolina African American ministers for money to rebuild Fairwold.[59]

The physical labor needed to build the new home was donated by State A&M. The SCFCWC decided to turn the new home into a girls' orphanage and received its funding annually from the southern-based philanthropic Duke Foundation. The new home, renamed the Marian B. Wilkinson Home for Girls, inspired African American clubwomen in other southern states to pursue similar goals, as seen with the formation of the Virginia Home for Delinquent Negro Girls.[60]

Marian Wilkinson also helped organize the Sunlight Club on "June 29, 1909 at Trinity Methodist Church," where they planned programs to help feed and clothe needy African Americans. By 1928, the Sunlight Club had thirty-five active members, generally composed of upper-class women mixed with some upper-middle-class women. Despite its benevolent acts and philanthropic philosophy, the Sunlight Club was an elitist organization, selective in its membership even though it professed an open-door membership policy. Generally, membership consisted of the upper-class chartered members, while the daughters of members belonged to the Marian B. Wilkinson Club, a junior service club that also helped the financially less fortunate.[61]

Also in Orangeburg in 1928, Marian Wilkinson managed to get the first YWCA building constructed on an African American college, where she served as the chief YWCA advisor. Even though the YWCA was a national organization engaged in interracial affairs, white and African American members worked separately in their racially segregated structures. Finally, in the 1930s Wilkinson helped set up a Works Progress Administration (WPA) training school and day nursery under the auspices of the New Deal.[62]

Meeting in each other's homes, these women actively "furnished food for the sick and needy, made sheets, and donated supplies to the 'old folks' homes." The Sunlight Club earned a reputation as one of the main organizations, other than the churches, that helped African Americans in Orangeburg. In fact, the Sunlight was "the only club in the state that [had] the distinction of owning a club house." Cecelia Daniels Fleming recalled how the Sunlight Club raised money successfully by having its members' children travel around South Carolina to perform plays and recitals. The club also had booths for various things, including a doll contest, at both the local white and African American fairs.[63]

The Sunlight Club donated a substantial amount of money annually to help support the Fairwold School for orphaned girls since racial discrimination prevented state and county funds from being used to support the institution. Also, since the state and county provided very few funds toward the building and support of the segregated African American schools, these clubwomen took it upon themselves to fill the void. Focusing on rural Orangeburg, where there were fewer schools for African Americans, the Sunlight Club raised money to build the Rosenwald School in the Great Branch area of the county. Julius Rosenwald of Sears and Roebuck, a white, northern philanthropist and staunch supporter of southern African American education, matched the funds raised by the Sunlight Club to fulfill this goal. A school, which later became a community center, was built. The club also developed an employment "help directory" for both males and females. One of its advertisements in the local newspaper read "Help Wanted: The names and addresses of colored women, girls, men, boys, who are seeking employment. The Sunlight Club."[64]

White clubwomen also noticed the impoverished community or the "Negro problem," since they were concerned it would gradually impact whites adversely. In 1938, a member of the Dixie Club appealed to Orangeburg's white women through a newspaper article, calling on them to help improve conditions in the African American community, since this indirectly affected the white child's welfare:[65]

> If you have not done so, permit me to suggest that you ask your husband to drive you through the communities called "Quicktown," "Black Bottom," "Sunnyside," and some other not so well or euphemistically named, but where conditions are almost identical. But you say, "What is this to me? These are negro suburbs." If you have any such idea, permit me to say that you are entirely mistaken. No longer than yesterday, I drove through one of those so-called negro settlements in the city of Orangeburg and saw white and negro children playing together on the same front porch. . . . "If you will only take the time to investigate for yourself, I believe you can in one afternoon convince yourself that housing conditions in these outlying suburbs of Orangeburg must be improved or your child or mine will suffer. You must lift them in self-defense."[66]

Whether any white women's group responded to this plea is not known. But this type of paternalistic attitude toward the African American community was not uncommon during the Jim Crow era, as many saw this community as inferior and its people incapable of taking care of themselves properly and living decently.

Throughout the New Deal era, South Carolina continued its racially discriminative practice of distributing unequal amounts of funds to segregated white and African American programs. However, the Sunlight Club benefited from the assistance of the WPA when it successfully opened and managed a government-supported community center to serve the African American community. The center was one of several government agencies that had set up a youth program that followed the guidelines set by the New Deal's National Youth Agency. The city of Orangeburg provided "the rent for the building and repairs were made by students from State [A&M] and Dunton Memorial, while various supplies were generously furnished by numerous business concerns and individuals in Orangeburg. The work at this center was to provide worthwhile instruction in various fields [and] . . . office recreation and training, both for juveniles and adults."[67]

Besides the Marian B. Wilkinson Club, the Sunlight Club, and the campus sororities, there were a few other women's clubs on the college campuses involved with service-oriented work. The YWCA in 1928 at State A&M functioned as an organization that extended a cordial welcome to its new students. The Criteria Club not only promoted "the spirit of higher education, created and developed good fellowship, and encouraged the enrichment in character education" but also made monetary donations "in the way of material for the beautification of the buildings and grounds" of its campus.[68]

Racial uplift work was seen as the *naturalis opus* of upper-class and well-educated African American women in Orangeburg. It was believed that these elite women, by virtue of their greater privileges and opportunities, were prepared to lead their people, especially other women. The criticisms of upper-class activists as being a "self-serving elite" was justified, as some in Orangeburg did "assume . . . a paternalistic, even patronizing attitude toward the less fortunate of their race,"[69] but whether or not they were snobbish, they all contributed to the social uplift of the Orangeburg African American community.

3.

Upper-Class Women's Work inside the Home

In general, work inside the home was "housework": cleaning, washing, ironing, cooking, and caring for children. Whether family members or hired servants performed these tasks depended mainly on the family's class position. In the antebellum years, upper-class white women's work inside the home had largely been a matter of supervising their slaves or servants. These genteel women did not spend their lives lazing under a magnolia tree, sipping on a cool glass of lemonade; on the contrary, sometimes they were engaged in rather heavy work.[1]

Like wealthy white women, elite African American women, realizing that "the cult of domesticity . . . was a distinct and important social vocation," employed household servants, purchased modern commodities, and busied themselves with their club work.[2] During the antebellum era, their life-style was similar to that of their white counterparts. In her study of free women of color in rural Georgia, Adele Logan Alexander describes how Susan Hunt, a light-skinned free woman of African American and Cherokee heritage, operated more as the "southern lady" or "plantation mistress" at Pomegranate Hall in rural Georgia rather than as a mere house servant for the wealthy white Judge Nathan Sayre. She oversaw "the panoply of domestic functions," including "everything from providing food and clothing for the entire household to caring for both the physical and spiritual well-being of her own family as well as that of Sayre's slaves. Supervising the work of the domestic servants—household maintenance, cooking, cleaning, and laundering at the least . . . Susan routinely . . . negotiated with trades people, gardened, smoked meat, preserved fresh fruits and vegetables, nursed the sick, mended, and made candles, soap, and household linens."[3]

The role of upper-class white women changed substantially in the postbellum years. Although still responsible for managing and supervising the domestic sphere, they no longer engaged in heavy work, and, when they did perform modest tasks, they were assisted by their domestics. No longer working supervisors, they were ladies of charm and leisure.[4] Like white upper-class women, postbellum elite African American women also managed their households and usually hired more than one servant to assist with housekeeping. They organized social functions in their homes, including parties, receptions, and other events. Down South, these elite African American women employed African American domestics; up North, their counterparts complained that either they could not secure African American servants or those they could hire did not show the proper deference. Thus, like women of the white upper class, northern elite African American women hired Scandinavian and German female immigrants.[5] Having white servants most likely added to their social status and gave them greater prestige in the larger African American community during an era when most African American women worked as domestics for white households.

Between 1880 and 1910, some upper-class African American married women in Orangeburg chose to work outside the home, but most did not (see table 3). The luxury of having household servants, of owning modern household commodities, and of having the time to pursue social and cultural activities was also a reality for these women. Marian Birnie Wilkinson of Orangeburg, one of the busiest African American women in South Carolina, was generally unavailable to perform the many household tasks needed to maintain a family. It was especially important that the home of State A&M's president remain orderly, clean, and comfortable, since it too, like the Atlanta home of Lugenia Hope, wife of the president of Morehouse College, was a "guest house" for visitors. In Orangeburg, there were no African American hotels and Jim Crow laws prevented African Americans from staying at the local white-owned St. Joseph Hotel on Russell Street. Thus, the Wilkinson home also served as surrogate hotel for select quests associated with the college.[6]

Lacking the advantages of having an extended family in Orangeburg, Marian Wilkinson hired an older African American woman, Aunt Jane, to cook breakfast and dinner (or "lunch") and work as nursemaid, with full responsibility for disciplining the children. In addition, a Miss Steel was hired to assist with the cooking and minor washing and ironing, but most

Table 3

Upper-Class Married African American Women's Occupations in Orangeburg, 1880–1910

Occupation	1880	1900	1910
At home	32	25	24
Teacher (college)	0	0	2
Teacher (other)	2	0	2
Dress maker	0	2	6
Trained nurse	0	0	1
Beauty culturist	0	0	1
Total	34	27	36

Source: Bureau of the Census, *Census of 1880 on Population. Orangeburg Town, Census of 1900 on Population. Orangeburg City,* and *Census of 1910 on Population. Orangeburg City.* *Note:* The total number of African American households in Orangeburg for 1880 was 266; for 1900, 535; and for 1910, 708.

of the washing and ironing was done by a washerwoman or the campus laundry.[7] Supper, the last meal of the day and the lightest one, was usually prepared either by the children or by Marian Birnie Wilkinson herself. The children's chores included setting the table, doing some minor washing and ironing of their personal clothing, driving the car to do family errands, and bringing in firewood or "coal gates." Marian Wilkinson did little or no housework. Her husband, Robert, did none, with the exception of "winding the several clocks throughout the home, especially when the boyfriends were at the house too long."[8]

Marian Wilkinson hired college students to clean rooms and drive the buggy (later, the car) to transport family members or run errands. According to her daughter, Lula Love Wilkinson, her primary reason for hiring these students was to help them earn extra money to pay for their schooling. While some elite women were snobbish and promoted blatant social divisions between their family members and servants, Wilkinson taught her children that they "were not better than anyone else. When college students did chores in the house, [she] dared the children to refer to them as servants."[9]

Wilkinson was not the only college president's wife to employ student labor. Lugenia Hope also ran her household "with assistance from family members, hired help, and student workers. Students from Spelman and Atlanta Baptist [later called Morehouse] colleges were assigned to work in the president's house." One male student arrived at 5:45 each morning, awakening the family. Interestingly, his duties included the traditional female tasks of dusting and sweeping the house. Lugenia's husband's nephew was responsible for making the bread, while her own children, including the sons, had the task of dishwashing.[10] Unlike Marian Wilkinson's husband, Lugenia Hope's husband, John, Sr., "contribute[d] . . . to the kitchen detail . . . sporadic[ally]."[11]

Cora Ransom Green taught for one year in the Normal Training School at Claflin until she married Seibels Remington Green, a physician, in 1917. She became a successful seamstress, working from a separate sewing room in her home, and was the mother of three children, an active community civic worker, and a member of the women's "bridge" card social club. Like the Wilkinsons, the Greens also had no extended family ties in Orangeburg to lend support. Thus, Cora Green's household African American staff included a washerwoman, a cook, a nursemaid, and a cleaning lady up until 1932.[12]

The washerwoman worked in the Green's back yard, except during the winter months, when she worked at her home. She usually came to wash once or twice weekly on a Monday and Wednesday and was paid meager wages, especially during the Great Depression. Dr. Green made the lye soap necessary for washing both the household goods and his medical office supplies. After washing, the washerwoman hung the items up to dry and then ironed them, using an iron heated "atop the cook stove."[13] The Greens' cook was usually a married woman herself, with children at home. She stayed all day, from 7:30 A.M. to 3:00 P.M., having dinner ready by 1:00 P.M. She did not shop for groceries because Cora Green did the shopping and Dr. Green often received food in lieu of cash for medical services. The cleaning lady came twice a week to do the heavier cleaning and scrubbing. She also cleaned the indoor toilet once it was installed, but prior to that the outdoor toilet was cleaned by a special wagon that serviced select residential areas.[14]

The live-in nursemaid, or "nanny," traveled with the Green family whenever they moved. She was usually a single young woman from rural Orangeburg who received pay and free room and board. Her primary task was to take care of the children, since the parents were generally gone during the day. She, in fact, was like an older sister. As the children grew, the need for a nursemaid declined as the Greens' eldest child began to take on greater responsibility. With Dr. Green constantly making house calls and Cora Green either busy with sewing or attending meetings, the house servants generally spent more time with the children than their parents did. On holidays and Sundays, Cora Green canned food and cooked for herself.[15]

Judy Rollins, in her study of domestics and their employers, points out how white women displayed their superior class status through maternalistic attitudes, giving their servants "second-hand items that were not expected to be returned but, instead, received with expressed gratitude." African Americans such as Cora Green also provided their servants with castaway clothing and a "servant pan" or "tote pan" of leftover food for their family. Furthermore, the Greens demonstrated their commitment to their upper-class status by "providing all their servants with separate eating facilities." This elitist attitude regarding dining separately was definitely held by southern white employers. One southern woman stated that "whether the servant was black or white, employers and servants did not dine together. . . . The president in the White House is served by blacks and whites, and he doesn't have them come and sit down at the table. They're there in the capacity to serve."[16]

Some upper-class African American homemakers in the 1920s and 1930s participated in the housework, even though they had domestic help. Bessie George Sulton continued to help cook and do some of the light housecleaning. She had a live-in nursemaid to take care of the children, to do some cooking, and to clean. Like a second mother, this middle-aged woman also disciplined the children when necessary. Later, a younger maid, between the age of fourteen and fifteen, was hired to cook and clean. Beginning work at 8:00 A.M., she first washed the breakfast dishes and then prepared dinner. While dinner was cooking, she would clean the house and finish all her work by 2:00 P.M.[17] Bessie Sulton also prepared the light daily supper while her daughters made beds, dusted, or cleaned the silverware. The boys were responsible for bringing in the firewood and doing the yard work. In 1914, the Sulton house was one of the few in Orangeburg to have both electricity and indoor plumbing, including running water and toilets, making some tasks less difficult.[18]

At the Sulton home on Mondays, the housekeeper washed clothes in the bathroom during the winter months. In the summer, sometimes Bessie George Sulton herself, with the help of her children, washed clothes in the back yard in tin tubs. Tuesdays were reserved for ironing, for which there was an electric iron, while Fridays and Saturdays were for general housecleaning. Aside from helping with domestic chores, Bessie Sulton still worked actively in the Sunlight Club and with Trinity Methodist Episcopal Church's women's societies.[19]

Bessie George Sulton was active in the Sunlight Club, a service organization serving the African American community in Orangeburg, and assisted her servants with domestic chores. Here she is pictured in the 1960s with her husband, McDuffie. Courtesy of the Sulton Family.

Her sister-in-law, Daisy Hume Sulton, on the other hand, enjoyed doing her own cooking. Once or twice a week a young housekeeper performed light duties, such as sweeping, dusting, changing linens, and occasional cooking, and on certain days, she did the heavier work, such as cleaning the woodwork and windows. At one point, when Sulton's health was poor, the housekeeper came in daily to do all the cooking and cleaning. Otherwise, Daisy enjoyed cooking and canning food for both her family and the church.[20]

Like Daisy Sulton, Sadie Fordham Smith also preferred to do her own cooking. Unlike Marian Wilkinson, with her organizational duties, and Cora Green, with her sewing career, Daisy Sulton and Sadie Smith lived less hectic lives. Like Sulton, Smith had more time to pursue cooking and fund raising. She baked goods and sent them to people in need, such as the sick or elderly. She grew a successful vegetable garden, canned and preserved food in the summer, cooked for her family, raised chickens, and tended to her flower garden. She even exhibited her canned goods at the Orangeburg County Fair.[21]

Smith always employed an African American domestic, who washed, ironed, and did the general housekeeping that she did not do herself. At one point, Smith even recruited a WPA worker who had been doing "hoe work" to clean for her. Even though her husband gave her an allowance during the Depression, she not only took in boarders but also cooked and sold dinners daily to couples or transit people to earn extra money.[22]

It was not unusual for upper-class African American children to be given light chores in the home. Carmen Sulton Thomasson remembers how in 1928 at age five she stood on a bench to wash dishes. She also would help make beds and clean the bathroom sink, the bathtub, and the commode. She described how she "had brushes . . . [and] would boil a kettle filled with water and then put a little soap powder in the toilet." Then she "would pour the hot water in the commode or warm water in the winter since during those days, there were no cleaners or toiletries to put in the toilet for cleaning." She earned an allowance of $1.50 weekly for these chores. During the Depression, she recalls that her father, a successful lumber businessman, instilled in his children the need to work in order to earn money for an allowance.[23]

When her eight children were younger, Daisy Williams had an African American washerwoman come once a week to do the laundry. She also had a day houseboy who not only helped in her husband's blacksmith shop but also would do light household chores. As the children grew older, they were given chores, replacing the help of the servants. When Daisy Williams returned to teaching, the older children attended school while the younger ones went out to a babysitter.[24] Sallie Daniels, too, hired a washerwoman to come once a week when her four children were small. Even then, the children would assist in bringing in the dry clothes from the clothesline. At one point, Daniels's poor health necessitated that the washerwoman do some of the cooking. As the children aged, they were taught other chores, such as washing dishes, sweeping, washing clothes, and even cooking.[25]

Daniels's husband generally did the grocery shopping and performed household repairs with the help of the boys. Sally canned the vegetables grown in the garden and worked as a seamstress for both African American and white families. As she sewed on her machine, she would train the children "to cook by having them bring food to the sewing machine for her to taste." Cecelia Daniels Fleming recalled how her mother washed her own clothes in the back yard:[26] "Mom trained the girls in how to wash clothes. She would use a scrub board, a black boiling pot, three tin tubs, and octagon or lye soap that was usually given to her. She would first wash the clothes in the tub to get the general dirt out, then she would let them sit in a second tub to soak until the water was very hot in the black pot to disinfect them and purify them, using soap. Afterward, she would put the clothes into three separate rinse tubs, using some bluing liquid in the first rinse. She had a wash shed with tubs in it."[27]

Hazel Pierce, on the other hand, did all of the cleaning and housework herself, despite her active participation in the Sunlight Club and the private preschool she held in her home for the children of the elite. Like Sally Daniels, she also had a wash shed set up in her back yard; fortunately, she had a pump on the back porch that made preparations somewhat easier. She reserved Mondays for washing, placing her clothes on the line to dry before dinner at 12:30. On the same day, she sent her husband's shirt collars to the laundry for cleaning while she washed his shirts. She ironed on Tuesdays, "using the cookstove to heat the iron before she had electricity." Fridays and Saturdays were her general cleaning days, including any light yard work not done by her husband. Like many elite women, she was not burdened with grocery shopping but instead wrote the grocery list and gave it to her husband, who shopped for the household. Usually, he gave her twenty-five dollars a month "to run the house."[28]

Pierce's three children, including Geraldine Pierce Zimmerman, were given light household chores to do on the weekends. They attended Claflin's grammar school Tuesday through Saturday; there were no classes held on Mondays, since the Methodist-oriented Claflin restricted its students from studying on the holy day, Sunday. Thus, Pierce wanted her children to focus solely on their school work during the weekdays. On Saturdays after school, their chores included helping in the kitchen and with the yard work. According to Zimmerman, her brother was chiefly responsible for "killing the chicken every Saturday for Sunday's dinner," while her assignment was the much-hated task of "dressing the chicken," or plucking out the feathers and cleaning the bird inside.[29]

Even though upper-class African American households could afford outside servant help to free wives and daughters from housework, some elite women opted to do their own housework. Perhaps a certain work ethic their parents had instilled in them as children led them to do some, if not most, of their own work. Even if they did not do any housework, they were still far from being idle, as they actively pursued their careers or worked zealously in clubs or in church work. Whether they did housework depended on how committed they were to their personal careers or volunteer work. Those who were more active usually hired servants; women with children, on the other hand, generally remained closer to home, performing many of the tasks themselves and sometimes training their children to do them.

Elite African American women were very conscious of their upper-class status in the larger Orangeburg African American community. Although their life-style resembled that of the white middle class more than that of the white upper class, they consistently strove to maintain their attractive homes and employed servants to assist them in this task. While some had paying jobs working inside or outside the home, their earnings were not necessary to maintain the household. They had time to groom their children in the arts, busy themselves with civic club work "to uplift the race," and entertain themselves through their proper social clubs.

Part II.
The Ebony In-Betweens:
The Middle Class

4.

Middle-Class African Americans

Middle-class African Americans in Orangeburg, although larger in number, had much in common with upper-class African Americans. The middle class also lived comfortable lives. In preparing their children for their stations in life, they stressed schooling and the arts, often providing music and dance lessons. Education and cultural refinement thus further distanced the middle class from the larger working class. Because of their greater wealth, the white middle class as a whole was more financially stable than the African American middle class. In addition, whites benefited from the various social and economic opportunities denied African Americans. Characteristically, the white middle class lived more comfortably than the African American middle class and were among the first, after the white upper class, to enjoy modern conveniences.[1]

The African American middle class emerged from an earlier well-to-do Reconstruction African American community. Members of this class were well off compared to the majority of African Americans and "exhibit[ed] considerable race pride" as they "strove to be respectable." While many sought an even higher class status or greater financial security through education, professions, and businesses, few managed to enter the close-knit upper class, as they did not meet certain social criteria, frequently including a respectable family history. Their middle-class status was usually the result of jobs held by both husband and wife. At times, a husband's or wife's job determined the family's class position, especially if one or the other had attained a degree in higher education and as a result entered a well-paid profession.[2]

The middle class could be divided into the upper middle class and the lower middle class. The upper middle class was more financially secure and identified and associated more intimately with upper-class African Americans, consciously separating themselves from the larger middle class. They were generally better educated and worked as teachers, ministers, or clerics. The majority of middle-class African Americans, however, belonged to the lower middle class and struggled to maintain their status despite their meager standards of living.

Members of the lower middle class held the traditional service jobs that the majority of African Americans performed—janitor, nursemaid, cook, maid—but they had different employers: white establishments, public institutions, and influential, upper-class whites. Their jobs generally paid more, had better perquisites (such as a larger quantity of leftover food or better quality castaway clothing), and were even considered more prestigious since they were associated with upper-class white society, successful white-operated businesses, or coveted public service jobs in the courthouse or post office.[3]

Conscious of itself as a class, the African American middle-class community struggled endlessly to differentiate itself from the larger, impoverished working class. Its members sought to identify or associate with those in the upper class, either socially or culturally, in order to enhance their own social standing in the community. E. Franklin Frazier argues that the middle class, like the elite, perceived themselves as superior to the masses.[4] As "a sign of [this] superior social status" in the larger African American community, some families took pride in showing that their women did not have to work outside the home. Mamie Garvin Fields of Charleston recalled the reaction of some white women to a beautiful white dress crocheted by her mother and trimmed with yellow ribbons: "The white people stopped her [mother] in the street to ask where she got [the dress]; they thought maybe she was a laundress and stole it from some white women." In Fields's recollection of the incident, she responded by saying, "A laundress? Never! After being married to George Washington Garvin, mother didn't have to work. Although he didn't have much money, my father put it down: she would be a housewife; his wife would 'never' go out to work for white people."[5]

Education was very important among the African American middle class. Their children's graduation from a Normal Training School program or a college qualified them for reputable jobs that would further sustain their middle-class social status. These families worked hard to save money for their children's education, especially before the emergence of public schools. Because middle-class parents had to pay for both primary and secondary education, there was sometimes such financial hardship on the family that children were not able to attend school all at one time. For example, Mamie Garvin Fields recalled how she had to sit out school for one year since her parents had "two children already in high school . . . [and] didn't have the money for [her]." Thus her mother, for the first time, traveled to the North "to work in a white woman's house" in New York and New Jersey for the summer to earn money. Pauli Murray of Baltimore, on the other hand, lived in poverty, as she depended on donations from various family members, charity clothing from her college, and working on whatever type jobs she could find to finance her education at Hunter College.[6]

Middle-class African Americans lived in comfortable houses, usually nicer than those of the majority of African Americans. However, most in the middle class still could not afford amenities such as indoor plumbing, electricity, or telephone services. It is important to note that within the middle class there were some who enjoyed greater comfort and wealth than the majority: members of the upper-middle-class. They were mostly affiliated with African American colleges and earned sizable salaries, or were hardworking and skilled in relatively profitable trades. Upper-middle-class families generally resided in neighborhoods near the colleges, where the early African American well-to-do communities were established.

When Mamie Garvin and Robert Fields, a newlywed upper-middle-class couple, left Charleston, South Carolina, for Charlotte, North Carolina, where Robert accepted a well-paying bricklayer job, Mamie did not have to work. Her husband surprised her with a new "little cottage" he built himself in the nicest neighborhood, "[by] the campus of Johnson C. Smith University." According to Fields, her "perfect honeymoon house . . . was lovely from the outside. Set back from the street, . . . [it] had a good-sized yard in front and a planted path leading up to the door, which was between two windows with flower boxes. Very romantic, like a picture out of a magazine. A dream house." This couple opted to join the Methodist church over the "upper crust" Presbyterian church and the "lively" Holiness church. They were able to afford health care, as they chose a college-trained physician over the traditional midwife. They lost their first baby due to hiring an inexperienced doctor, but they still had the choice to seek better health care, while those in the lower middle class or working class had no choice but to hire a midwife. When the couple returned to Charleston, they were among the first to purchase a Model T Ford in the city.[7]

As discussed previously, South Carolina's constitution of 1895 enforced the customary Jim Crow laws, which segregated public, residen-

A middle-class home on Treadwell Street, 1997.

tial, and job facilities. Hence, African Americans' social and economic options remained limited.[8] In Orangeburg, the founding of Claflin University and, later, State A&M provided African Americans with new experiences and training that allowed them to advance within their own communities. However, this exacerbated any existing social divisions within this early financially secure community, as some vigorously pursued an education, which further enhanced their status and alienated them from their class of origin. Largely due to higher education, the Reconstruction well-to-do community gradually diverged into two distinct classes—the previously discussed upper class which was more financially secure and well educated by 1880, and the middle class. Orangeburg's middle class then further divided into the upper middle class and the lower middle class.[9]

Overall, in 1880, the middle class had increased in numbers but was not yet an economically strong, viable class. The lower middle class, in particular, had not severed all ties to the working class and was, more or less, a small but growing group that resembled a stable upper working or artisan class whose members did not generally have professional training. Like the upper class, the middle class was restricted from reaching its full potential in the larger Orangeburg community

Homes of the middle class on Treadwell Street, 1997.

due to racial discrimination and segregation. Its advanced class position shone only within the African American community.[10]

In the early twentieth century, a degree from Claflin or State A&M
and employment in a well-regarded job with a suitable income were criteria for belonging to the middle class. Other social factors, including
residential area, social club affiliation, middle-class background, and
church affiliation, further defined or enhanced middle-class status.
Overall, the middle class was less affluent than the upper class, as
middle-class families had to rely on the incomes of two adults to sustain their life-style. There were some in the middle class who had
sufficient money to be associated with the upper class but lacked the
appropriate cultural refinement and the prestige that came from belonging to an old family of notable political history or free ancestry.[11]

Education played a major role in determining class in Orangeburg's
African American community. For members of the middle class, education varied; some had very little, others held higher degrees. The
middle class grew as more working-class African Americans graduated
from college and worked as skilled professionals—teachers, dressmakers, carpenters, and barbers. But because of Jim Crow restrictions, they
served only the African American community instead of the all-white

community that some members of the African American upper class serviced. Middle-class African Americans lacking higher education usually held semiskilled or entrepreneurial jobs, such as hotel waiter, farmer, restaurant keeper, midwife, or shingle maker.[12]

Orangeburg's African American middle class was not a homogeneous one. Differences in wealth, education, and family origin and history created significant social divisions. The financially comfortable upper middle class, usually more educated and skilled, were more successful at emulating and identifying with Orangeburg's upper-class elite. The less financially secure lower middle class, however, the bulk of Orangeburg's middle class, were not as successful. Although skin complexion was not as obvious a distinguishing mark among the middle class as it was among Orangeburg's elite, a sizable number of light- and brown-skinned middle-class African Americans consciously socialized and identified with similar-looking upper-class African Americans.[13] The social achievements, heritage, and economic comforts of this upper middle class placed them in a higher category and gave them a more prestigious social status in the community as compared to the lower middle class, but these advantages still did not qualify them for upper-class status.

Overall, African Americans of the upper middle class, like those of the

A middle-class home on Treadwell Street, 1997.

upper class, sought to wed spouses of similar or higher class standing. This did not mean, however, that educated middle-class women did not marry men with less education, as in the case with the upper-middle-class Mamie Fields of Charleston, who married a man who stopped his bricklayer training in eighth grade in order to work to support his mother after his father had died. Besides being particular about whom they married, the upper middle class was also conscious of which church they attended or where they lived. In Orangeburg, the upper middle class usually attended the Episcopal, Methodist, or Presbyterian church. They resided with their families in attractive, comfortable homes, usually in neighborhoods near the colleges, where the more affluent African American families lived, on Treadwell Street or the Goff Avenue Extension. While the homes of the upper middle class were not as large as those of the upper class, they usually had the amenities associated with middle-class households, including indoor plumbing, electricity, modern appliances, and attractive yards.[14]

Upper-middle-class African American children dressed well and attended the primary and secondary schools at the colleges. Some parents also managed to allow them to study music or dance to acquire a taste of upper-class culture. More important, parents placed a high value on the education of their children. However, unlike their peers in the upper class, most upper-middle-class women had to work to earn money to help pay tuition for their sons and daughters to attend the Normal Training School or college program at Claflin or State A&M.[15]

The majority of middle-class African Americans in Orangeburg belonged to the lower middle class and usually came from agricultural or working-class families. As children, they attended Sterling, the original African American public school in town, and, afterward, other public schools, including Riverside, Dunton, and Wilkinson. For those who attended the private schools at the local colleges, both they and their parents worked diligently to raise the money for decent clothes and school fees by doing seasonal jobs such as picking cotton or harvesting crops.[16] These lower-middle-class children were not as well dressed as upper-middle-class children, and their parents could not afford to educate them in the arts.

Lower-middle-class African Americans in Orangeburg were either skilled or semiskilled, less sophisticated than the upper middle class, and lacked the cultural refinement found among upper-class African Americans. Conscious of their higher class position in relation to the working class, they were zealous, however, in their efforts to sustain their precarious middle-class status. The more stable middle-class families usually were more skilled and had either graduated from college or attended college but did not complete the program due to economic reasons. Those trained in the Normal Training School were prepared for teaching careers, which gave them the opportunity for upward mobility. Those who did not have any higher education were entrepreneurs—operating restaurants, farms, beauty salons—or were midwives. When they were successful, they in turn placed a high value on the education of their offspring, managing to send at least one child to college.[17]

Skilled or semiskilled, lower-middle-class African Americans dreaded the notion of regressing to their previous economically deprived backgrounds. Unfortunately, their proudly earned ministerial or teaching degrees or their skilled manual jobs provided them with incomes insufficient to sustain their middle-class life-style with ease, especially since they sometimes contributed financially to needy relatives. Unlike their peers in the upper middle class, those in the lower middle class did not generally marry spouses of similar class standing or with prestigious jobs. For example, Georgia Swett of Orangeburg had working-class origins but was educated and worked as a teacher, placing her in the lower middle class. She married a man also from working class origins but with little education who eventually took a factory job in New York City that paid quite well.[18] Even with her education and respectable teaching job, his tenuous factory job and their close ties to the working class disqualified them for upper-middle-class status. Compared to upper- and upper-middle-class African Americans, those in the lower middle class were more likely to marry someone from the working class.

Members of the lower middle class normally attended the Methodist or Baptist church. Their families were not usually concentrated in any particular residential area in Orangeburg as were those from the upper middle class. A few families of the lower middle class were scattered in the more respectable African American communities along Treadwell Street or the Goff Avenue Extension, where some Methodist ministers with their families lived due to their direct or indirect association with the Methodist college, Claflin. Most, however, lived along the fringes of these nicer areas, while some occupied the nicer houses found "on the other side of the tracks" in the poorer African American communities. Their homes varied in size and lacked ostentation. Their humble dwellings had fewer rooms but did have a separate living room, usually a nice flowered yard, and crude indoor plumbing and electrical fixtures once they were able to afford such amenities.[19]

Middle-class African Americans lived between two different socioeconomic groups. They attempted to mirror the atypical life-styles of the more elite African Americans, yet they did not ignore their less fortunate neighbors and relatives in the working class. The lower middle class still inter-married, attended church, and socialized and lived with those who belonged to this economically depressed class.

The Middle-Class Female

Middle-class white families, like aristocratic white families, believed that women had a special role in society, that of "ideal mothers" who were "efficient caretaker[s] in relations [*sic*] to children and the home." They believed that the "true woman" was "emotional, dependent, and gentle—a born follower." Whenever these women ventured into the public sphere or were in the private sphere, they were expected to behave properly as ladies. The education of middle-class white females in the various "ladies courses" in domestic economy further imbued them with the idea of domestic femininity and trained them to become skilled wives and mothers.[20]

Accepting domestic femininity as the proper role of middle-class females, both African American men and women believed that once married, their "wives [should] stay home" and "train the children" while their husbands supported them. These African American middle-class housewives were to maintain clean, orderly homes, get involved in civic work in the community and church, be "champion[s] in cooking," and, when they went out in public, even to visit a neighbor next door, to conduct themselves like ladies and dress properly. Mamie Fields reflects her middle-class upbringing as she posits that a lady was "never to go out anywhere in [her] apron." She added that "[if] you see [an African American] woman in the street wearing an apron, that says something. If she has her hair rolled up or house slippers on, then that says something too. 'Keep those things in the house' was the point." As a young girl growing up in Charleston, these rules were constantly emphasized and clearly demonstrated her family's middle-class consciousness, self-perceptions, and how they wished to be perceived by others in the community.[21]

To be a housewife and not have to work was a status symbol in the African American community in the late nineteenth and early twentieth centuries. Sharon Harley argues that it was a reality that really could not materialize, since middle-class African American men were not afforded the same economic opportunities as white middle-class men to support their wives. Thus, Harley argues, half of these married women were gainfully employed as compared to one-fourth of white middle-class women. Because of economic necessity, middle-class men were not in a position to oppose their wives' employment, even though some did. On the other hand, some African American females were taught "to prioritize . . . finding a career, an occupation," over entering into a "foolish marriage through the lack of occupation."[22]

Education was equally important among middle-class African Americans, whose social status was often a result of acquiring higher education. The educational opportunities for middle-class African American girls, however, were not equivalent to those of white middle-class girls, as they could not attend the same private schools and thus had to rely on attending the few schools available to them. Before the introduction of public schools, middle-class African American females were educated by private classes held in upper-class or upper-middle-class homes or in the church, where the minister or his wife served as the teacher.

Because the early private schools charged fees, the financial stability of upper-middle-class families allowed them to take greater advantage of this early education. Once African American colleges were established, their schools commonly included fee-paying primary and secondary schools. Since few high schools for African Americans existed in the early twentieth century South, it was not uncommon for middle-class females to leave home to attend these college-operated high schools, boarding on its campuses. As in middle-class white families, raising the necessary school fees created a financial hardship on both upper- and lower-middle-class African American households, frequently resulting in the mother and daughter working extra jobs, including domestic work.[23]

The young middle-class girls who went away to school either boarded on the college campus or were given permission by the college to stay in the community with relatives or friends of the family. Mamie Fields left Charleston in 1905 to attend Claflin's high school. Fields lived off campus with a few other female students attending Claflin and State A&M at a boarding house operated by some of her relatives, "the Abrams Middletons." They "all . . . had certain duties before they left in the morning." Getting up early, they "made the beds, swept the rooms, and drew water from the square-top well outside." At school, they "were escorted by a matron or an upperclassman" when they went into town to shop or for church.[24]

Most students chose to attend Trinity Methodist Church across the street from Claflin University. Each morning on campus, female and male students went to chapel, for attendance was compulsory. For fun, they went for long walks or held Friday night socials. Following the standards set for middle-class white culture, dancing was not permitted, but they were permitted to march in "single file and make figures, everybody turning left or right, taking a step back or sideways, according to the leader." Other females joined the various clubs on campus, which included a sewing group, the college choir, and the Friends of Africa. Fields remembered that when she moved on campus to live in the dormitory, "the campus routine was strict. Rising at 5 A.M. each morning, they had to wash at the pitcher and washstands in [their] rooms, clean up the rooms, dress, stand for inspection by the matron, report for the morning devotions at the chapel, and then go to breakfast." After each main meal, their matron escorted them to the outdoor bathrooms. At night in their candlelit dormitory without plumbing, they all bathed at the same time in their own rooms, after carrying the heated water and bathing tin tubs upstairs to their rooms.[25]

Education greatly enhanced the growth of Orangeburg's African American middle class. Middle-class females pursued teaching degrees, as increasing numbers continued to graduate from both the preparatory school and the college. The majority studied the mandatory women's courses in music, sewing, dress making, and domestic economy. In 1918, while male enrollment declined at Claflin and State A&M, probably due to men either joining the military or taking advantage of wartime jobs in the North, female enrollment remained the same. In the 1920s, middle-class female students continued to study the conventional female courses. Whether they chose to teach or to become homemakers or entrepreneurs, these traditional courses prepared them for their occupations.[26]

5.

Middle-Class Women's Work
outside the Home

In her book *Women and the American Experience,* Nancy Woloch examined the frustration many white women who graduated before 1900 eventually experienced. Some of these women saw themselves as being in "limbo" or at a "dead end" once they graduated, since all they had to look forward to was marriage and life as a housewife. They confronted extreme gender discrimination, which excluded them from many jobs in the labor market, because the larger society deemed the home women's proper sphere. Finding appropriate jobs became problematic for these white, college-educated women, particularly before 1900, when "more than 75 percent" of them opted to remain single and seek employment. They eventually found jobs as office workers, teachers, nurses, librarians, lawyers, and entrepreneurs. While most married middle-class white women did not work outside the home before 1940, the Great Depression of the 1930s forced many to seek temporary or part-time outside work.[1]

Middle-class African American women's reasons for seeking higher education were different from those of middle-class white women. For them, education was not a liberating achievement that freed them from marriage and housewifery but a means of escaping the drudgery of domestic work. African American women experienced both gender and racial discrimination in the labor force: even when qualified, when they possessed the required training and skills, they were not hired. It was only during various crises such as World War I and the Great Depression that they were finally able to work—as bookkeepers, stenographers, and so on—in places that historically had hired only white women.[2]

Paid Work

According to Orangeburg's 1880 census, the majority of that town's middle-class African American women stayed home and kept house, although they most likely were engaged in some form of gainful employment at home. The few who worked outside the home were domestic servants and washerwomen. Most single African American females lived at home, and less than one-third were in school. The jobs held by middle-class men ranged from farmers and firemen (tending fires at white-owned saw mills) to the more skilled bricklayers and house carpenters. A few worked as well diggers, tinners, railroad mail workers, porters, or hostlers for white businesses or wealthy white families. Although non-agricultural jobs were considered good, reputable positions, their paucity enabled only a minority of men to take advantage of them.[3]

In late-nineteenth-century Orangeburg the earliest professional group of middle-class African American women working outside the home were teachers, the majority of them graduating from the Normal Training School teaching program at Claflin University. Like upper-class African American females, they too studied the traditional female subjects and taught in the town of Orangeburg, in rural Orangeburg, or elsewhere in South Carolina.[4]

The middle class had now bloomed into a distinct group sharply differentiated from the nineteenth-century middle class and the impecunious working class. Vocational skills, gained either through higher education or less formal training, were crucial in setting this class apart from the larger, unskilled working class. By 1900, the majority of middle-class women in Orangeburg's census were still listed as being "at home." Most who worked outside the home were washerwomen and were most likely lower-middle-class women. Perhaps lower-middle-class women gravitated toward this work because of the limited employment opportunities afforded educated or skilled women in Jim Crow Orangeburg. Even though this was hard, back-breaking labor, it gave them greater control over their work hours, allowed them to employ family members or friends if needed, and provided them with greater input when selecting their employers. These middle-class washerwomen usually sought families to wash for, but on occasion families pursued reputable washerwomen to hire, thus providing the women with a certain authority, allowing them to accept or reject a potential job.[5]

A number of lower-middle-class women worked as cooks in private homes, as house servants, or as farm laborers while their spouses held higher status jobs. Although only a few women worked as dress makers and midwives, these nondomestic and non-agricultural jobs reflected a gradual change in the type of employment African American middle-class women began to pursue. Even though some of these jobs became available, racial discrimination prevented African American women from having the same access to these jobs as white women. Thus, when certain jobs became available in the city, they were reserved for white women of lesser or equal training. A South Carolina law of 1915 prohibited interracial workplaces, and businesses in Orangeburg adhered to these Jim Crow restrictions.[6]

There were limited teaching opportunities in the city of Orangeburg once public schools were built for both whites and African Americans. As in Charleston, teaching positions were held by single white and African American females; thus as most middle-class, single African American females from Orangeburg graduated, they had little choice but to relocate in search of respectable jobs, since the few available to African American women were usually offered to upper- or upper-middle-class women first.[7]

The majority of middle-class, single African American females were listed in the census as being either in school or at home. The few who worked outside the home were teachers, dress makers, or domestics. Those working as domestics were most likely from the lower middle class. As for middle-class females enrolled at Claflin or State A&M, most were in the Normal Training School pursuing teaching careers. There were, however, a few middle-class women employed in the more prestigious teaching and lower administrative positions at Claflin.[8]

Like middle-class white women, middle-class African American women also faced gender discrimination in the labor force. According to Sharon Harley, who examined African American women employed in Washington, D.C., in the late nineteenth and early twentieth centuries, it was African American men who initially held the top-level clerical positions in the city. As increasing numbers of trained white women entered the labor force, however, various factors, including racial discrimination, led to their gradually replacing African American men in clerical positions. Harley argues that in D.C., sex-segregated jobs seemed "to have been widely accepted," reflecting African American attitudes favoring the "traditional sex-roles." Educated upper- and middle-class women who worked were expected to hold the traditional female jobs, not compete for positions normally held by men. It was men who became "dentists, embalmers, . . . tailors, post mail carriers, . . . or ministers." While many men and women argued that "women made better elementary school teachers," the debate as to whether married teachers should continue to teach or quit to become homemakers persisted.[9]

It appears that in African American middle-class households in Orangeburg there was little tension between husbands and wives regarding the wife working outside the home. Even in the case of Mamie Garvin Fields of Charleston, who had trained to be a teacher but did not have to work once she married in 1914, there appeared to have been little or no problem with her working outside the home. During the economically depressed time in 1923, when there was very little work for bricklayers in Charleston and her husband had become temporarily unemployed, she still did not have to seek a job. After living in Charleston, Charlotte, and New York City, the Fields returned to settle in the Charleston area in 1924, where they both began to substitute teach in town for three years. Once the Rosenwald Foundation and Jeanes Program started to build more African American schools in Charleston County, Mamie Fields received her first teaching assignment, and her husband was thrilled and supportive. As in Washington, D.C., and other cities, Fields was confronted with both racial and gender discrimination, for she had no choice but to work in Charleston County, since only "maiden ladies," usually white, were permitted to teach in town.[10]

Other middle-class African American women in Orangeburg were employed as dress makers and seamstresses, working for both white and African American families. Unlike elite African American women, a few upper-middle-class women in South Carolina worked as domestics, not usually for whites down South but for those living up North. In the North, white employers paid more and were assumed to be free of degrading southern "rebel" attitudes and other prejudice when relating to their African American domestics. The few upper-middle-class African American women who took such menial jobs in the North did so temporarily, until they had raised the money they wanted. While on these jobs, these upper-middle-class women seemed to display less tolerance for degrading treatment from northern white employers. In the case of Charleston's Rebecca Garvin, she refused to be submissive before her white employers when she worked in New Jersey one summer to earn money for high school fees for her daughters.[11]

During the summer, other middle-class females, especially Orangeburg's college students, worked to earn money for school fees in the few factory jobs reserved for African American women in the North. While middle-class white female college students were usually able to find respectable jobs that were relevant to their training, African American female students worked at servant jobs reserved only for African Americans. They were generally overqualified for these jobs, as they worked as chambermaids, nursemaids, and factory laborers.[12]

Some middle-class African American women worked outside the home before and after marriage, while others stopped work once they married. It was common for upper-middle-class women to teach while single and to withdraw from work once they married. Felecia Sasportas Bythewood taught in Orangeburg County after graduating from Claflin in 1898. When she married in 1905, she stopped work to become a homemaker. Another Claflin graduate, Ella Govan Middleton, taught at Sterling School and in Orangeburg County at different times when she was single. Like Bythewood, she retired from teaching once she married.[13]

Before 1910, there were upper-middle-class women who continued to work once married. Others stopped work once married but then returned, usually because of some form of financial hardship or some unexpected circumstance. Janie Walker Harrington, a graduate from Claflin's Normal Training School program, became a homemaker once married, but after her husband's untimely death, she returned to teaching.[14] It was typical for lower-middle-class African American women to work outside the home before and after marriage; they seldom withdrew from the workplace once married. Even while pregnant, and during their childbearing and breast-feeding years, many lower-middle-class women continued to work. Once the baby was born, they still engaged in some form of gainful employment, often taking in washing and ironing until the midwife felt it appropriate for them to return to work.[15]

Women who worked as domestics or farm laborers were from the lower middle class. During the first decade of the twentieth century, Sheldonia Wilmington Brown, married to a minister who pastored at his own church, worked for years for two white families on separate occasions, cooking and cleaning. Such work was not genteel and was considered unthinkable for upper-middle-class African American women.[16]

A significant number of lower-middle-class women were quite skilled before 1940, despite their lack of professional or educational training. Midwifery, practiced by southern African American women since slavery, was a respectable occupation in the African American community. It was not the most lucrative occupation in Orangeburg, but it conferred a respectable status. Millie Jamison Felder, married to a shingle maker, learned midwifery as a teenager from her former slave mother. She delivered many babies, both African American and white, sometimes with the assistance of a doctor if complications occurred. Felder's daughter, Ella Felder Wilson, explains her mother's routine of delivering babies:[17] "When a woman started showing, [my] mother would check on them once or twice a month. She would give information on what to eat, their weight, and the type of grease to use on their skin. When it was time to deliver, she washed the mother up and delivered the baby. After three days, she turned the birth license into the state. For nine days afterward, she checked the mother for fever or infection. If there were any complications, she would then call the doctor."[18]

Felder earned thirty dollars per baby for the "hard work" of delivering the babies and for the after care of both mother and baby, since the women were bedridden for about ten days after giving birth. those who could not pay money paid Felder with "chickens, hog meat, or with things out of the garden." Later, in her career as a midwife, Ella Felder Wilson points out that at some point her mother did go to Columbia, South Carolina, to obtain a license in midwifery. Aside from midwifery, she also cooked at Baptist College in Orangeburg, an all-white female school. She served the students breakfast promptly at 7 A.M., and their dinner at 12:30 in the afternoon.[19]

Around April and May, Felder picked strawberries and, afterward, cotton each year. Her shingle maker husband also did yard work and other odd jobs for a prominent white lawyer, supporting the family with his income along with hers. She generally used her earnings "for clothes, house things, and for taking over when his money was short."[20] Using their money for household expenses, however, was common among both African American and white middle-class women who were generally employed.

Orangeburg's African American middle class, now firmly established, increased from 53 households in 1880 to 143 in 1910. African American men in this class either had domestic or agricultural jobs working on the college campuses or were skilled or semiskilled artisans, working as harness makers, barbers, tailors, builders, or merchants. The more financially successful upper-middle-class artisans, businessmen, or professionals continued to work for both African American and white customers or only white customers. The pay for work as a waiter or cook in white-owned business establishments, as a janitor in a white-owned public facility, as a maintenance man at the courthouse, a laborer in a public office, or a farmer or fireman in charge of the furnace at one of the colleges was considered good at this time. Such positions enabled their families to enjoy a relatively comfortable lower-middle-class life.

Lucy Pearson Simmons's father earned four hundred dollars monthly in the 1930s, working as the maintenance man at Orangeburg's courthouse. His salary enabled him to provide a middle-class life for his family and to send his children to college.[21]

The work of middle-class African American women in 1910 ranged from homemaking to domestic work to farm labor. Some women's middle-class status resulted directly from their husband's occupations, particularly those who were in the lower middle class. Some lower-class women continued to work as cooks or house servants for private families, but their peers in the upper middle class continued to perceive such work as degrading. Furthermore, there was no evidence to show that Orangeburg's upper-middle-class women ever worked as domestics in the North for white families, even temporarily, as in the case with Mamie Garvin Fields and her mother, Rebecca, from Charleston.[22]

Lower-middle-class women working as domestics usually attributed their middle-class status to the more prestigious or well-paying jobs held by their spouses, who worked as clergymen, house painters, or domestics in respectable white establishments. In turn, lower-middle-class men who worked as day laborers, sooty fireman feeding black coals into hot, burning furnaces, or domestics for private families had a middle-class status due to their wives' respectable or profitable jobs as dress makers or teachers.[23]

The number of African American dress makers increased in 1910. Perhaps as the demand for dress making increased, more women pursued this course of study in school in order to prepare themselves for a career as opposed to marriage and homemaking. About this time, the number of female students studying sewing and dress making at Claflin and State A&M also rose.[24] Dress making, after all, was a desirable alternative to domestic labor. It was work that was both available to African American females and an acceptable, genteel profession for middle-class single or married females. Dress making was done in the privacy of the home and permitted upper-middle-class and middle-class women to fulfill the traditional role in the domestic sphere by simultaneously caring for their children and the home. More important, it permitted middle-class women whose incomes were indispensable to the family to earn money while staying at home.

In Orangeburg, middle-class families attempted to educate their daughters and train them in some career so that they would escape the drudgery of domestic work. A growing number of young middle-class women pursued college degrees beyond the Normal Training School program for teachers. By 1910, most middle-class, single African

American females in Orangeburg worked as teachers, most likely in rural Orangeburg. This is not surprising, since like other African American colleges in the South, the curricula of Claflin and State A&M "included academic [liberal arts] subjects . . . [and a] large dose . . . of industrial arts courses, particularly homemaking [for women] and an environment that enforced codes of morality and thrift." When State A&M combined its domestic economy courses into a distinct Home Economics Department, this further prepared these young women for respectable jobs, especially teaching, since African American women were expected "to teach in order to uplift the masses."[25]

It was not unusual for middle-class college students to work while enrolled in school. Some began working while they were students in the primary schools. These young students who worked came from the lower middle class and had to work not only to help their parents pay for their books, clothing, and school fees but also to help support their families. Unlike upper-middle-class female students, lower-middle-class female students generally performed domestic tasks to earn money.

Ella Felder Wilson had to work to make weekly contributions to her family's lower-middle-class household when she attended State A&M's grade school. She walked every day to the white female school, Baptist College, to pick up the soiled cloth napkins the students used at mealtime. Each day she returned a clean, ironed, neatly folded pile of napkins and left by hauling off another heavy bag of soiled ones to prepare for the next day. She gave her weekly earnings of twenty-five to thirty cents to her mother, who in turn gave Ella a few cents for spending change. The exploitation of young Felder was reflected in the meager pay she received for performing this time-consuming and heavy labor. Non-exploitative job opportunities were few for African American girls, and because their financial contributions to the family were so important, they had little choice but to accept menial, low-paying jobs.[26]

While in high school, Lucy Pearson Simmons worked several jobs to earn money for her schooling and to assist her family. She worked at a local white-owned floral shop, cleaning up and arranging the flowers, for $2.00 weekly. She also earned $5.50 weekly by cleaning the apartment four days a week for an African American couple who taught at State A&M. Aside from these two jobs, she washed and ironed blouses and dresses for various African American school teachers.[27]

Another young girl, Marian Gregg, attended Claflin's elementary school. Since school started in mid- to late September, she spent August working as a fieldhand on white-owned cotton and peanut plantations: "Dr. Dixon would pick up a load of people on either Sunday night or early, early Monday morning. We would stay on his farm until Friday afternoon. We went to the cotton field early in the morning and picked cotton until noon. Then, his wife, Mrs. Dixon, would fix our dinner. Afterwards, we would pick peanuts from her peanut patch. In the evening, they would boil some peanuts in the big wash pot for everyone to eat and we would play 'hide 'n go seek' while the peanuts cooked." Cotton worms frequently stung the pickers but did not deter them, as they felt the pain was worth the "good" money they earned. Each person had a sack and, aside from free meals, was paid one dollar for every one hundred pounds of cotton picked. According to Gregg, she usually picked 110 to 150 pounds daily and gave everything she earned to her mother.[28]

Some lower-middle-class female students from rural Orangeburg County boarded with relatives or friends of the family in the city of Orangeburg so that they could attend grammar school. Two young girls, Georgia Waymer Swett and Anna Mitchell Colter, moved to Orangeburg in the 1920s to attend Dunton and Sterling Schools, respectively. While both girls' families "sent food up from the country" and the necessary money for additional food and boarding fees, they both had to do household chores such as sweeping the porch, mopping the kitchen, and helping with the general cleaning as a part of their boarding fee.[29]

During the summer, both Swett and Colter returned to their respective rural homes to work on the farm, hoeing and picking cotton. Aside from her schoolwork at Sterling and her household chores at the boarding home, Anna Colter also worked to earn money to help support herself. At 9 A.M. every Saturday, she worked for an African American professor at State A&M and his wife, washing their breakfast dishes, scrubbing the kitchen, sweeping, and dusting.[30]

Most middle-class female students worked while in high school or college. The lighter administrative jobs were generally held for upper-middle-class female students. In 1926, one such student, Edith Wilson Vaughn, was enrolled in State A&M's high school and lived on campus. Her parents paid her tuition, but she worked in the campus bookstore, earning ten dollars a month. Upon graduation, she enrolled in the college, continued her job in the bookstore, and earned twelve dollars a month for her personal spending money. Another student, Bernie Bryant Middleton, worked correcting papers for an English instructor during her four years at Claflin in the late 1930s. When Claflin experienced serious cash-flow problems as a result of the Depression, the college paid Middleton by waiving her tuition fee.[31]

Only a few lower-middle-class students held the more desired administrative jobs. Most performed menial tasks in the dormitories, laundry rooms, or the dining rooms on the two colleges. At Claflin University in 1930, Janie Harrington Pearson was responsible for setting up the tables in the dining room and, afterward, cleaning them. She also washed and ironed shirts for her brothers who were also in college as well as caring for her own clothes.[32]

One of the more fortunate lower-middle-class women who escaped such domestic tasks was Susie Alexander Hubbard, the daughter of a rural farmer and homemaker. The summer before entering State A&M in the late 1930s, she worked in Orangeburg County as a mangle operator in a laundry room, ironing linen. Once in college, a friend of the family, who also happened to be a trustee at the college, made certain that Hubbard found employment on campus. During her first year, she was assigned to work in the newly formed college YWCA program in the Y-Hut Building, operating the canteen that sold sandwiches and snacks in the evening. By her senior year, she was the student director of all the Y-Hut activities.[33]

Mamie Williams Alexander (shown here in the 1950s), a homemaker and farmwife, helped save money to send her daughter, Susie Alexander Hubbard, to Orangeburg to attend State A&M. Courtesy of Susie Alexander Hubbard.

Mamie Williams Alexander in her Sunday clothing, c. mid-1950s. Courtesy of Susie Alexander Hubbard.

Some middle-class students worked part time while in college but not in campus-affiliated jobs. Such students generally lived off campus with their families, guardians, or relatives and earned money from washing and ironing for individuals or families in the community. Lucy Pearson Simmons, for example, worked part time, washing and ironing blouses for twenty-five cents and dresses for fifty cents.[34]

From the 1870s to 1932, Claflin and State A&M enforced rigid rules regarding the mobility of its female students living on the campus. Thus because their contact with the larger community was limited, they were prevented from freely pursuing part-time work in town. A few middle-class girls were fortunate to receive scholarships and did not have to work. Others accordingly relied on their colleges for jobs. As mentioned earlier, the colleges' faculty and staff frequently hired male and female students for part-time or temporary domestic work. Felicia Sasportas Bythewood and Marian B. Wilkinson consistently employed students to work at their homes at odd tasks, enabling them to raise money for their school expenses.[35]

Anna Colter, a student who boarded in Orangeburg beginning with her grammar school years at State A&M, always worked part time as a domestic to earn money. While attending the State A&M normal school, she stopped work since her mother had relocated to Orangeburg and now received a government pension check. After two years, she stopped attending State A&M altogether in order to enroll in the Judy Breland Beauty School. There she worked her way through school, earning twenty-five cents a day after the school hired her to do the general cleaning, maintain the records on the hair customers, and open and close the shop daily.[36]

Students who lived off campus continued to work part time, washing and ironing clothes or serving as nursemaids. They worked for both African American and white families, but as middle-class women, seldom did they commit to doing this type of work full time in Orangeburg during their summer vacation. If so, they strove to work for wealthy white families whose homes increased their knowledge of middle-class life, initiating them into the preferred soaps, detergents, and even lingerie used by the upper classes. Once they graduated from college, these middle-class women did not continue with their work as domestics. Those who did work as domestics most likely had never attended college or, at most, attended college at some point but did not complete it.[37]

Usually middle-class female students, particularly those from the lower middle class, worked during their summer vacation to earn money

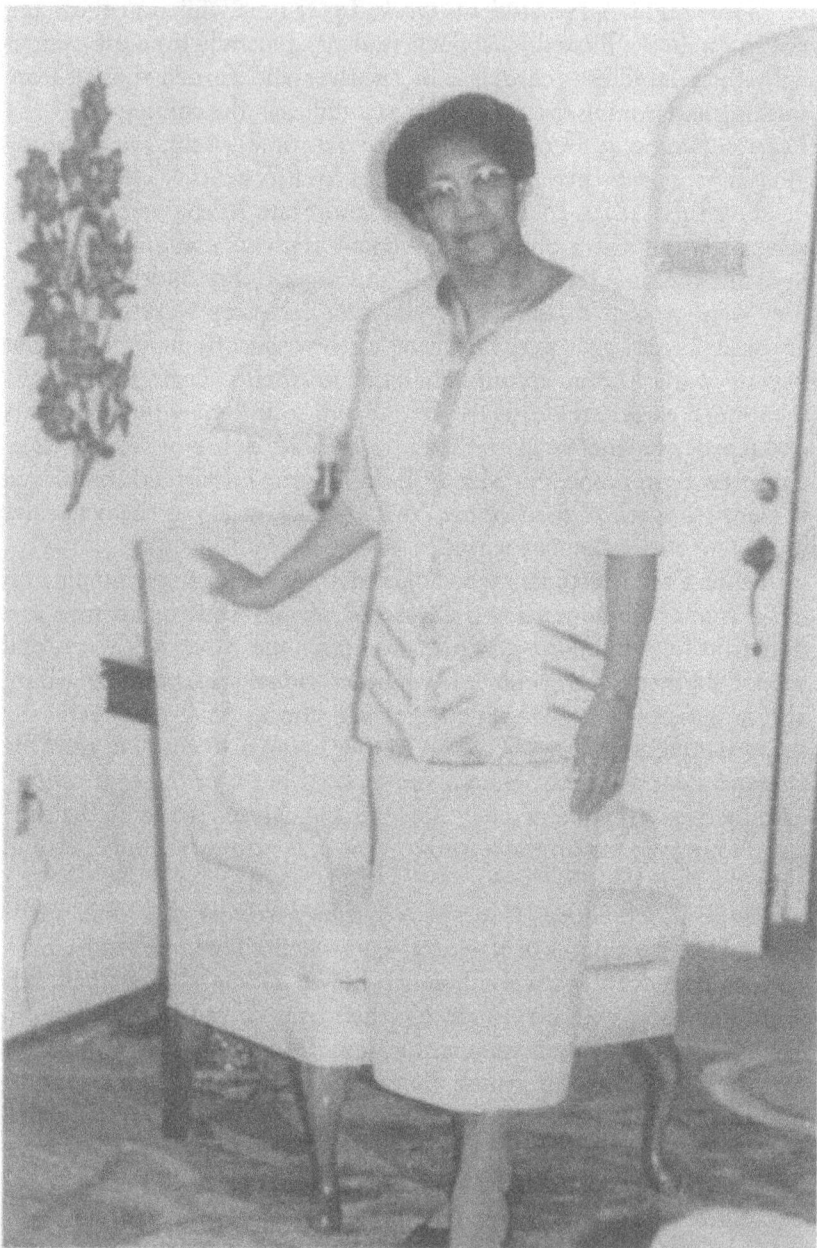

Susie Alexander Hubbard (shown here in 1997) recalls how the dean at State A&M encouraged girls in home economics to take summer domestic jobs in wealthy white homes to learn about modern conveniences and genteel culture.

for school. Some returned to their rural homes in Orangeburg County to work on farms. Maude Haigler Lawrence, a student at Claflin University in the late 1920s, returned home every summer to supervise her grandmother's fruit farm in Orangeburg County. Her grandmother owned a cane mill that made syrup products for the community. Lawrence was paid a small amount of money for every gallon of a syrup product sold, allowing her to save a sizable sum for her schooling. On the other hand, Susan Alexander Hubbard worked on her family's farm during her first summer as a college student. Afterward, she started working for a wealthy white family during her summer breaks, cooking and cleaning. Since the family had a washerwoman to wash the clothing and linen, Hubbard was freed from this laborious task.[38]

Other female students who worked during the summer chose domestic jobs in northern cities. Because these jobs paid much more than domestic jobs in Orangeburg, lower-middle-class students preferred them. Not only was the pay of $2.50 to $3.00 a week much less in Orangeburg than the $12.50 to $15.00 paid in New York City or Philadelphia, but the opportunity to do domestic work for white families in the North was still seen as less demeaning. These college students assumed that northern whites' attitudes toward them differed from that of southern whites, who still saw "all [African American] people . . . [as] ignorant, . . . and still slaves."[39]

Sometimes these female college students were actually encouraged by their college administrators or faculty to seek domestic jobs with wealthy white families. This experience provided them with the opportunity to use modern electrical machinery or appliances, like vacuum cleaners, refrigerators, or cake mixers, and gave them greater insight on how well-to-do, genteel ladies should live. Such jobs imbued them with both bourgeois ideology and Euro-American culture, which further prepared them for the life-style they aspired to live.[40]

While enrolled at Claflin, Marian Gregg traveled to New York City for two summers to work to earn money for college. She worked as a "mother's helper" for a white family, earning $50 a month. Her pay was later reduced to $35 monthly when her employers experienced some financial difficulties. Gregg cooked, cleaned, washed clothes, and served as a nursemaid to the children. She sent her mother some money each month to save toward her school tuition. Another student from State A&M college, Lucy Simmons, worked in the summer at a resort in New York City as a housekeeper. She earned $18.75 plus tips weekly, along with three free meals a day. She saved enough money to pay her entire tuition.[41]

Some female students acquired their jobs through advertisements. Many went to work in northern urban centers as a result of direct recruitment from community African American women who annually carried small groups of female college students on the train to known summer job positions, particularly at summer resorts. Others found jobs by visiting relatives already working on domestic jobs for white families. These relatives either coaxed their employers into hiring their kinfolk as temporary help for the summer or referred them to their other relatives or white families for employment.[42]

Georgia Waymer Swett left State A&M in 1935 for one year to find domestic work in Philadelphia that would enable her to earn money for school. She stayed with an older sister who already worked as a domestic for a white family and eventually took a "sleep-in" job advertised in the newspaper not far from her sister's job. While there, she cooked, cared for the children, and learned to use the electrical vacuum cleaner, the iron, and the washing machine. Her day began at 7 A.M. and ended at 6 P.M. The seven dollars a week with free room and board that she earned permitted her to pay most of her school fees for the following years.[43]

Between 1920 and 1940, a growing number of middle-class women continued to work outside the home. Some even worked double jobs in order to earn money toward their children's education or to make contributions to their families' income. These jobs continued to be restricted to working in the African American community, interacting with whites only when sewing for them or working as domestics. For example, Carey Tucker Pearson taught in Orangeburg County during the day. In the evenings and on weekends, she worked full time as a seamstress in her home, sewing for both African Americans and well-paying, upper-middle-class whites. This double employment was not unusual for skilled middle-class women, who worked as dress makers, teachers, and domestic workers. On the other hand, the few middle-class white women who worked outside the home were in skilled, respectable positions reserved for white women only: clerks in banks, secretaries, teachers, bank tellers, nurses, or business partners with their husbands.[44]

Unlike white women, many upper-middle-class African American women chose to either continue working after they married or return to the workplace once their children reached a certain age. Collin Robinson Embly, for example, continued to teach in Orangeburg County after marriage while her children's grandmother, a live-in relative, or a hired maid watched the children. According to one daughter, Clemmie Embly Webber, after her mother "stopped teaching, she was the first insurance agent in South Carolina to sell insurance for the African American–owned North Carolina Mutual Life Insurance Company which was an unusual job for a woman." Rather atypical, "she was very aggressive, ambitious, assertive, and business-minded." On the other hand, a few middle-class women, such as Marian Gregg and Beatrice Thompson, chose not to marry at all for various reasons but instead pursued successful teaching careers after their schooling. Thompson chose education and a career over marriage so that she would remain financially independent to care for her aging parents.[45]

Between 1910 and 1940, as more middle-class women studied business administration, increased numbers of upper-middle-class females employed in low-level administrative jobs at Claflin and State A&M worked as stenographers, clerks, secretaries, dietitians, and, sometimes, department heads or deans. African American colleges and businesses were the only places African American women could find such work since Jim Crow segregation and racial discrimination excluded them from similar jobs in Orangeburg. For example, Gertrude Dangerfield Bryant, also married, first worked as a teacher at Claflin's high school. She eventually became "directoress" of the Business Department at Claflin and later secretary to the president of the college. The children's grandparents resided with her family, watching the children while she and her husband worked.[46]

While still studying at State A&M, Edith Wilson Vaughn worked in an administrative position to earn money to pay fees. Upon graduation, she continued to work at A&M as a clerk in the Admissions Office. Overall, women's job positions were usually clerical and wielded little power and influence as compared to those of men, who held the more prestigious, decision-making administrative positions. Even though by 1940 more women were working on African American college campuses, because of gender discrimination at these schools they still remained a minority population on campus, despite the efforts of the National Association of College Women to bring gender equality in employment and promotion (see table 4).[47]

Aside from gender discrimination in college administrative positions, the number of middle-class women who taught at Claflin and State A&M also reflected gender discrimination in its hiring practices. On the college faculty, the women were outnumbered by men. These women usually taught only the courses traditionally studied by female students, such as home economics or education (see tables 5 and 6).

Between 1920 and 1940, married lower-middle-class women continued to teach in the public rural schools. While most women who taught in the public African American schools in Orangeburg County were still single, more married women now taught. Besides teaching, some lower-middle-class women still worked as full-time domestics, not only for white

Table 4

Administrative and Faculty Positions at Claflin and State A&M by Gender, 1880–1940

Year	Claflin		State A&M	
	F	M	F	M
1880	2	10	—	—
1885	6	16	—	—
1890	14	44	—	—
1895	20	42	—	—
1900	19	50	—	—
1910	29	50	—	—
1911	—	—	15	34
1918	—	—	22	53
1920	7	29	16	38
1925	34	47	36	68
1930	—	—	32	72
1931	23	36	—	—
1936	20	31	33	82
1939	—	—	37	92
1940	23	39	—	—

Source: Annual Catalogues of Claflin University, 1880–1940, and *Catalogues of State A&M, 1911–39.*

Note: State A&M catalogs were missing for 1880, 1885, 1890, 1895, 1900, 1906, 1910, 1931, 1936, and 1940. Claflin University catalogs were missing for 1911, 1918, 1930, and 1939.

families but also, in a few cases, for African American ones. Willard Gatewood discusses how well-to-do African Americans living in the North complained of problems they had in securing African American servants. This appeared not to be a problem in Orangeburg. However, lower-middle-class women who worked as domestics were selective in choosing their employers as they attempted to work for well-to-do white and, in a few cases, African American families. Beginning in 1934, Mamie Haigler worked as a domestic for the elite family of Helen Wilkinson Sheffield, the married daughter of State A&M's president, Robert Shaw Wilkinson. She worked from 7 A.M. to 3 P.M., Monday to Saturday, doing all the

Table 5

Teachers at Claflin University by Gender and Subject Taught, 1900–1940

Year	College and Normal M	F	High School M	F	Grades 1-8 M	F	Manual Training M	F	Music M	F	Domestic Science M	F
1900	1	15	–	–	7	11	4	13	2	4	–	–
1906	4	12	–	–	9	9	11	11	2	2	3	3
1910	5	11	0	0	7	8	0	12	3	3	3	3
1916	6	13	–	–	7	7	0	10	2	2	2	2
1920	6	12	–	–	6	6	0	8	1	3	–	–
1925	5	13	–	–	7	7	7	9	4	4	–	–
1930	4	14	3	6	–	–	–	–	2	4	–	–
1936	5	12	5	7	4	4	–	–	4	5	–	–
1940	11	22	–	–	–	–	–	–	–	–	–	–

Source: Annual Catalog of Claflin University, 1900–1928; Claflin College Catalogue, 1934–40.

Note: Catalogues for 1905, 1915, and 1935 were missing.

Table 6

Teachers at State A&M by Gender and Subject Taught, Sample Years, 1911–39

Year	College & Normal		Prep/High School		Academic Dept.		Agriculture		Business/ Commercial		Home Economics		Domestic Science		Mech./ Industrial	
	F	M	F	M	F	M	F	M	F	M	F	M	F	M	F	M
1911	0	7	–	–	7	1	0	6	2	1	–	–	4	12		
1918	3	12	4	7	–	–	–	–	–	–	6	6	–	–		
1920	5	16	–	–	–	–	–	–	1	5	5	5	–	–		
1924	5	12	–	–	–	–	0	9	1	4	9	1	–	–	0	15
1925	11	20	5	13	0	0	0	9	1	3	9	9	0	14		
1926	4	9	5	0	–	–	0	8	1	1	7	0	–	–	0	12
1927	8	10	3	4	–	–	0	8	1	1	7	0	–	–	0	12
1928	7	12	4	4	–	–	0	9	1	1	9	0	–	–	0	12
1929	7	10	5	4	–	–	0	11	1	1	8	0	–	–	0	12
1930	5	17	7	11	0	0	0	11	0	0	8	8	0	13	0	12
1936	14	48	0	0	0	0	0	0	0	0	0	0	0	0		
1939	37	92	0	0	0	0	0	0	0	0	0	0	0	0		

Source: Catalogues of State A&M, 1911–39.

cooking, cleaning, washing, and ironing. On Sundays, she only worked early in the morning, preparing the family's breakfast, while Helen Sheffield prepared Sunday's dinners. Since she worked for the founding family of the Sunlight Club, she also cooked the food to help raise money for the club's activities.[48]

Lower-middle-class women also took domestic work in public places. Since jobs on the college campuses or in white business establishments paid well and were considered "good jobs," many sought them. Both Mary Elizabeth Thompson and her husband held domestic positions at Claflin in the 1920s and 1930s. Unlike State A&M, apparently Claflin, with its largely white administration and faculty, were consistent in recognizing and abiding by the existing Jim Crow practice of racially segregated facilities in that it had an all-white dining room on campus. It was there that Mary Thompson worked essentially as the cook. Despite her domestic position, her job at the college offered higher wages than the average cook made working for a private family. Also, being affiliated with the college carried greater prestige.[49]

Another woman of the lower middle class, Sheldonia Wilmington Brown, ran a café that supported her family successfully after her husband's death. Previously, she had worked as a cook for a white family, but when her husband died, she rented three rooms in a building from a white proprietor and served meals to a largely African American working-class clientele. Other lower-middle-class African Americans dined at her place daily. On Saturdays, when rural poor white families traveled to Orangeburg to shop, she also served them. Since these poor rural whites could more easily afford her restaurant's ten-cent meals as opposed to the twenty-cent ones at the local white establishments, they frequented her restaurant more. Following the appropriate tradition of Jim Crow segregation, they dined in a separate room, which Brown had set aside for her "white only" customers. She earned a comfortable income that eventually enabled her to buy a small home in the working-class community.[50]

While the majority of middle-class women in 1910 were homemakers with some kind of gainful employment within their homes, World War I and the Great Depression forced many to seek outside work to help alleviate the rising financial pressures threatening their life-styles. As the Depression subsided in the late 1930s, most remained in the labor force. Subsequently, increased numbers of female college graduates augmented the female presence in the work force, although many still hoped to retire once they married to engage in some form of paid work from their homes. However, the single middle-class women who worked and later married generally continued to work rather than become permanent homemakers.

Unpaid Work

Many middle-class southern women, African American and white, were engaged in the same progressive reform work as their northern middle-class peers. These women were not necessarily "conscious feminists" but social activists imbued with the ideals of the "cult of true womanhood" as they worked to change their communities. White women, in particular, focused on transforming their "corrupt and unjust cities," correcting the "chaotic and fragmentary world" their "selfish and corrupt men had created." They busied themselves in helping to improve the work conditions, vocational training, and general home life of their poorer, wage-earning white sisters. [51]

Middle-class African American women's volunteer work focused on both racial and social issues in their community. Perhaps due to the combination of being both class and race conscious, at times the pride of some middle-class African American women led them to confront and reject racial discrimination. Such discrimination was either overt or subtle, but usually faced on an individual level. For example, Rebecca Garvin of Charleston reacted immediately and negatively to a white shoe salesman when he called her "auntie." Feigning ignorance of the Jim Crow title bestowed upon older African American women, Garvin asked him whether she was his mother's or father's sister. She refused to be "treated . . . like a slave servant." Her daughter, Mamie Fields, refused to enter the back door of a white home where she was invited to teach cross-stitching to the mistress of the home. She asserted she was entering the home "in the capacity of being an invited cross-stitcher and not a servant."[52]

Several clubs were formed throughout South Carolina that included upper- and middle-class African American women. Some club memberships consciously excluded lower-middle-class women, while others included lower-middle-class women whose jobs ranged from being teachers and seamstresses to housewives, domestics, and beauticians. It was not uncommon for clubs to be named after Marian Birnie Wilkinson, the founder of the African American club women's movement in South Carolina. Several clubs founded in Charleston included the Marian Birnie Wilkinson Club in 1927, the Elite Art and Social Club in 1936, the Volkamenian Club in 1938, the Poinsetta Club in 1939, and the Azalea Beauticians in 1940. Clubs that emerged in Columbia were the

Culture Club in 1910; in Florence, the Eureka Club in 1916; in Hartsville, the Helping Hand Club in 1921; in Spartanburg, the Golden Rule Club and the Wellford Mother's Home Demonstration Club in 1924; in Union in the late 1920s the Marian B. Wilkinson Club; in Chester, the Marian Birnie Wilkinson Federation Club in 1928; in Walterboro, the Marianette Federated Club in 1935; in Georgetown, the Better Home and Garden Club in 1936; in Barnwell, the Uplift Club in 1937; in Aiken, the Civic League of Aiken in 1939; and in Seneca, the Mary McLeod Bethune Club in 1940.[53]

Middle-class African American women formed self-help societies to serve various community needs. In Charleston, for example, they formed various "parlor societies," such as the Lily Club and Esther Club, to raise money to help the sick and "to give a little bit for the dead." The Monrovia Society was responsible for raising money to bury people and maintain its cemetery. Other light-skinned, upper-middle-class women joined the elite, "colorphobic" Brown Fellowship Society or St. Mark's Episcopal Church and engaged in church-related social work.[54]

Other middle-class women in Charleston engaged in volunteer work through their racially segregated branches of the YMCA. By 1907, these women had managed to raise enough money to build an African American branch of the YWCA. Through this new chapter and their churches, these middle-class African American women busied themselves doing volunteer work to raise money and improve conditions at the local African American hospital and its nurse training program. A branch of the South Carolina Federation of Colored Women's Clubs was established in Charleston in 1916, the Charleston City Federation. They successfully won some funds from the city to help build a new housing project for poor African Americans and worked with the state chapter in financially supporting the Wilkinson Home for Girls in Cayce, South Carolina.[55]

Mamie Garvin Fields recalls how women's snobbish attitudes held back progress in Charleston, since many members in the Charleston City Federation supported a more "exclusive" club so that certain women would not be invited to join the individual clubs, even if they had the ability and education and were ready to serve. As a result, Fields and some other middle-class women established a new organization in 1925, called the Modern Priscilla Club, with an open membership. While most members were teachers, other members included "housewives, a domestic worker, businesswomen, and beauticians." The Charleston City Federation was comprised largely of Charleston's aristocratic and upper-middle-class women. They snubbed the Modern Priscilla Club and attempted to relegate its members to performing the tasks of "cooks and maids" when working together at various club-related functions. Modern Priscilla refused to submit, however, and emerged to become a well-respected and productive chapter of the SCFCWC.[56]

Most of Orangeburg's white women's clubs concerned with social uplift work involved both upper- and middle-class women and were usually affiliated with their churches. However, they also had secular clubs working on projects to improve their community, such as building a home for the white elderly. But most of the secular clubs, like the majority of African American women's clubs, were more socially oriented than service-oriented.[57]

In Orangeburg, middle-class African American women were also involved in some form of volunteer work, usually with the upper-class African American women. However, the extent of their involvement and the type of volunteer work they performed varied, according to whether they were upper or lower middle class. Upper-middle-class women were active in the church missionary societies or committees, particularly at Trinity Methodist Episcopal, St. Luke's Presbyterian, and St. Paul's Episcopal Churches. They raised money to support the church, collected clothing and

Members of the Charleston City Federation Club, a volunteer organization serving Charleston's African Americans. From *Fiftieth Anniversary. South Carolina Federation of Colored Women's Clubs.*

food for the less fortunate, and visited the sick and elderly. They were also very active in civic activities in the African American community. Like upper-class African American women, they too belonged to the Sunlight Club and strove to uplift the race by improving the educational conditions and creating new economic opportunities.[58]

There were a few lower-middle-class women who were teachers, seamstresses, and housewives who belonged to the Sunlight Club. The extent of their active participation as a group, however, lagged behind that of upper-middle-class women, due to family and, sometimes, work obligations. Child care, cooking, and housework diminished their free or leisure time and thus interfered with their volunteer work. Yet many lower-middle-class women were not members of the club before 1940, even if their schedules permitted. As seen in Charleston, there was internal discrimination and an awkward alienation that existed within some of these women's clubs.[59]

Sharon Harley found in her study of African American club women in Washington, D.C., that "through their exclusive club membership, these socially prominent and educated women sought to bring to the white public's attention, cultural and intellectual differences within the [African

Members of the Modern Priscilla Club of Charleston. Established in 1925, this service club opened its membership to African American women of all classes. From *Fiftieth Anniversary. South Carolina Federation of Colored Women's Clubs.*

American] community and, thereby, to enhance their image as culturally and socially superior race members." While Harley points out that after the 1920s, these groups included women from different social and occupational backgrounds, this was not the case for Orangeburg's social and civic clubs. Nor was it the case in Orangeburg that when it came to working toward "racial and individual betterment, . . . [that their class differences] diminished in importance," as Cynthia Neverdon-Morton argues. Even though the Sunlight Club's "membership . . . consist[ed] of all interested women in Orangeburg," in actuality, women without the "preferred background" were excluded from its ranks. The club's membership was not open until long after 1940.[60]

Lower-middle-class women in Orangeburg who held certain jobs were not considered for membership in the Sunlight Club. The lower-middle-class status of Mamie Haigler, the dark-skinned domestic servant for Helen Wilkinson Sheffield, was attributed to her husband, Franklin Preston Haigler. He received his licentiate instruction degree from Claflin and taught in Orangeburg County. Because Sheffield was inextricably involved with the Sunlight Club alongside her mother, Marian Wilkinson, Mamie Haigler attended all the Sunlight Club meetings in a domestic capacity to cook, serve, and clean. She was never invited to join the club before 1940, most likely due to her status and position as a domestic.[61]

Other women of the lower middle class did not attempt to join the Sunlight Club or any other social clubs whose members were from the elite or upper middle class. They believed that the lack of certain social criteria, such as job position, light-skinned complexion, family background, residence, and education, would affect their membership application. For example, Frizell Brown Bowman, a light-skinned woman with long, straight hair from lower-middle-class origins, attended Allen University in Columbia after finishing the Sterling School in Orangeburg. She stopped school once she married her light-skinned boyfriend from upper-middle-class origins, Robert Bowman, who attended State A&M but stopped to work as a professional embalmer in a local African American funeral home. His mother, Antinika Brown, was a chartered member of the Sunlight Club and insisted that her daughter-in-law also join. However, when Frizell Bowman and her friend, Rosa Gaffney, a well-respected woman in the African American community with a "spotless reputation," applied for membership, she was refused. In turn, Bowman declined her invitation to join and attributed Gaffney's refusal to "color prejudice," since Gaffney was "too dark, . . . black-skinned."[62]

The volunteer work of most lower-middle-class women who were able to be active was usually church-related. They attended the regular meetings, cooked, and sold goods to raise money for the church. Although Mamie Haigler was not a member of the Sunlight Club, she was still an active member at Trinity, "baking and cooking to raise money." She "sold cakes, cookies, and dinners" for the church and on the first Sunday helped serve the communion. While some lower-middle-class African American women attended the Methodist church, most in Orangeburg attended Baptist churches and did their volunteer work there. According to Evelyn Brooks-Higginbotham, the efforts of middle-class African American women organizing through both the Baptist conventions and churches to uplift and improve conditions for African Americans persisted from 1880 to 1920. But in Orangeburg, the "lower" middle-class African American women persisted in their church work long after 1940.[63]

Some elite and middle-class women were also engaged in the suffrage movement. Paula Giddings points out that little research has focused on their contribution, and she argues that African American women "had a more consistent attitude toward the vote than whites." Rosalyn Terborg-Penn adds that they "maintained a political philosophy of universal suffrage, while whites . . . advocated a limited, educated suffrage." White women fought to gain white women's suffrage, and once both white and African American women formed coalitions to fight for women's suffrage, racial prejudice prevailed. Racism and segregation within the suffrage movement was demonstrated in Chicago in the 1913 suffragists' parade, when African American club women had to agree to march at the rear.[64]

African American men were supportive of suffrage for both men and women. Jacqueline Rouse adds that southern African American club women also saw "the urgent need for the ballot." They saw women's suffrage as promoting gender equality within the African American community, since it "would change the role of [African American] women in society . . . as they aimed at solving specific problems uniquely theirs." While few, if any, southern African American women's clubs focused solely on female suffrage, there were attempts made to organize both African American and white women in the South to work together on the suffrage question. For example, at Tuskegee Institute in 1920, two white representatives from the Methodist Women's Missionary Council joined the African American female giants "Margaret Washington, Mary McCrorey, . . . Mary McLeod Bethune" and others at a NACW meeting to discuss "suffrage and other mutual concerns." In Orangeburg, many of the white female instructors who taught at Claflin were from Boston and were "white suffragettes very involved in organizing to get the vote for women." According to Clemmie Embly Webber, her mother, Collin Robinson Embly, was a suffragist. Embly, an upper-middle-class student at Claflin, was active in the women's suffrage movement between 1906 and 1907, working with the different white Boston suffragists employed at the college. Her activism continued after school, when in 1909 she became one of the chartered members of the Sunlight Club.[65]

Middle-class African American women attempted to mirror the atypical life-styles of upper-class African Americans, yet most did not ignore the economically depressed conditions of their less fortunate neighbors or relatives. They shunned the notion of living in such dire poverty, and some engaged in activities to help improve living conditions in the larger African American community. The majority of upper-middle-class women were active in volunteer work in churches and clubs. They were socially intimate with upper-class African American women and thus could be found in the same social, religious, and civic circles.

With few exceptions, women of the lower middle class were excluded from social circles. In any case, their work and familial obligations usually restricted them from full-fledged volunteer work. Thus, they busied themselves in helping the African American community through their church organizations. Lower-middle-class women remained in a somewhat precarious economic positions, often due to the tenuous nature of the jobs they or their husbands held. Although these women lived better than the working-class majority, many of them were no more than a few steps away from this lower status. It was a struggle for them to sustain their middle-class position in the African American community, knowing they did not have the same financial security as their upper-middle-class peers.

6.

Middle-Class Women's Work inside the Home

Any middle-class white household that could afford domestic help hired someone to free "the lady of the house" from the drudgery of housework. Having servants enhanced and sustained a white family's middle-class status in the community. In her study on housewives and domestic servants, Phyllis Palmer points out that even "lower middle-income families" managed to hire domestics, because there existed a sizable pool of African American women who would work for meager wages. Jim Crow segregation and racial discrimination excluded them from the better-paying jobs, and thus they were forced to work for low wages in whatever job they could find. Jane Stafford, a middle-class southern white woman, recalled the days she had African American house servants. She remembered how "even the poorest [white] person had servants. . . . They use to say if a southern man had two dollars, he gave one to the blacks to wait on him. Everyone had servants. It was just the way." While lower-middle-class white households were financially limited to hiring only one, most likely overworked, domestic, upper-middle-class white households usually had several.[1]

Domestic servants were not as common in the homes of middle-class African Americans as in the homes of the upper-class. Although a small minority of upper-middle-class African American families could afford full-time domestics, most could not. Instead, they hired part-time domestic help to assist in the everyday work of the household, such as cleaning, washing, and ironing, or to help on a temporary basis until a certain job was completed. As poorer white households struggled to hire at least one domestic to do the laundry, lower-middle-class African American households, too, attempted to hire a part-time domestic. Phyllis Palmer's study found that among African American households in Indianapolis, there were examples of "wives working as maids or domestics and . . . [their] husbands as janitors, laborers, and servants" who managed financially to hire a domestic to do their laundry. Perhaps their employers paid them reasonable wages, placing them in a lower-middle-class bracket despite their positions. Regardless, a family's ability to hire any kind of domestic help in an African American household created certain perceptions of social status in the larger African American community.[2]

Middle-class African American women generally performed their own housework, including cleaning, cooking, canning, sewing, and care of their children. Rebecca Garvin of Charleston was a housewife and dress maker, trained informally by her aunt and formally through schooling at Wesley Church and Claflin. Besides making beautiful dresses for her daughters, she was also a "champion cooking ordinary things." She cooked creative and delicious meals in, first, the chimney hearth and, later, on the stove her husband bought her. According to her daughter, Mamie Garvin Fields, she cooked "fancy things in that chimney—beautiful pastries, fruitcakes, . . . and cakes," by "using a 'spider,' a cast-iron pot they put in the fireplace with coals on top." As for middle-class children, they too had tasks, including going to the public well or the nearest spigot to get water and assisting their mothers in their chores.[3]

Census records for the city of Orangeburg between 1880 and 1910 reveal that, despite the increased numbers of middle-class women working outside the home, the majority of middle-class women were still at home (see table 7). The number of African American households increased from 266 in 1880 to 708 by 1910, or by 117 percent, as more African Americans migrated to search for better economic opportunities, to further their education, or to seek employment other than agricultural work.

Whether working outside the home or not, middle-class African American women still were responsible for coordinating the housework or arranging for grandparents or hired nursemaids to care for their children. Most children, in turn, had daily chores: the boys brought in the wood and coals for the stoves, the girls swept the floors, made the beds, washed the windows, fed the chickens, or helped their mothers rinse the washed clothes.[4]

A few upper-middle-class women who were employed outside the home had help with some, if not all, of their domestic tasks. In the early 1900s, while Collin Robinson Embly taught school in Orangeburg

Table 7

Middle-Class Married African American Women's Occupations in Orangeburg, 1880–1910

Occupation	1880	1900	1910
At home	32	75	79
Teacher	0	1	5
Dress maker	0	3	12
Trained nurse	0	0	1
Midwife	0	2	1
Merchant/grocery	0	0	1
Sick nurse	0	0	1
Washerwoman	3	11	30
Day laborer	1	1	0
Farm operator	0	1	1
Farm laborer	0	2	1
Total	36	96	132

Source: Bureau of the Census, *Census of 1880 on Population. Orangeburg Town*, *Census of 1900 on Population. Orangeburg City*, and *Census of 1910 on Population. Orangeburg City*. Note: The total number of African American households in Orangeburg for 1880 was 266; for 1900, 535; and for 1910, 708.

County, she had a live-in maid who cooked, cleaned the house, and assisted Embly's mother in watching the children. In 1939, Edith Wilson Vaughn, who worked as an administrator at State A&M, did her own housecleaning, but she contracted a washerwoman to do her weekly washing and ironing.[5]

Some upper-middle-class women working outside the home chose to do their work inside the home. Some did so because family members helped them with the housework, while others did their own housework because they enjoyed it. Gertrude Dangerfield Bryant worked at Claflin University, first as a teacher in the high school and later as an administrator in the University. Her children helped with the household cleaning, but she still cooked at home for her family, washed clothes in her back yard on Saturdays, and ironed those clothes on Saturday nights.[6]

Generally, however, between 1920 and 1940 it was upper-middle-class housewives and not lower-middle-class ones who usually had some form of domestic help. The kind of housework these upper-middle-class women engaged in depended largely upon the type of help they hired. It was not unusual for them to employ female students to work as live-in housekeepers, especially those students who moved to Orangeburg to attend either the local high schools or colleges. These live-in students did the general housekeeping in exchange for room and board. This, in many instances, was the only choice these less fortunate students had, since their parents could not afford to pay for on-campus room and board in addition to the fees for enrollment, books, and uniforms. The students cleaned house, tended to the garden, and washed and ironed clothing, exempting the "lady of the house" from doing housework.[7]

In addition to hiring students, a few upper-middle-class women hired regular domestic workers, who usually worked as day workers, not live-ins. They washed and ironed, assisted in canning or gardening, and tended to the children. These day laborers were generally responsible for performing the heavier household tasks. While Clarissa Dozier Dickson's domestic helper did the general housekeeping, she spent her time tending her garden, raising chickens to sell eggs, and raising cows that provided milk for her family. Other middle-class women sometimes employed temporary help to assist in seasonal tasks such as canning or gardening, but they more or less relied on their older children to help with the various household chores.[8]

Women of the lower middle class who worked outside the home usually did their own housework with the assistance of their children. When Sheldonia Brown's husband was alive, she was a housewife who did her own housework. After his death, she opened a successful café that served mostly working-class patrons, while continuing to do her own housework as she could not afford domestic help. Her daughter, Frizell Brown Bowman, on the other hand, was a lower-middle-class housewife who spent her days tending to her flower garden and doing minor repairs around the house. She hired various school-aged girls to do her cleaning chores in exchange for small fees or clothing.[9]

Unlike Frizell Bowman, most lower-middle-class housewives did not only the general housework but also other significant tasks necessary for the family's survival. Janie Walker Harrington cooked, cleaned, did the washing and ironing, and sewed practically all the clothing her family wore. Ella Felder Wilson recalled that in addition to cleaning, cooking, and sewing, her "mother and father made everything that their family used, except for coffee and salt." Her mother, Millie Jason Felder,[10] "pieced quilts for the family or sold them to people . . . crocheted all the sweaters, knitted shoes for the babies, and made most of the clothing. She tended to her garden, but never canned, since she did not like canned food. She wanted things fresh. She cared for the chickens and hogs, cured hams, made sausage, grew rice, made flour, and grew sugar cane for syrup."[11]

Some lower-middle-class housewives also were engaged in some form of gainful employment at home for extra money. In addition to doing the house cleaning, gardening, and cooking for a family of eight, Ella Govan Middleton washed and ironed the table cloths from Claflin University's dining hall. Another housewife, Leila Summers Harrison, sewed, crocheted, and did hair dressing for others.[12] She operated a small home business, making little girls' dresses, complete with bonnets, aprons, and bloomers, for thirty-five to forty cents; boys' pants for twenty-five to thirty cents; and women's dresses for a dollar. She also crocheted "lap robes" for beds, baskets for flower jars, and scarves for tables. These items ranged in price from twenty-five cents to five dollars. Harrison "washed and pressed" women's hair for twenty-five to fifty cents. Like most middle-class women, she used her money to help maintain the household.[13]

While both upper- and lower-middle-class women worked outside the home, upper-middle-class women held the more respectable and desirable jobs, generally hiring part-time domestics to help with the housework they could not handle. The majority of middle-class women, however, did their own housework. Few upper-middle-class women had full-time domestic help, and none had a full-time staff of workers, as some in the upper class did.

Like upper-class African American women, both upper- and lower-middle-class housewives also engaged in volunteer work. In addition to working outside the home, middle-class African American women were active in volunteer work through their churches and, in the case of the upper middle class, the Sunlight Club. Middle-class women in Orangeburg were influential in improving the lives of less fortunate African Americans. Contrary to Evelyn Brooks-Higginbotham's findings that African American middle-class women were generously immersed in their Baptist church work,[14] in Orangeburg most lower-middle-class housewives experienced a conflict between their housework and volunteer activities. Because their work as housewives was more indispensable to their families, they had less time for volunteer work. In addition, the intraclass discrimination among African Americans, even in social uplift work, prevented women from different classes from working together for the general good of the African American community.

Part III. The Toiling Ebony Drudges: The Working Class

7.

Working-Class African Americans

Between the mid-nineteenth and early twentieth century, middle-class white social crusaders focused most of their efforts on raising the living standards of average working-class whites in the United States. European immigrants and rural whites were migrating to the city in increasing numbers, creating a slew of new problems: overcrowded streets, slum dwellings, poor diets, and meager health-care services. Various poverty-relief organizations, such as the YMCA, the YWCA, the Children's Aid Society, and the Salvation Army, were established to alleviate poverty among the white working and lower classes.[1]

Most working-class white men and women held unskilled jobs, working long, hard hours in sometimes unsafe conditions for low hourly wages. They hoped one day to acquire the skills that would enable them to earn far more than what they made now as "common laborers." When opportunities for such advancement arose, it was white workers, especially men, who were able to take advantage. African Americans were excluded from participating in the training open to working-class whites. In both rural and urban white working-class households, families depended on the cooperation of all members for economic survival. The white working class was aware of itself as a group, as members consciously identified and sought to socialize with one another.[2]

Regarding the African American working class in the United States, Mary Frances Berry and John Blassingame argue that "the economic history of [African Americans] proves conclusively that America

failed on practically all fronts to guarantee them a right to life and the
pursuit of happiness" due to "the racial caste system which prevailed."
After slavery, the majority still lived in the rural South in "virtual peon-
age," working as sharecroppers, farm laborers, and tenant farmers. The
urban African American working class engaged in the most menial jobs,
working as domestics, day laborers, laundresses, firemen maintaining
furnaces, sewage diggers, cooks, and draymen. They earned low wages
and lived in the poorest areas of towns. Even poorer still were those in
the lower working class, who held seasonal or casual jobs and were
barely able to subsist on what they earned.[3]

Overall, the majority of African Americans in the United States continued to live in destitution between 1880 and 1940, depending "heavily
on their [neighbors and] extended family members [such as grandparents,
cousins, aunts, and uncles] for help and support." The usual consequences
of poverty, including poor health care, illiteracy, back-breaking labor, poor
sanitation, powerlessness, and ignorance plagued their communities. They
held "the heaviest, dirtiest, lowest-paid unskilled jobs." They rented their
homes but still had dreams of one day becoming homeowners and educating their offspring. Conscious of their class position, they strove to achieve
bits and pieces of the "material and cultural" things associated with the upper and middle classes.[4]

In South Carolina, the status of African Americans was the lowest
in the state, and most African Americans occupied the lowest rung on
the economic ladder. Working-class families required the income of
both adults and children living in the household. Orangeburg's African
American working-class community can be divided into two groups: the
regular working class, who more or less lived on a subsistence level, and
the lower working class, who lived on the wage-earning fringes of life
and appreciated extra occasional jobs and charity. Lower-working-class
women usually depended on occasional agricultural or domestic jobs,
such as planting and harvesting, or on assisting upper- or middle-class
women in canning, heavy washing, or spring cleaning. Within the more
impoverished lower-working-class families, incomes were even smaller
due to inconsistent employment or lack of two parents in the household.[5] While the typical working-class African American family in
Orangeburg before 1940 was headed by two parents, there were some
single-parent households, primarily due to one parent leaving to work
in another city or state, death, separation, or divorce.[6]

Orangeburg's working-class community was conscious of its inferior
class status and admired and envied the wealth and achievements of those
in the upper and middle classes. Because of the kind of jobs they held, they
had the greatest contact with the larger white community in Orangeburg

and thus were constantly reminded of their inferior economic and racial status. They stayed in their "proper places" as they performed their work, but they were not without pride, confidence, or motivation.

Sharon Harley argues that even though white society and the African American upper classes tended to deny the African American working class an "elevated social status," some working-class members nevertheless enjoyed positions of esteem within their own families and neighborhoods. "A clean house, good meals, and well-mannered, responsible children were major sources of pride and status" in working-class communities. Other factors greatly enhanced social status: having the reputation of being a hard-working and honest family; being perceived as a leader in the community, playing an active, respectable role in the church; being kin to a well-respected senior citizen in the community; or having a family member who had accomplished something out of the ordinary, such as graduating from college or purchasing a home.[7]

In the 1880s, African Americans continued to migrate from the countryside into the town of Orangeburg, as well as to other southern, western, and northern states. Even with President Woodrow Wilson's executive order to segregate government civil service jobs, migration to the North continued to increase during World War I, as working-class African Americans sought jobs generated by the war. Migrations slowed during the Depression, as fewer jobs became available. Overall, white Orangeburg and a minority of the city's snobbish, elite African Americans viewed these African American masses as a degrading bunch who were locked in poverty and who occupied an undesirable socioeconomic position in the city.[8]

As more poor families left rural Orangeburg, where they normally produced their own vegetables, meats, and dairy products, to migrate to the town of Orangeburg, they experienced greater racial discrimination and poverty. Now they struggled to adapt to the consumerism that required them to have more money to purchase items from stores—items they had once produced themselves. According to Jacqueline Jones, these "urban women had to rely almost exclusively on wage labor in order to provide for their families or supplement their husband's income."[9]

The working class' disadvantaged social position forecast for its members a life of drudgery and, at times, severe economic hardship. Most worked as domestics, day laborers, and farmhands for low wages. African Americans working these menial jobs at the colleges, however, enjoyed a more respectable status, and their positions—ranging from dining room cook to campus farm operator—were coveted in the working-class community.[10]

In her discussion of the antebellum Civil War homes of well-to-do and middle-class families, Christine Stansell illustrates how class distinctions were further "dramatized" in the types of homes people lived in. For example, the homes of the more financially secure consisted of an upstairs and a downstairs, which separated the "work" area from the "leisure" area. Also in these homes were separate living spaces for the family and servants. On the other hand, the homes of working-class white families did not reflect such comfort. In large, urban cities, working-class whites lived in slum tenement buildings that Stansell describes as being "incubators of disease and vice." Few skilled working-class whites were able to escape from the city to the outlying suburbs to buy a home like their middle-class peers. Poor white families in rural areas continued to live in their self-sufficient farmhouses without plumbing, electricity, and other relatively modern conveniences.[11] According to Leslie Woodcock Tentler, most working-class white women "lived in congested, poorly maintained housing that even in the 1920s often lacked hot running water, set laundry tubs, and private indoor toilets. Working-class neighborhoods were usually located in the dirtiest parts of the city, adjacent to mills and factories. Few working-class families could afford home appliances. Marketing in the working-class household was a daily activity, for iceboxes were small and inefficient. Laundering, without a washing machine, typically consumed several evenings a week."[12]

On the other hand, W. E. B. Du Bois described the housing of the poor working-class African Americans in rural Georgia as either being a few "new neat frame houses" or a "cluster of farm houses with fields." These farmhouses were "primitive" and usually had two and a half rooms made of "old dirty log[s]." Those who lived in Atlanta scarcely had furniture. "Perched on wooden or bricked pillars," these houses usually had a "bed or two, a few chairs, a table, a stove or fireplace, a trunk or chest." Their floors were "bare and there [were] no pictures. Sometimes six or eight persons live[d] in two such rooms and pay[ed] $1.50 a month or . . . as much as $4.00." According to Du Bois, "These houses [had] water outside in a well or street hydrant; the outhouses [were] used in common by several tenants."[13]

Maggie Comer recalled how most of the houses they lived in while in Memphis were like barns:

> If they had any windows, they were open in the daytime. They let them out on a string. One [house] didn't have any windows. You opened the doors, no screens. I can't remember any that didn't have floors that you couldn't jump across from one plank to the other.

There were holes in the floors of some. My sister said that she used to sit in one house and count all the chickens under it. . . .

There were no lights, just lamps with coal oil and wicks in them. We were so poor we didn't own but one lamp . . . [and] . . . you had to go from one room to the other with this lamp. We cooked on a coal or wood stove, mostly wood. You just pick up a board or plank or what have you around, and cook your meals. . . . At some places where we lived, there was simply no wood unless you pulled a board off the house to make fire.[14]

Asa H. Gordon described the poor living quarters of slaves in South Carolina and pointed out that after the antebellum era, these same slave cabins or huts were rented to former slaves to live in while the more well-to-do African Americans rented the large plantation houses. The homes of poor African Americans still had the same "curious bareness and roughness" as their former slave relatives. In describing the homes of the poor, who mostly resided in rural South Carolina shortly after slavery, he said there were "few chairs with backs, no sheets on the beds, no books, no newspapers, no closets or out-houses, no bedrooms, no tablecloths and very few dishes." He added that there were also "no carpets and usually no floors, no windows, no pictures, no clocks, no lights at night save that of the fireplace, little or nothing save bare rough shelter."[15]

In Orangeburg, working-class African Americans in 1880 were usually not homeowners but rented dilapidated housing on unpaved dirt roads without sidewalks, such as Sunnyside, Calhoun, and Cannon. Their homes were unpainted wood, also "perched on . . . bricked pillars." There were three- or sometimes four-room houses with outhouses in their back yards, since their homes were the last to receive indoor plumbing, if they received it at all. One of the rooms was a kitchen, which contained a wood-burning cook stove and an icebox, and the other two served as bedrooms, one of them having a "pot belly" woodburning stove used to heat the house. There were no closets or a separate living room or sitting room. Guests were entertained on the porch or in the dirt yard during warm weather, or on chairs and, maybe, a makeshift sofa placed in one of the bedrooms during cooler months. A few of the under-occupied four-room houses might use one of the four rooms for a living room.[16]

Members of the working class had the least amount of education. When their children attended school, it was at first at the Sterling School in Orangeburg and later at Riverside, Dunton, or Wilkinson.

A working-class African American home in rural Orangeburg, 1898. From *Annual Catalogue of Claflin University and College of A&M, 1898.*

Unlike parents in the upper and middle classes, most working-class parents in Orangeburg appear to have attached more importance to their children completing their chores or doing well on their jobs rather than to getting a good education. Working-class children were not usually clad in the nicer clothing nor exposed to bourgeois Euro-American cultural arts, music, or ballet during their leisure time.[17]

These families could not afford to shop at the exclusive, white-owned dress shops or department stores. Very infrequently could they purchase goods from these businesses, and when they did, it was usually done through a credit-purchase plan. Instead, they shopped at the inexpensive dry goods stores in the African American shopping district on Railroad Avenue in Orangeburg or at inexpensive white-owned stores, purchasing poorer quality items at affordable prices. Moreover, they, like elite and middle-class African Americans, were not allowed to try on clothing but had to follow customary Jim Crow restrictions. They were confronted with racial discrimination and poor treatment, sometimes to the point of physical abuse.[18]

Eloise Tyler Williams recalled how in the late 1930s the "poor, [African American] people" usually shopped for "cheap shoes" and other items at I. Silver's, a store most African Americans at the time commonly called

A working-class residence in Orangeburg. This 1997 photograph and the following six illustrate examples of residences of working-class African Americans built prior to 1940.

A working-class residence in Orangeburg.

"the Jew store," since it was owned and operated by a Jewish white couple. While still a school-aged girl, Williams recollects entering the store one day with her older cousin, Josephine Morgan, and two other female relatives to shop for shoes. After trying on a few pairs and deciding to leave without purchasing any shoes, the woman "became furious, started yelling obscenities at [them] and immediately ran after them" to chase them out of the store. The woman managed to "kick Josephine, the last one, as hard as she could in her behind," causing her great pain.[19]

Scared and confused, Williams, Morgan, and the others wondered what might have provoked such angry and violent behavior from the Jewish woman whose store they had frequented so often. Williams pointed out that "that was how white people treated [African American] folks." In Jim Crow Orangeburg, there was nothing they could do, because "whites could do things like that to [African Americans] and get away with it."[20] Perhaps the young women broke an unspoken Jim Crow law that prohibited African Americans from trying on merchandise; or, if they were permitted to try on shoes at I. Silver's, maybe the owner was angry because they did not then make a purchase.

None of the working-class African Americans in Orangeburg attended the "high-cultured" Episcopal church, and only a minority at-

A working-class residence in Orangeburg.

tended the Methodist and Presbyterian churches. Most belonged to the numerous rural and city Baptist churches, including Bull Swamp, Old Mount Zion, Andrews Chapel, Williams Chapel, Macedonia, Mt. Pisgah, Mt. Carmel, and St. Paul's. Their social lives and little leisure time usually revolved around visiting nearby neighbors or attending church-related events at their grass-roots Baptist churches. Working-class women usually had little leisure time, however, as they spent most of their week working, with only Saturday afternoons and Sundays free. Rarely did those in the working class own any significant property—homes, businesses, or land—beyond their immediate meager furnishings and clothing. Their lives, nevertheless, were filled with hard work, illiteracy, and a lack of elite, Euro-American cultural refinements, such as eloquent language, dress, proper social mannerisms, and the various social activities that upper- and middle-class African Americans identified with and emulated.[21]

The Working-Class Female

Although the "cult of domesticity" permeated the working class as thoroughly as the upper and middle classes, the reality was that lower-class

A working-class residence in Orangeburg.

women could not fulfill the ideology's prescribed genteel role. Their wealth was not commensurate to that of some in the upper classes, who could afford a life filled with servants, leisure time, and financial comfort. Educating their female children was not a priority for working-class white families, because they realized their daughters would eventually marry and retire from paid labor. In the meantime, these families depended on the wages of all their children to help sustain the family.[22]

Many white women were able to withdraw from the labor force once married to pursue their "expected calling." They saw work outside the home as a temporary activity and looked forward to marrying, they hoped, "prosperous middle-class husbands" and living the life of a "lady." Many saw "marriage and motherhood" as being "the crowning point of their lives." To further encourage women not to work after marriage, various newspapers and reformers between 1883 and 1914 researched and argued the potential threat "wage work" had on "the possibilities of adequate mothering." In other situations, some working-class white women returned to work after marriage, since their households needed the two incomes.[23]

Working-class African American women did not have the option to retire from employment once they married. Their wages were far lower than their white working-class counterparts, since they held the menial jobs

A working-class residence in Orangeburg.

that working-class white women avoided. Jacqueline Jones rightly argues that working-class African American girls "might have indulged in romantic fantasies about marriage, but few . . . could count on a wedding to end their days of sustained wage earning." Working-class African American parents taught their daughters to avoid men who appeared shiftless or unable to keep a job, or whose vices included alcohol and "chasing women." Instead, they were encouraged to marry a "good, hardworking man who wanted something out of life and who would take care of his wife and children." Working-class females themselves were taught to also be "hardworking and honest," so that one day they would become good wives and mothers. Most working-class African American parents instilled a strong work ethic in their children when they were quite young by assigning them various household chores. They were constantly encouraged to do an excellent job, no matter how trivial the work.[24]

Formal education for poor, working-class African American families was much the same as that for working-class white families. Both families needed financial contributions from everyone in the household, so work took precedence over education. However, working-class white families did not suffer from racial discrimination when it came to making decisions regarding education. For African Americans, poverty, discrimination, segre-

A working-class residence in Orangeburg.

A working-class residence in Orangeburg.

gation, and alienation determined whether their children attended school and for how long. Adele Alexander describes how in Sparta, Georgia, the "free colored school stayed in session just three months per year during the 1880s." Short school years were set by "white officials who controlled public funds" and who, on the other hand, strongly "supported high schools for whites." These officials argued that African Americans "should be trained only for agricultural or domestic work and therefore needed but a few years of basic education." This notion of little or no education for African Americans was widely accepted by the average white person in the South between 1880 and 1940.[25]

Once education became legally available to African Americans during the Reconstruction era, some families still did not encourage schooling for their children. According to Adele Alexander, some had "understandably internalized . . . [the] low expectations" taught to them as slaves. For example, Treena Threatt Nelson's grandparents "had been slaves . . . who never had the vision to aspire further than domestics or servants in and around houses owned and occupied by white people." When their ten-year-old daughter was offered a job as a maid in a white home, they "readily agreed," placing "financial imperatives" over "book learning." Thus they

Makeshift cabinets or shelves were usually built to hold canned vegetables in working-class homes.

"pulled her right out of her fourth grade class and the girl never returned to school."[26]

Several scholars have argued that African American women worked hard and sacrificed a great deal to educate their children. Some no doubt did sacrifice their personal needs to save money to provide their offspring with an education that would one day hopefully improve their lives. For example, Mary McLeod Bethune's parents wanted to send all nine of their children to school, but "they could hardly spare even one for all the farm labor that needed to be done." Thus, it was Mary, the youngest, who was permitted to attend the newly opened country school. In turn, young Mary rushed home every day to teach her siblings whatever she had learned that day.[27]

However, as seen in Treena Threatt Nelson's family, there were other working-class African Americans who were not as supportive of educating their offspring. The novelist Richard Wright experienced negative support and resistance from his grandmother when he was a child attending school in Mississippi in the 1920s, even though he excelled in reading and writing. On the other hand, his grandmother applauded his wage-earning capacity, as it helped the family tremendously. Wright's grandmother and

St. Paul's Baptist Church, in the Calhoun Drive area of Orangeburg, a working-class neighborhood.

other poor, elderly African Americans usually were skeptical or pessimistic of the consequences of their young offspring achieving an education. They apparently saw education as a means to provoke the wrath of southern whites, who perceived literate African Americans as being "uppity." There were other working-class African Americans who had little faith in education as being a successful means to occupational mobility. Even with an education, they knew that racism would still prohibit and restrict educated African Americans from attaining certain job positions.[28]

The majority of working-class African Americans had respect for education and those who were educated. They, too, wanted the best life for their offspring and realized that through education, a higher standard of life was possible. But they realistically weighed the possibilities of their children actually attaining such an educational training, enabling them to become teachers, seamstresses, or tailors and live comfortable, middle-class life-styles. While a few working-class families did sacrifice and persevere to educate their children, most accepted the reality that the odds were against them economically and socially. These parents invested their time in emphasizing the one goal that was certain to have a definite end for their children: attaining wage-earning jobs.

Williams Chapel Church, in the working-class Calhoun Drive area of Orangeburg.

Eloise Tyler Williams (shown here in 1984) was often scolded by her grandmother, "Ducky," about putting schoolwork before her chores. For Ducky, housework came first.

Many working-class children spent their early morning hours in school and their afternoons working at a job or performing certain tasks at home. Even though Alice Kessler-Harris, Jacqueline Jones, Gerda Lerner, Dorothy Sterling, and others have argued that African American families, especially women, made education for their children "a high priority item," this was simply not the norm within the African American working-class community in Orangeburg before 1940. Nor, evidence suggests, was it in other working-class communities of the time.[29]

Elizabeth Clark-Lewis's study of African American domestics who migrated from the rural South to Washington, D.C., between 1900 and 1926 discusses how these women "did not have to learn to work" as this was "centrality . . . to their lives." Clark-Lewis found that of the twenty-three women she studied, while growing up as children in the rural South, "the education of all . . . was severely limited by the need to help support the family, which was recognized by them as their primary responsibility upon reaching seven years of age." This was not unusual. In fact, to complete seventh or eighth grade was a major achievement for African American rural children. Mamie Garvin Fields recalled how "most of the children . . . stopped school in order to work. Many never came at all." It was not uncommon for Fields and other teachers in South Carolina "to go out to find the school-age children who never came" because they were working or they lacked clothing to wear.[30]

In Orangeburg, this nonsupport for education could be very frustrat-

Table 8

Claflin University Grammar School Enrollments by Gender,
1869–1940

Year	Total Claflin	Total State A&M	Students from Orangeburg Total Claflin	Total State A&M
1870	128	181	—	—
1872	83	141	67	82
1878	78	142	—	—
1880	52	101	23	17
1884	125	159	62	53
1891	226	339	170	181
1896	235	256	—	—
1901	300	287	—	—
1905	233	276	98	73
1911	183	170	—	—
1915	185	158	—	—
1922	160	147	—	—
1937	24	16	1	3
1940	22	17	22	17

Source: Catalogues of Claflin University, 1869–1940.

Note: Statistics are for grades one to eight. Data on hometown origins were not available for 1870, 1878, 1896, 1901, 1911, 1915, and 1922.

ing for African American working-class females. One little girl, Eloise Tyler Williams, who worked as a nursemaid and washed clothes at home for others, was particularly fond of school. However, she did not receive her grandmother's encouragement and support. According to Williams, "There was a girl in my class who was very smart. One day, I asked this girl how did she become so smart. She simply said that she studied a lot at home. Therefore, so that I could get real smart, I would hide under my house near the chimney wall and do my lesson." Williams recalled that she "wanted to be real smart like that little girl in school," but that eventually her grandmother, Ducky, found out she "was under the house studying," and "she would throw the firewood under the house at me to make me come out. Ducky would not stop until I came from under the house." Her grandmother was not thrilled with the idea of her granddaughter attending school, preferring instead that she work full time. She saw book reading as promoting idleness and laziness.[31]

A small group of working-class parents in Orangeburg did sacrifice the economic contributions of their children so that they could attend school. In the late nineteenth century, the Sterling School was a small, dilapidated building built to hold a limited number of students. Even though it was always overcrowded, the working-class children enrolled represented but a tiny fraction of children from the working-class community. A small number of working-class parents struggled to raise money to send their children to the private, fee-paying school at either Claflin or State A&M.

Because it was such a huge financial sacrifice for working-class families to send their children to Sterling to complete the eighth grade and then on to the fee-paying high school at Claflin or State A&M, prior to 1940, the majority of African Americans never completed their grammar or high school education. Those who completed the first few years of grammar school did so while working part time to earn money to contribute to the household. They usually stopped around the second or third grade to work full time.[32]

It is important to note here that the majority of the African American children enrolled in school in Orangeburg were from the working class. However, the number of working-class children enrolled in school was disproportionately low in relation to the overall school-aged, working-class population. The number of upper- and middle-class children attending school was much higher and consistent with their overall school-aged population.

Jacqueline Jones argues that there were usually more African American girls than boys enrolled in the schools, but in Orangeburg this was not initially the case. Orangeburg's 1880 census listed more boys than girls between the ages of six and seventeen enrolled in school. This imbalance might have reflected the young girls' indispensable roles in their homes as mothers' helpers in caring for the younger children or assisting with the cooking, washing, or ironing. Or, perhaps, like Jean Wheeler Smith's fictitious character, Fannie Mae, many females attempted to attend school while holding jobs but eventually had to drop out because their numerous absences from class caused them to fall too far behind. On the other hand, perhaps some African American families, like white working-class ones, also had higher hopes for their sons gaining an education for better jobs that would allow them to contribute substantially to their families.[33]

After 1910, Jones's argument of more girls than boys also held true

Table 9

State A&M Grammar School Enrollments by Gender, 1911–40

Year	Total Females	Total Males	Students from Orangeburg Total Females	Total Males
1912	268	254	121	107
1922	192	184	54	31
1925	211	219	48	33
1928	216	182	60	59
1935	32	23	—	—
1940	47	38	—	—

Source: Catalogues of State A&M, 1911–40.
Note: Statistics are for grades one to six. Data on hometown origins were not available for 1935 or 1940.

for Orangeburg. While records were no longer available for the early public schools, where the majority of working-class children attended before 1940, Claflin and State A&M early records listed their students by names or gender. Before 1911, Claflin's grammar school enrollment of boys was always higher on the average than that of the girls, from its inception in 1869 to 1910. Table 8 shows that the number of girls enrolled at Claflin consistently exceeded the number of boys from 1911 to 1940. Even when State A&M's grammar school opened around 1910, its female enrollment, too, surpassed that of the males, as shown in table 9. In the colleges' two high schools, between 1923 and 1940, there were more females than males, perhaps due to their parents' attempt to ensure them of having a respectable profession and thus a brighter financial future (see table 10).

The majority of females who attended Claflin and State A&M primary and secondary schools were not from Orangeburg, as shown in tables 8, 9, and 10. Instead, most came from nearby cities and the surrounding rural areas in South Carolina. Some were daughters from the upper and middle classes, as seen with Mamie Garvin Fields and her relatives who came from Charleston to attend Claflin high school, but there was a significant number of working-class females attending these schools as well.

Table 10

Claflin and State A&M's High School Enrollments by Gender, 1923–40

	Claflin Total		State A&M Total		Students from Orangeburg Claflin Total		State A&M Total	
Year	F	M	F	M	F	M	F	M
1923	84	68	—	—	22	16	—	—
1929	108	60	—	—	24	17	—	—
1930	—	—	232	198	—	—	88	79
1932	82	36	129	122	40	25	54	50
1935	54	27	—	—	24	20	—	—
1937	97	67	—	—	55	31	—	—
1940	22	16	—	—	22	16	—	—

Source: Catalogues of Claflin University, 1923–40, and Catalogue of State Agricultural and Mechanical College of South Carolina, 1930–32.

However, having their daughters attend Claflin and State A&M's grammar schools full time was not the norm for Orangeburg's working-class families, since most could not even afford the relatively low fees charged by the colleges. More important, these families were not able to forego their daughters' labor power. Working-class parents in Orangeburg before 1940, mostly illiterate themselves, did not see educating their daughters past a few years of grammar school as a priority.[34]

The majority of working-class African American girls in Orangeburg who did attend grammar or high school did not go to Claflin or State A&M. Although it lacked the proper resources needed for effective teaching and adequate intellectual development, most working-class girls attended the Sterling School because it was free. Since its opening in 1899, Sterling had experienced severe overcrowding, much worse than that found in Orangeburg's free-paying white schools. In 1903, for example, enrollment was at 582, the school taking in students from both Orangeburg and the surrounding rural communities. Students were taught by a staff of 4, including the principal, which yielded a ratio of 1 teacher to 145 pupils. When enrollment increased in 1905 to 650, with only one teacher being added to the staff, the ratio was 1 teacher per 130 pupils. With the opening in 1922 of Dunton, the first African American public grammar school in Orangeburg, Sterling closed after several years of African Americans' pleading for a new school building to replace "the old and crowded wooden building," which was a "fire trap and incubator of disease."[35]

Tables 8 and 9 show that around the time that Dunton opened, Claflin and State A&M's student enrollments drastically declined. Most likely, working- and lower-middle-class students from both the city of Orangeburg and Orangeburg County attended the city's public school for African Americans. When another public grammar school, Riverside, opened in 1931, it relieved Dunton's overcrowded condition. The opening of another school further decreased working-class and lower-middle-class enrollment at Claflin and State A&M's grammar school program, and as a result, the colleges' academically superior grammar schools were mostly attended by the sons and daughters of the upper and middle classes. Only a few working-class females continued their education at Claflin and State A&M's grammar schools after 1922.[36]

Most students attending the high schools at Claflin and State A&M were not from Orangeburg, as shown in table 10. Of those who were from Orangeburg, most belonged to either the upper or middle class. However, a few working-class students completed the grammar school programs at Sterling, Dunton, or Riverside and made plans to attend high school at either Claflin or State A&M. A small number of working-class parents managed to save the necessary fees for them to attend these private high schools. Simultaneously, working-class African American females worked doubly hard, not only to succeed in grammar school to meet the requirements for high school but also to earn money to pay for their fees to attend the school.

The opening of the first public high school in South Carolina was in Orangeburg in 1937. Wilkinson High School, named after President Wilkinson at State A&M, made it possible for poor working-class females to advance their education beyond grammar school. As in the grammar schools, enrollment declined drastically at the private college high schools, as shown in table 10, again leaving the sons and daughters of the elite and middle-class families attending these schools. Even though working-class females no longer had to raise fees to attend school, Orangeburg's working-class parents still did not attach great importance to having their sons and daughters educated beyond a certain level. That their offspring perform excellently on their jobs and earn incomes continued to be most important. Despite the odds against them attending, let alone graduating

Table 11

Occupations of Parents Whose Children Were Enrolled at State A&M, 1918–19

Occupation	Number of Students	Occupation	Number of Students
Farmer	314	Insurance agent	5
Carpenter	39	Chauffeur	4
Preacher	39	Clerk	4
Seamstress	35	Harness maker	3
Teacher	28	Hotel proprietor	3
Housekeeper/maid	18	Trained nurse	3
Laundress	18	Undertaker	2
Cook	13	Florist	2
Brickmason	13	Butcher	2
Blacksmith	11	Doctor	1
Merchant	11	Detective	1
Porter	8	Editor	1
Barber	7	Watchman	1
Government employee	7	Butler	1
Mechanic	7	Hairdresser	1
Tailor	7	Lumberman	1
Postal clerk	6	Shoemaker	1
Painter	5	Soldier	1
Janitor	5	Drayman	1
Laborer	5		

Source: Catalog of State Agricultural and Mechanical College of South Carolina, 1918, 90–91.

from high school, significant numbers of working-class females did attend school, persevere in their studies, and graduate from Wilkinson between 1930 and 1940.[37]

A significant number of working-class females also went on to attend or complete the Normal Training School for teacher training or enroll in the college program for a baccalaureate degree. The majority of students attending Claflin and State A&M were from South Carolina, with a few coming from as far away as Africa and South America, Ohio, Maine, and Colorado. The majority of the African American

South Carolinians, however, were not from Orangeburg but from small towns and rural areas. Most of their parents did agricultural work, as shown in table 11, suggesting that, for the most part, both colleges' student bodies came from working-class families.[38] Thus between 1880 and 1940, the majority of State A&M's graduates (and probably Claflin's too, but data was not available) were not from Orangeburg.

Families who had working-class daughters attending Claflin or State A&M were challenged financially. At Claflin in 1872 board was $10.00 a month and the rooms were "$1 a month with a $1.50 fee for incidental expenses." While tuition was initially free, students were responsible for getting their own lights, towels, bedding, and books. By 1887, students had to "bring quilts, sheets, pillows with cases, spreads, mirrors, towels, soaps, lamps, books, Bible, napkins, teaspoons [and] tumblers." They also had to have money to purchase the required "navy blue uniform skirts and caps" and a "white dress in season."[39]

As at Claflin, State A&M had regulations that included how to dress and where to live, and this most likely created a greater financial burden for working-class students. For example, female students were required to bring the following items to school: "One pillow, two pairs of pillow cases two pairs of sheets, one pair of blankets, two counter paner [?], six towels, toilet soap, and comb, hair and tooth brush, six table napkins, one clothes bag and a spoon, knife, and glass, for individual use in the dormitory room, . . . umbrellas and overshoes." Regulations further stated that "senior girls will need two aprons, one pair of cuffs, and one cap for the Practice Home. . . . Officials will check each student for the named articles."[40] As working-class girls could not even afford most of these items in their homes, purchasing them for school was almost impossible.

State A&M also required that "all dental work be done" before school started, since students would not be dismissed from school if dental problems emerged later. Students also were asked to bring "an extra pair of eyeglasses." These added medical expenses, if applicable, further decreased some working-class girls' chances of attending school and added greater financial stress to the family. Similarly, like at Claflin, students at A&M had to purchase the proper uniform: "Two white and two blue suits" and a pair of low-heeled shoes, all consistent with the seasons. Even though the uniforms were required to avoid "embarrassments" arising from "different conditions," they actually created additional financial problems for these girls and their families. It must have been particularly frustrating when the college further required that all females had to live and board on campus if they were not from

Orangeburg. This decreased their chances of acquiring jobs in the community. However, most of Orangeburg's working-class female students were not affected, as they lived either at home or in a local boarding-house, where they worked to finance their schooling.[41]

Most working-class females enrolled in the Normal Training School instead of the College Program to become teachers. According to Nancy Woloch, it was "teaching that provided more African American women than men with professional work." Therefore, "families went to greater efforts to educate daughters than sons, reversing the priorities of white families." The working-class African American community, in particular, respected teachers. Sharon Harley notes that teaching was a "much sought after profession," since "it represented an acceptable extension of their domestic roles in the home. . . . [Teachers] performed duties commensurate with their professional training, . . . [and teaching] provided one of the best salaries available to [African Americans] in general, . . . and it carried considerable social prestige and status in the community."[42]

It was these working-class female graduates who made up the growing number of African Americans entering the middle class in the early twentieth century. Working-class African American women, on the whole, were the least educated and skilled, and their opportunities for upward social mobility were accordingly slim. Thus, when they did attain higher education and enter the middle class, their humble agricultural or working-class backgrounds followed them. Largely members of the lower middle class, they were not automatically accepted into the social circles occupied by upper- and upper-middle-class educated women. Even their newly acquired middle-class attitudes and life-styles were not enough for entry into the much-coveted upper-class or upper-middle-class African American community. Entrance usually required that they either marry someone already in an upper class or reach some unassailably high economic status in the community.

8.

Working-Class Women's Work outside the Home

Working-class white families "hovered near . . . [the] poverty line" and observed the upper white classes with envy. Most working-class white women who worked outside the home were single. In the North, before 1920, single women mainly worked as domestic servants in white homes, in factories, and, eventually, in department stores. While domestic service work was not the most sought after employment among working-class white women, it was the most easily available. Married working-class white women also earned money by working from their home. Down South, poorer housewives "sold [their] surplus produce" while their single daughters were "hired out to do housework or served for more prosperous neighbors. . . . [A] few work[ed] in small cotton mills."[1]

Paid Work

Between 1880 and 1930 South Carolina's textile industry prospered, largely due to the "abundant supply of [white] cheap, non-union labor." The labor supply remained abundant, particularly as more and more white males and females moved into town to work in the cotton mills. During World War I, when many farm youth and working-class white males joined the military, the mill superintendents hired "teenagers, women, and elderly men to keep the plants running." Even during the Depression, when many mills had to close, these working-class males and females preferred to work at reduced hours and wages rather than return to farming. In the South, "one measure of genteel employment" for working-class white women was "the absence of . . . [African American] women." In the mills and the factories, white women refused to work alongside African American women.[2]

During the colonial era until emancipation in 1865, the majority of African American women were slaves. As slaves, they performed all kinds of work, from unskilled, simple tasks to skilled, complex ones. In the rural areas, "whites . . . who might hesitate to assign white women to plant, plow, and dig the fields exploited [African American] women slaves shamelessly in these jobs. . . . They [also] laundered, cooked, nursed, and cleaned" their masters' houses. There was, of course, a financially secure sector of free African American women, usually of mixed racial heritage, who escaped the drudgery of domestic and farm work or who did not have to work outside the home at all. However, most free African American women in southern cities worked on "lowly . . . paid jobs as servants and in northern cities," such as New York, as "street peddlers, selling in particular their hot corn, Manhattan's special delivery." Others "found themselves confined to the most onerous jobs."[3]

After slavery, the majority of African American women remained unskilled and uneducated, and still had few job choices outside of agricultural, laundry, and domestic work. A few women were qualified to enter the professions, but because of the "discrimination in the semi-professional and blue-collar occupations," they too had little choice but to perform domestic work. Racial discrimination and segregation in the workplace restricted them to these menial positions. By the 1890s, working-class white women were beginning to enter office work, as secretaries, typists, and stenographers, having been allowed to acquire the necessary skills, but African American working-class women were denied such opportunities, even if they managed to acquire the skills. The northern unions that eventually included some working-class white female workers initially excluded African American females, as did unions formed by white women.[4] Protective labor legislation that focused on female laborers had white exploited females in mind, not African American wage earners.

The majority of African American working-class women were domestics. Many left the rural or urban South in search of better pay in the North only to find somewhat higher wages but the same long, grueling work hours and a more expensive cost of living. Most tried to become day servants, but due to competition from white female immigrants, they generally were hired at lower wages, working as "cooks, laundresses, scrubwomen, and maids." In the South, however, because of that region's "glutted labor market for [African American] women," they had no choice but to work long hours, sometimes "up to a seventy-nine hour work week with a half day on Thursdays and Sundays." If they complained or refused to work such hours, they were easily replaced.[5]

South Carolina did not hire African American men and women to work in its factories or mills. In a few cases, "foreigners," most likely northerners, relocated to the state and built factories that hired African Americans. These jobs "were never numerous," however, and according to Earnest Lander, African Americans were eventually "discharged from all but a few menial tasks." The majority of African Americans labored as sharecroppers in the early 1880s, as most still lived in rural South Carolina. A few families were able to save enough from sharecropping to buy their own farms. The family of educator Mary McCleod Bethune, for example, managed over the years to purchase five acres of land in Mayesville, South Carolina, on which they built a log house. For food, they caught fish in a nearby stream, trapped animals in the woods, and grew vegetables. They spent hours and days performing the back-breaking tasks of farming cotton for an income. If at harvest there was a good price for cotton, they paid their debts, bought supplies, and had a few dollars left.[6]

By the late nineteenth century, more than three-fourths of all African American households in Orangeburg were working class. Unlike upper-class and some upper-middle-class women, Orangeburg's working-class women had no option but to work. The working class earned the lowest wages in the city, and it was mandatory that all family members contribute financially to the household. Working-class women were largely unskilled and uneducated, and they earned meager wages from their arduous labor.[7]

In 1880, there were 266 African American households in Orangeburg and 175 of them were working class. Of these, only 50 were two-parent households. Jacqueline Jones argues that while most African American households had a husband and wife, a significant minority did not. She points out that there existed a "relatively large proportion of female-headed families," due mainly to "20 to 25 percent" of the women being widows because of the "high death rate among [African American] men." Orangeburg had an even greater percentage of female-headed households. Out of a total of 175 working-class households in 1880, 95 were headed by women and 10 were headed by men.[8]

More than two-thirds of Orangeburg's working-class households in 1880 were headed by women. This sizable number might have reflected an increase in the number of unmarried women with children migrating from the rural countryside to the town seeking better jobs. Although interracial relationships in Orangeburg were uncommon and illegal, the 1880 census listed one "concubine" as living with a white "brickmaker" and working as a "farm worker." In contrast to African American females who headed single-parent households, most of whom worked, most single white women were listed as being "at home," perhaps supported financially by some form of home employment or wage contributions from their children.[9]

Most of Orangeburg's African American working girls under age seventeen worked as domestics and served as nursemaids for white children; many others were live-in servants. Historically, young girls, not the stereotypical "aged mammy who remained in her ante-bellum place out of loyalty or for other reasons," were hired as servants in white households. To use young African American females as live-in domestics was a continuity from slavery to freedom. In fact, it was not unusual for girls in Orangeburg as young as age nine to work as nursemaids or live-in domestics. Young males under age seventeen generally were listed as farmhands, domestic workers, or students.[10]

The majority of working-class African American adult women worked as domestic servants in 1880; a small number were listed in the census as washerwomen. Their husbands worked as farmhands or farm laborers, while others were "day laborers." As larger numbers of rural southern African Americans migrated to towns and cities between 1880 and 1915, it was not uncommon for African American males to work in "sporadic wage-earning opportunities [that] guaranteed husbands and sons low wages and long periods of enforced idleness." Hence, because of the low pay and, at times, sporadic employment of both the women and men, many in the working class traveled back to the rural areas to perform seasonal agricultural work on large private plantations to supplement their incomes.[11]

The Orangeburg census indicated that by 1900, the majority of working-class African American women were "at home." They still engaged in some form of work at home, however, as their economic contribution to the family was imperative. Most working-class women between the ages eighteen and eighty-one were listed as washerwomen and cooks for private white families. Most men were day laborers, while a minority worked as farm laborers, railroad laborers, farmers, raftsman, draymen, cooks, or firemen operating the furnaces at the mills. A minority of women worked as day laborers at odd jobs and as domestic house servants. The day work of washerwomen and cooks enabled them to work shorter hours than the live-in servants and spend their evenings

A majority of African American working-class women worked as domestics cleaning the homes of middle-class whites. Here a model, using the straw broom she made, portrays a domestic in the early 1900s. Model: Catherine "Neely" Fowler.

doing odd jobs or tasks for their families. The majority of girls under age seventeen were listed as being in school in 1900, even though most probably still worked either before or after school to contribute financially to the family. Those who were not listed as students worked as nursemaids, cooks, laundresses, farm laborers, and house girls. Nursemaids were as young as seven and laundresses as young as nine.[12]

In 1900, approximately 184 working-class African American households were female-headed, out of a total of 379. These women, who labored as cooks and washerwomen, were usually among the city's poorest, since their single incomes supported the entire family until a child was old enough to work. As working single parents, their day work was especially convenient as they were able to care for their young children and family themselves in the evenings, instead of exclusively relying on older children or live-in relatives. Washerwomen worked at home and were normally assisted by their children who were not in school. Other single-parent women worked as house servants, nursemaids, or farm laborers, or they took in boarders or peddled chickens. While most were domestics or farmhands, a few working-class women were entrepreneurs who served a largely working-class clientele or made dresses for other working-class families.[13]

Like other working-class African American women in the South, Orangeburg's African American women too depended almost exclusively on wage labor to support their families or supplement their husbands' income, generally working as domestic servants and washerwomen. In 1910, an overwhelming majority of working-class African American women in Orangeburg worked as "laundresses" for private families. Most women washed clothes for their employers at their own homes; a few washed at the employers' homes. The second largest group of women were cooks who worked in private homes. While a small minority worked for upper- and upper-middle-class African American families, the majority worked for white middle-class families. A few women were listed as nursemaids, saleswomen on the street, operators of boardinghouses, and restaurant keepers. By the early twentieth century, even fewer women worked as farmers or farm laborers, perhaps due to the ever-increasing demand for domestic labor in the city, which was seen as more desirable than agricultural work.[14]

The majority of working-class men continued to work as unskilled day laborers doing non-agricultural work, while the next largest group of laborers worked as farm laborers. More men now worked as firemen as Orangeburg's infrastructure developed to include more factories, businesses, and buildings. These men constantly fed coal into hot, burning furnaces, providing heat for buildings and energy for industries. A

It was common practice for working-class girls, portrayed here by two models, to pick cotton in rural Orangeburg to earn money for school supplies or clothing. Models: Sibongile and Abikanile Mack-Williams.

smaller group of men were employed in other unskilled jobs, including house servant, drayman, hackman, and painter.[15]

The majority of girls under seventeen who worked were listed in the census in 1910 as cooks or nursemaids. The overwhelming majority of single females were over seventeen and worked as washerwomen and cooks. As in 1900, there were only three live-in domestics listed in the census reports, but unlike those in 1910, they all worked for African American families. Although girls as young as twelve worked as cooks and nursemaids, the average young female worker was fourteen.[16]

In 1910, single-parent African American female heads of house continued to work as domestics for private white families. The majority were cooks and washerwomen, while a few performed menial labor in public places such as hotels, boardinghouses, or steam laundry rooms. Orangeburg's census shows that a few single-parent women—midwives, women running boardinghouses from their homes by taking in students, or owners of small restaurants—continued to work as entrepreneurs. Such employment allowed them greater control over their labor.[17]

Between 1880 and 1900, several droughts and crop failures caused much suffering among African Americans in the rural areas. As a result, more families migrated from rural Orangeburg to the city, increasing the pool of urban domestic workers in Orangeburg. Later, African American women from various southern cities, including Orangeburg, gradually began leaving the South on "an average of 6,700 . . . annually" to go to northern cities, especially to Philadelphia, New York, and Boston, between 1870 and 1910. The majority who remained in Orangeburg still worked as domestics for extremely low wages.[18]

By World War I, large numbers of African American women were leaving the South for jobs in the North, causing "some alarm" among whites. A few came up with means to retard or halt the migrations, such as arresting white northern agents who recruited African American labor or dragging African American men and women from the trains. In the North, "a laundress or cook could earn $1.50 to $2 a day plus carfare and meals," that is, earning in one day almost a week's worth of pay down South. In northern factories or industrial jobs, they earned $3.00 a day as compared to the 50 cents they made picking cotton in the South. Yet even with these increased wages, working-class African American women faced racial discrimination as they continued to earn less than working-class white females and were confined to the "dirtiest and most difficult tasks" in "the most-heat intense" positions in the factory.[19]

Few, if any, working-class African American households in the South relied on the income of one adult to support the household. In working-class African American households, all had to work, including "wives, children, and [any] relatives" residing in the home. As in working-class white families, African American children, in particular, were expected to find some type of wage-labor work and help the family. In Orangeburg between 1880 and 1940, the census showed that it was also a common practice for young African American girls under seventeen to work.[20]

For most working-class African Americans in Orangeburg, attending school was, more or less, a privilege rather than an immediate necessity. Hence, before 1940 it was more common to find young working-class girls working instead of attending school. Susan Tucker's research revealed several examples of elderly domestic women in the South who began working as young girls. One domestic, for example, began work at the age of twelve as a nursemaid for fifty cents a week. She also had to "wash dishes and clothes." Emma Jane Parler of Orangeburg dropped out of Sterling School in the fourth grade to work. Her mother both encouraged and supported this decision.[21]

In 1922 at age fourteen, Parler worked as a nursemaid, watching the two young children of a white physician. She earned $1.25 a week and a dinner meal daily. Her responsibilities included playing with the children, changing diapers, giving them a bath, and feeding them a "supper of butter sandwiches with sugar sprinkled over the butter." At first she was too young to perform many of the major tasks, but after eight years' work she had learned to cook dinner, clean up, serve the man of the house his dinner, and prepare the bath water for the lady of the house. Like working-class white daughters who worked, African American daughters also turned in their entire wages to their parents. For example, except for an allowance of 5 to 10 cents a week, Parler's entire earnings, which had increased from a $1.25 to $1.50 a week, went straight to her mother to help pay rent and buy food.[22]

While many had to stop school completely to work, some continued with their schooling, working either full time before the school year began or part time after school ended each day. Thus, school opening was generally delayed, sometimes as late as October, enabling students to participate in the crop harvest. It was common for both working-class boys and girls to pick cotton or other crops in rural Orangeburg to earn money for school supplies and clothing. Whenever news circulated that the "cotton wagon was coming up the different streets to pick up cotton pickers, children and adults waited to be picked up at 4 A.M. each morning on the streets, carrying their lunches and returning daily around 6 P.M." Catherine Livingston gave all of her "cotton money" to her mother when she was paid on Fridays. Her mother, in turn, gave her a small allowance, saved a portion for school needs, and used the rest for the household.[23]

Generally, working-class African American girls worked as nursemaids or laundresses after school in the 1920s and 1930s. Even before these children started school, some white families sought their services as nursemaids. Between the age of six and seven, Flossie Williams was hired to play with the granddaughter of a white woman who lived nearby in her neighborhood. She earned fifty cents a week to play from 10:00 A.M. to noon daily. However, when Williams's mother found out, she made her young daughter quit work after two weeks. Because during the antebellum era it had not been unusual for white males to harass and exploit African American female domestics sexually, Williams's mother feared that her child would fall victim to such sexual abuse. Not limited to Orangeburg, this "fear of rape by white male household members was a factor . . . in the South," as families warned young female kin about the threat of rape. According to Ona Fisher of North Carolina, "Nobody . . . was sent out before you was told to be careful of the white men or his sons. Girls were counseled [on] how to run or not always be in the home alone with the white man or big sons."[24]

Most nursemaids were young, school-aged girls who were hired to take care of younger white children each day after school. Eloise Tyler Williams was paid fifty cents a week to work as a nursemaid from 3:00 to 6:00 P.M. daily after school. In nursing the children, she not only had to play with them but, before leaving for home, she had to bathe and feed them their supper.[25]

Many young girls also worked as laundresses or washerwomen. They either assisted their mothers or grandmothers or they did the laundry themselves while their mothers worked outside the home. White families, as well as the few African American families who could afford such services, either delivered their dirty laundry to the laundresses or had them pick it up. Since most families averaged two to three large loads of clothing, which included everything from their house curtains or bed linens to their underwear, the job was heavy and distasteful.[26]

While still in school, Pearl Green Johnson washed and ironed clothes for the family her mother worked for as well as for other families seeking her service. She normally had at least two families she washed for, earning sometimes as much as $2.00 to $2.50 per family. She would wash one family's clothes at a time to prevent them from getting mixed up. She washed her clothes on Mondays, and after they dried, she "sprinkled them down with water" on Tuesdays to decrease the wrinkles. Then on Wednesday nights she ironed them, returning them on Thursdays. Aside from

To earn money to help support the family, working-class women and girls worked as washerwomen for both white and African American upper-class families. Here a model demonstrates clothes washing with a washboard and tub. Model: Abikanile Mack-Williams.

Domestics washed one family's laundry at a time to keep from getting laundry mixed up. After drying, as demonstrated by the model, the laundry was pressed with a hot iron, folded neatly, and returned to the family within days. Model: Sibongile Mack-Williams.

washing and ironing, she would wait for the cotton truck to come down Sunnyside Street at 6:00 A.M. during cotton-picking season. Returning around 6:00 or 7:00 P.M., she sometimes earned between $10.00 and $15.00 a week. All money, however, was given to her mother, who in turn gave Johnson 50 cents to keep.[27]

It was not unusual for these poor, working-class females, both young and old, to marvel over or admire the fine linens and clothing they washed and ironed with great care. In fact, Eloise Tyler Williams, a school-aged laundress, would wash and iron clothing on a Monday or Tuesday, then actually wear the beautiful clothes from the laundry to school during the week, rewashing them so that they would be ready for return on Friday with the other laundry. For a few days each week at school, she happily replaced her homely, secondhand dresses with the finer, attractive ones she borrowed from her wash load.[28] Such actions were among the subtle ways African American females found pleasure and rewards from their tedious, back-breaking labor.

It was also common practice for both the African American upper class and upper middle class to hire school-aged girls of their own race to watch their children. While in the seventh grade, Mattie Mack Jeffcoat watched the young children of a couple teaching at State A&M every day after school. Wearing a white uniform, she babysat the children, washed the baby's cloth diapers and clothes, and prepared their supper, earning four dollars a week.[29]

Even though the number of live-in female domestics had decreased drastically between 1920 and 1940, those few who worked as live-in servants were usually young and single, sometimes with children. They commonly left their children at home under the care of other relatives, usually working from Sunday to Saturday evening. In 1924, Mattie Jeffcoat was a single parent at the age fourteen. She left her infant son with her mother in Rowesville, South Carolina, and took a live-in domestic job in Orangeburg for three years, watching the young children of a physician and his wife. She earned $3.00 a week and sent $2.50 of it to her mother to help care for the baby.[30] It was not uncommon for grandparents to raise their single-parent grandchildren while the children's mothers took jobs away from home. The practice was especially common among poorer, working-class families for which the extended family ties were often the basis of economic and social survival.

Before 1940, working-class females who attended school full-time still had to work to help support their families. Before age sixteen and while a student in high school, Flossie Williams worked after school as a nursemaid for a white family, playing with their daughter and preparing her supper. Williams earned three dollars a week, which she gave to her mother, who in return would always give her a small allowance. In addition to her wages, she was given both used and new clothing by her employers.[31] Catherine Davis Livingston, a student at Wilkinson High School in the late 1930s, washed, ironed, and cooked for a middle-class African American family. She worked each day after school between 3:00 and 6:00 P.M., earning three dollars a week. Even as a young child, she either babysat in the afternoons for white families or played in the yard with their children, earning seventy-five cents a week and sometimes an additional small gift bought by the family.[32]

Eloise Funchess Amaker boarded with an African American family in Orangeburg while attending Dunton School in 1929. After school, she worked for a family during the week earning seventy-five cents a week for cleaning the house, washing the dishes, sweeping the kitchen, and emptying the trash. From her seventy-five cents, she paid fifty cents for her room and board, using the remaining twenty-five cents to buy paper and pencils. On the weekends, her mother, who lived in Orangeburg County, furnished her with "peas, sweet potatoes, and other things off the farm" to help toward her room and board. She boarded with the family for five years until she finished school. During summer months, however, she returned to her family "to pick and hoe cotton until time to go to school." All the money she earned during the summer was contributed to the family's earnings.[33]

Some high school working-class girls had to work but did not necessarily earn a wage. Frequently, female student boarders earned their room and board by doing housework. Even though Florrie Jones Malichi moved to the city of Orangeburg in 1939 to stay with her sister and attend Wilkinson High School, she had to assume all the chores, such as cooking, shopping, cleaning, and washing the lighter clothing. When Eloise Tyler Williams's grandmother moved to New York City to seek a better job during the Depression years, Williams stayed behind and boarded with one of Orangeburg's respected middle-class families. Her room and board was free in exchange for cleaning the house and sharing the cooking.[34]

Usually, the few working-class female students from Orangeburg who attended Claflin or State A&M college could only afford to go if they themselves worked to earn the moderate tuition fees. Florrie Jones Malichi worked as a domestic during the day for a white family and nursed an elderly white woman during the night, earning enough money to begin taking nursing classes at State A&M. Another woman, Helen Reese Thompson, also worked as a domestic for Orangeburg's first educated African

American registered nurse, Florella Fordham, who strongly encouraged her to study nursing at State A&M. Hence, Thompson enrolled in the nursing program at the college while continuing to work on her domestic job, earning enough money to pay tuition.[35]

Some working-class young women were fortunate enough to get menial jobs on the campus, as the more respectable ones were taken by upper- or upper-middle-class students. Flossie Williams, a student at State A&M studying home economics, worked in the laundry room and the cafeteria on campus during her first two years of college. Her wages were applied directly to her tuition. During the summers in the late 1930s, Williams, like so many other lower-middle-class and working-class female students, traveled to New York City to work as a domestic for a private white family. She saved enough money to buy school supplies and contribute to her family's household income.[36]

Between 1920 and 1940, like other southern cities, Orangeburg had its "oversupply of female labor . . . always available for domestic jobs." At different times, domestic jobs in the North opened up to them, particularly during the war. For example, during World War I, according to David M. Katzman, the number of white domestic servants decreased as more and more white maids, cooks, and laundresses preferred the temporary war jobs to their regular domestic work. He argues that the decrease in the number of European immigrant women who usually worked as servants, an increase in industrialization, and also the increase of education for women further decreased the number of available white female domestics. Hence, for the first time southern African American migrants were sought to fill many of these positions vacated by white European immigrant women. Even though African American female domestics were now being hired more readily, some white housewives still expressed their prejudices by insisting that agencies only send over "light[-skinned] colored girls with straight hair," despite the fact that the majority of applicants did not fit this description.[37]

Between 1920 and 1940, many working-class African American women still worked as washerwomen, despite Carter G. Woodson's warning in 1930 that due to mechanization, these laundresses were "rapidly" becoming anachronistic. Yet in Orangeburg before 1940, the growth of the laundry industry and the acquisition of washing machines in private homes apparently lagged behind those changes in the other southern cities. Thus the services of laundresses were still, on the whole, an integral part of Orangeburg's upper- and middle-class households.[38]

The majority of these laundresses washed and ironed clothes for upper- and middle-class white women, a job requiring a tremendous amount of time and patience. The work "was exceedingly heavy . . . and especially unpleasant in the South's already steaming climate." At times, it was even frustrating and demeaning. They did it nonetheless, as this was the only type of work available to them. According to Sadie Bodrick Fair, "Black people have done something for white people for a little bit of money. One woman named Miss Essie used to wash clothes, including the filthy, soiled cloths used by white women during their menstrual cycle. She would wash those dirty, bloody cloths by boiling them and getting them white as snow. She couldn't refuse them since she needed them as customers. We were some hard workin' women back in those days."[39]

They boiled the clothes in a big, round black wash pot in the back yard, usually with soap powder furnished by the white family, cleaned them on the washboard, and then rinsed them out several times, hanging them on the clothesline to dry. To iron the clothing, the "smoothing" or "flat" iron was heated by placing it on top of the chimney coals. "If anything was scorched or burnt," according to Eloise Tyler Williams, "black people usually had to pay for it."[40]

While most of these women's customers were white upper-class and middle-class families, there were others. Frances Muller Ferguson washed for poor white families who lived near her and worked in the cotton factory. She earned twenty-five cents to fifty cents per family for the washing and ironing of two or more loads of clothing. Some washerwomen washed for both African American and white families. Thelma "Sissy" Reed, for example, washed for both white families and the professional African American families associated with State A&M. In fact, many of these African American families insisted that they "didn't want anyone else to do their laundry but Sissy."[41]

While most customers dropped their clothing off and picked them up at the laundresses' houses, some laundresses had family members who picked up and returned the clothing. Sadie Bodrick Fair recalled how her Uncle Ed would drive his wagon and mule around to five or six different families, picking up clothes to be washed and ironed by his wife. On the other hand, Alice Gaines Mack would walk from house to house to wash clothes for two to three families, African American and white. She would wash and hang out clothes in one yard and while they dried, she would walk to another house to wash and hang out clothes. When the clothes dried, she would again walk from house to house to take them in, leaving them for another domestic servant to iron. She earned sometimes as much as $1.50 per day.[42]

Some women worked full time as washerwomen, while a few others saw this as temporary work until "something better came along." When Lillie Tingsey Moody first moved to Orangeburg County in 1931, she used to help an African American woman wash clothes every Monday, earning eighty cents each time. She did this until she became a full-time nursemaid for a white family. Pearl Green Johnson washed and ironed for families when her husband, a shoemaker, became an alcoholic and refused to support her. She did this until she was able to migrate to Connecticut to work as a domestic live-in. Mamie Sims Rufus washed clothes for several white families until she was able to go to New York City and get a better-paying job. In New York, she was a live-in domestic for a white family. She sent money and hand-me-down clothing to her mother in order to care for her young daughter, Fannie.[43] Despite the threat of mechanization and the coming of steam laundries, manual washing and ironing remained a form of work that was still available for working-class African American women long after 1940.

Nevertheless, the onset of mechanization did have a gradual effect on these washerwomen by replacing their arduous, manual labor with machinery; yet the demand for domestics in Orangeburg persisted, in both private homes and public businesses. Between 1920 and 1940, uneducated and unskilled poor African American women continued to be confined largely to domestic employment, working as washerwomen, cooks, and maids. In addition, some of their poor white counterparts lost their jobs during the Depression in the few factories or mills in the city and competed with African American women to work as washerwomen for white families.

It was not unusual for African American women to work as both domestics and washerwomen for different families. For example, Betty Jamison worked as a domestic for one family and washed and ironed for another one. Each morning, she walked several miles to work as a domestic servant for a white family. After walking the long distance back home on a Monday or Tuesday, she boiled the other family's clothes in a big, black iron pot in the back yard. After washing and drying them, she ironed them so that they would be ready for pick up on Thursday or Friday.[44]

Usually, these overworked domestics worked for one family and performed all the washing, ironing, cleaning, and cooking as well as watching their children. However, both upper-class white and African American families, as in the case with the elite African American family of Cora Ransom Green, usually hired different domestics to perform different tasks. For example, after Lillie Williams Thomas cooked, cleaned, and nursed the children for each of her white employers, she did not worry about washing and ironing, since each of these families had hired a separate washerwoman. In either case, these domestic drudges lived in poverty, earning low meager wages and bringing home leftover food daily in their servant pans, sometimes referred to as "anxious pans," to feed their families. While some women refused "to tote or accept food," most working-class African American women did not. Emma Parler, for example, not only depended on the tote to feed her parents but also looked forward to receiving the old nylon stockings and other castaway clothing given to her by her "boss lady." Because domestics were paid extremely low wages, employers felt satisfied in giving their servants what they themselves considered "nice presents and things." Some even "gave presents to their [servants'] families," as they felt obligated to give food, clothing, or gifts "to stay in good standing" with their help.[45]

The work of domestics was much more demanding than that of laundresses, who generally had greater control over their labor. It was also common practice to hire domestics to do one type of work while, in actuality, they performed several other tasks, especially in the case of nursemaids. When Lillie Tingsey Moody was hired as nursemaid to the children of a white family, she at first only tended to the children but later had to clean the house as well. Florrie Malichi's sister, Lil, was hired as a "sleep-in" nursemaid who not only nursed the children but eventually had to "wash, iron, cook, and clean" as well. Daisy Graham asserted that in the 1930s, "when you went to the white folks' house, you did everything. You didn't make nothing around them times. People were just working for little of nothing."[46] Even though they were not paid for the extra work, castaway clothing, tote pans, free rent, and "positive praise to other families regarding their work" presumably served as compensation.

Sadie Bodrick Fair, "was hired to work as a nursemaid, but . . . did everything else. After the family ate breakfast around eight o'clock, [she] cleaned up the kitchen and then worked around the house making beds, ironing, and other things." Afterward, she "had to give the kids lunch and then take them to the playground until sometimes late in the evening. After returning from the playground, [she] went home." Fair made $2.50 a week.[47]

It was not unusual for these nursemaids to congregate together at the playground, discussing the trials and tribulations of their jobs while their white charges played. Generally, they were required to wear uniforms to work. Sadie Fair recalls that they consisted of white aprons with white or green uniform dresses and white bands or sometimes white caps around their heads:[48] "Out at the playground, you could see all the [African American] nurses on the Ellis Avenue playground with their freshly washed or starched uniforms on, bought by their own meager earnings. We would all talk about our bosses, the kids, or all the ugly things that go on. This was a time to fraternize and discuss common problems experienced. It was something to look forward to. After all, we could not speak up to the boss honestly since you feared losing your job." Frequently, regular domestic servants were also required to wear some form of uniform dress. Even though Betty Jamison walked long distances every day in the 1930s to get to her domestic job, she wore a long dress with a freshly starched, bleached white apron and tied up her hair with a cloth band.[49]

Like laundresses, some domestics also worked for two families at a time. Daisy Salley Graham worked early in the morning, cleaning up for a white family for a $1.50 a week. Then between noon and one o'clock, she worked as a cook at a boardinghouse, walking to and from each job daily. Sadie Fair worked as a domestic for one family, but during the cotton season, she would request a few weeks off to plant or pick cotton, returning to her regular job afterward.[50] Most domestics, however, worked for one family, since it usually took all day to do the work.

In the 1930s, most African American women in the Southeast continued to work as domestics. Increased competition developed between African American and white women for these jobs during the Depression years.[51] Julia Kirk Blackwelder has argued that in a few places, such as San Antonio, competition for domestic jobs did not increase since these jobs outnumbered the available African American domestic workers. As in the larger South, Orangeburg's African American domestics often did lose their jobs to poor white women who had been laid off from their regular jobs at the local cotton mills or factories. Even with the later jobs created through New Deal legislation, African American women continued to face exclusion and discrimination as South Carolina and Orangeburg reserved the best jobs for whites. The poverty of Orangeburg's African American working-class women was alleviated only by the government's relief program coupled with the wages contributed by everyone in their households, including their children.[52]

During the Depression, over half of African American women lost their jobs as compared to "three out of ten working white women." Unemployed African American women in New York City, for example, congregated "at street corners," commonly referred to as "the Bronx slave markets, . . . early in the morning, seeking day's work and bargaining with customers for rates as low as 10 cents an hour." Even in the South, where most worked as domestics, half lost their jobs, and in many instances, they were replaced by white women who needed employment. Those African Americans who did not lose their jobs worked at lower rates.[53]

From the late 1920s to 1940s, working-class men struggled to hold on to their jobs as yardmen or domestic servants in either factories or private white households in which they worked as chauffeurs, butlers, or day laborers, doing odd cleaning or repair tasks. Others worked as day laborers for private businesses or for the city of Orangeburg, digging wells, cleaning streets, or constructing railroads. A few even used some rather unconventional and illegal means to make money. The National Prohibition Act, passed in 1919, prevented the sale and distribution of alcoholic beverages and was not repealed until 1934. Prohibition, however, did not stop illegal underground sales. For example, during the week, Roosevelt Kearse bought as many pints of liquor as he could afford from a bootlegger, hid them in the ground in his back yard, and on the weekends sold them to others at a higher price. Sometimes Kearse earned as much as one hundred dollars in one day.[54]

Most working-class African American women during the Depression continued to work as domestics in private homes or public businesses. It was not unusual for the classified ads section in the local newspaper to advertise domestic positions that specifically sought "colored women." One live-in job requested a "Colored Housekeeper: to take charge of house for elderly couple; living quarters provided." Others advertised for cooks: "Experienced colored cook. Apply Orange Cut Rate Drug Store" and "competent colored women for cook." African American nursemaids were in great demand, as well: "Colored nurse for two year old child" and "Wanted at Once-neat, experienced, colored housekeeper by working couple with three children. Salary $18 per month, room and board."[55]

Some white families in Orangeburg also chose to hire white female domestics until the end of the Depression era in order to help poor, working-class white women during this economic crisis. Some advertisements specifically sought to hire white domestics. One ad requested a "white girl, age 25 to 40 years to keep house, cook, and help work in store. Must be neat with good qualifications, and a lively person." Another sought an "intelligent white girl to help keep house and assist in operating small business."[56]

It was not unusual for poor African American and white females seeking domestic work to advertise themselves for jobs in the newspaper. For example: "Experienced Cook Wants Job. Mary Thornton, 31 Maple Court"; "Wanted: to do your Washing and Ironing. Edna Utsey, 127 W. Glover St."; "White lady desires work, housekeeping, or companion(ship)";

"Wanted-work: I want job washing and ironing. Emma Dash, 35 Inabinet Quarters"; and "Young white lady desires work as housekeeper." Less common were ads that sought employment for more than one family member: "Colored man and wife want job as cook and housekeeper. Edgo Huggins, 21 Dunton St."[57] In seeking employment through advertising, African American women did not usually refer to their race, whereas white women did, perhaps to let potential employers know that they were not typical "colored" women.

Although poverty continued to plague their lives during the Depression years, working-class women managed to survive by working as maids, cooks, laborers, and washerwomen. Rarely did they get work in Orangeburg's factories or businesses, except at the most menial levels. Jobs in Orangeburg's cotton mills or other factories were usually reserved for working-class white men and women.[58] African American working-class women continued to be overworked drudges trapped in a form of neoslavery. They often perfomed numerous tasks, and sometimes rather heavy ones, in jobs that should have been performed by more than one person. Particularly during the Depression era, these unskilled women bore the burden, since they knew that they could easily be replaced by other African American women seeking "a good family to work for."[59]

Beginning in 1929, Eloise Funchess Amaker, a single woman of nineteen, worked seven days a week for seven years for the same white family from 7:00 A.M. to 5:00 P.M., receiving one Sunday out of the month off. First, she prepared breakfast for a family of nine. After setting the table and serving them their breakfast, she would clean the pots and pans and only then sit in the kitchen to have her breakfast. By 8:00 A.M., the table was cleared and the dishes were washed. Between eight and eleven o'clock, she cleaned the five bedrooms by making beds, sweeping, and dusting each room.[60] By eleven o'clock she had prepared dinner so that it would be ready for the family when they came home at noon. Since they served themselves, she now only had to set and clear the table. After her dinner, she spent the remaining time "watching the 'devilish' little boy who had a habit of sneaking outside while she was in the midst of cleaning the rest of the house." She was also responsible for ordering the groceries, which were delivered by a porter from the store, and making the necessary accommodations for the family's guests during visits and holidays.[61]

Her employers hired a washerwoman to do the clothes and an African American school boy to prepare the supper since she left at 5:00 P.M. She was paid $2.50 a week with meals for her services, allowing her to pay her board, insurance, and church dues. She was also allowed to bring home a sandwich for her supper and, at times, was given used clothing if other family members did not want them. Hers ranked as a "good-paying" job, as during the Depression, many "grown men with families were making only twenty-five cents a week. They were lucky to get a job making that, but they made it."[62]

In the 1930s, the average domestic in Orangeburg earned from $2.00 to $2.50 a week, although a few fortunate ones, notably those who worked for employers relocating from northern areas, earned almost twice as much. Emma Jane Parler's weekly earnings increased from $2.00 to $4.00 when she accepted a job with a business family who moved to Orangeburg from Virginia shortly before 1940. By 1940, her wages had increased to $4.40 a week, enabling her to save money in the local bank for the first time.[63] T. K. Bythewood recalled the controversy created by another business owner who moved to Orangeburg before 1940 and paid "his domestics $6.00 a week. [The employer] felt that by paying them higher wages, this would prevent them from stealing other goods," suggesting that stealing was prevalent. According to Bythewood, other white families expressed their anger with him over this act since their workers had started asking questions about their pay. However, this particular businessman's reply was that "they steal that $6 amount away from you every week anyway, while at my house, they don't steal from me."[64] Perhaps, stealing was how some women rebelled subtly against their exploitative plight.

Perhaps the best domestic jobs in the city were those held with the wealthier or more socially prestigious white families. Daisy Salley Graham, for example, worked for the mayor of the city, cooking, cleaning the house, and performing other relevant domestic tasks. She earned five dollars a week and brought home as much food as she liked. She did not have to do the washing and ironing, as the family had hired a separate servant for that, but she did earn extra money from washing and ironing the uniforms of one white policeman in the city.[65]

Not all African American female domestics worked in private homes. Some working-class women also held domestic jobs in public businesses, which were considered very good jobs. For example, Alafair "Ducky" Morgan cooked in the nursery school at State A&M. Another woman, Elizabeth Darby Bonaparte, was a cook who worked in a public, white-owned boardinghouse from 7:00 A.M. to 3:00 P.M. daily. This boardinghouse provided accommodations for white travelers or its white permanent residents.[66]

Nora Gardner Smalls cooked in a white boardinghouse daily but later accepted a job at the St. Joseph Hotel that paid six dollars a week. There, she worked as a cook and cleaned the kitchen and the rooms. Eva Mosely

Davis also cooked, but in the city's hospital, which admitted African American patients through the back door, where they could be nursed to health in an isolated room near the kitchen. Unlike the cooks in the boardinghouse, she did not have to work on Saturdays and Sundays.[67]

During the Depression, the conditions of thousands of African American working-class women in the South worsened. Although New Deal federal work relief programs created jobs for thousands of unemployed men and women, most African American women were purposely excluded from these jobs, and those who were hired held the least desirable jobs. Relief programs also provided limited clothing and other goods to each family. According to Dorothy Scott Mack, "We went over to the white school called Thackston on Sellers Street to get those plain, straight dresses, canned fruits, canned juices, and dry milk and this really helped to feed our family. My great grandmother also received a small relief check and a coupon booklet. You always had to present those stamps or coupons in the booklet to get your supplies since everything was rationed out."[68]

African American domestics in the Depression years depended even more on servant pans from their jobs. This leftover food, supplemented by the vegetables grown in their small gardens and the eggs laid by their chickens, allowed them to feed their families. Even the castaway clothing provided by white families was considered, by many, a luxury. Despite their poverty-stricken lives as children, Dorothy Scott Mack and her brother, John, were perhaps among the "best-dressed" poor, working-class children in their school. Their mother, Julia Maude Scott, was a domestic for an upper-middle-class white family who constantly gave her children clothes that were not only "well kept but usually were quite expensive and of high quality."[69]

Many Orangeburg African American women migrated to New York, since domestic jobs in that city paid much more than those in Orangeburg. One woman, Alafair "Ducky" Morgan, initially migrated to Orangeburg from a smaller town in South Carolina in the 1930s to seek better economic conditions with her seven small grandchildren, but during the Depression she gathered her grandchildren and moved to New York City to find a better job. While some, like Flossie Williams, went to New York City in the 1930s to work as a live-in nanny to earn money for college,[70] most working-class women, like Morgan, sought jobs to earn money to support their families.

Pearl Green Johnson, tired of the low wages and the hard work of washing and ironing, moved to Connecticut in the 1930s to find better work. She first worked as a domestic and then found work in a laundry room. After paying her room and board, Johnson sent her mother ten dollars a month, since she "did not want her poor mother begging on the streets." Many early immigrant working-class European single women also sent their wages back home, to "Russia or Italy," to help maintain their households. [71]

During the Depression, "women from poor households . . . could count on help from their friends and neighbors. Grandmothers cared for their children's children," so that they would be "free to search for jobs elsewhere as the children lived under the watchful eye of a relative." Single, young working-class mothers, in particular, took advantage of available domestic jobs in New York, Philadelphia, Washington, and other northern, urban centers. Their strong, extended family ties in Orangeburg enabled them to leave their children, usually with their mothers or other close relatives. Once they found work, they sent money and castaway clothing to Orangeburg. When Alafair Morgan first moved to Orangeburg in the early 1930s, she brought all seven of her grandchildren with her. Of her four single-parent daughters, three had never been married and the fourth was separated from her husband. All four mothers found work outside of Orangeburg, two eventually in New York City. [72]

While many African American women migrated to other areas in search of better economic opportunities, the majority stayed behind in Orangeburg. Despite South Carolina's practice of distributing most of the WPA jobs to white men and women, some African American working-class women received jobs. Each day these workers had to report to the nearest WPA office, which was usually a public white school, to get their assignments. It was not unusual to see both African American men and women working together, sometimes even with a few poor whites, in small "chain gang-like" groups, cleaning the yards of buildings and churches. [73]

Daisy Salley Graham and Bertha Perry were fortunate to work in one of the several WPA segregated sewing rooms around Orangeburg that made clothing for poor people on relief. While they both sewed in all–African American female settings, Graham was eventually hired to work in an all-white WPA sewing room. There, she did not sew but worked as a cleanup maid who also "folded and packed garments, helped to cut the cloth, ran errands, picked up scraps, and swept the floor." She preferred this type of domestic work to the usual domestic housework, "since the WPA paid more even though it was every two weeks." As soon as she received her new WPA job, Alafair Morgan assigned her grandchildren to the task of continuing to do "the washing and ironing that she took in from white families." While the children washed and ironed, she worked as a domestic, cleaning a public white junior high school. [74]

Many African American women who worked on WPA jobs not only performed domestic tasks but also worked outside doing either agricultural work or general yard cleaning. Besides her WPA sewing room job, Daisy Graham also did seasonal work on government farms. She planted and picked beans, earning fifteen cents per hour. Nora Gardner Smalls made fifty cents each day by "hoeing grass, washing the inside of windows, cleaning schools and houses." At times, her son would come to help his overworked mother "hoe the grass" because it was too much for one person, even though he was not being paid.[75]

Some working-class women during the Depression still struggled as small entrepreneurs trying to earn money for their families. A few took in one or two boarders, "a favorite means of earning additional income" among both working-class white and African American women. The boarders were usually students or single-parent women whose rent money supplemented the working-class household earnings. Eva Mosely Davis took in as many as five or six boarders who were either attending high school or college in the city. Most of them did not pay her with money but with food, such as "fresh meat, meal, potatoes, and fresh vegetables" brought to Orangeburg on the weekends by their parents.[76]

Upon returning from her domestic job in Connecticut in 1937, Pearl Johnson opened a small community store in the midst of a poor, working-class African American neighborhood on Sunnyside Street. She had saved enough money from her Connecticut job to rent both a house for herself and a small place for a store for a $1.25 a week from another African American woman. Although she mainly served the poor African American community, she also occasionally served poor white customers who lived nearby. Her income enabled her to support both her ailing mother and her unemployed, alcoholic husband.[77]

A small minority of female entrepreneurs attempted to support their families based on their acquired skills. Julia Maude Scott, a single-parent, attended the Judy Breland Beauty and Culture School to study hairdressing. After taking her two young children to school, she worked as a domestic servant, cooking and cleaning for an upper-middle-class white family in the morning. She, too, relied on the servant pan to help feed her son and daughter. On some evenings, however, she would leave the children with their great grandmother while she visited various African American families "to do hair." Her hairdressing skills also afforded her some opportunities to prepare the hair of the corpses at the African American–owned Bythewood Funeral Home. These occasional, sometimes frequent, jobs allowed her to earn enough money to help support her children and her grandmother and to meet other household expenses.[78]

Working-class African American women worked arduously, no matter how numerous or strenuous their tasks. Seldom did these women lose their jobs. Even "during emergencies or following childbirth," they still managed to hold onto them by "having a sister, mother, friend, or even an older child, take over the job" during their absence. But these domestic jobs were not void of stress and tension, particularly when it came to employer-employee relations. Some white female employers, in particular, showed "all kinds of harshness and meanness in the kitchen" or home. In turn, the domestic "retaliated with strategies perversely appropriate to the domestic background." One woman from rural Charleston boasted to Mamie Garvin Fields of how domestic women in the area retaliated against ill-tempered whites. "When we cook the dinner, we spat in 'em. . . . Oh, yeah, stand over their pots and one would say 'Spit!' and all would spit. . . . Not just spit . . . hawk and spit. We did that to them people. They were too mean to us."[79]

John Rivers recalls how his mother, Julia Maude Scott, would have him and his sister, Dorothy Scott Mack, come by the house everyday after school where she worked as a domestic in order to get their dinner. On one occasion, young Rivers was in the kitchen talking to his mother when the white female employer entered and angrily scolded Scott for having her son in the house and then made him go outside. Once her employer left the kitchen, Scott "fixed her and her children's food and served it to them on the back step." She then "hawked and spat several times" in the remaining food to be served to the white family. Spitting, stealing, and other similar deviant actions were various subversive ways that African American women used to rebel against their mean-spirited bosses.[80]

Lower-middle-class and working-class women both had to work, whether at wage-labor jobs or at home. In either case, working-class women had fewer choices. Their need to work and their few skills forced them to accept whatever employment was available, regardless of its degradation or difficulty. Even when they worked as domestics in private homes or businesses, many still returned home to earn a few more dollars by washing and ironing or taking in boarders.

Although most African American domestics worked for whites, a minority worked for upper- and upper-middle-class African American families, receiving the same equitable pay. They did not experience the same awkwardness or social discontent that arose from intricate Jim Crow rules they had learned as youths growing up in Orangeburg, such as calling at the back door, avoiding direct eye contact, or yielding the sidewalk or conversations to whites. While they felt more relaxed and comfortable working around those of their own race, in some cases both racial and class differences between African American employers and employees caused dissatisfaction. For example, some African American female employers with their alleged "good hair," "good looks," and "light skin color" took pride in their appearance, transmitting an attitude of superiority toward their more "African-looking, dark-skinned" domestics. In fact, some of these domestics themselves believed that their own racial characteristics of darker hue, kinkier hair, and broader noses and lips were ugly and inferior to their employers' white-like physical features.[81]

African American women's contact with well-to-do, lighter-skinned African American women reminded them of their social inadequacies, and thus they further internalized feelings of racial inferiority already promoted by the larger white community. These female domestics constantly compared what they perceived to be "their inferior cultural skills and material goods associated with working class culture" to the more superior cultural and material means associated with their African American bosses' upper- or upper-middle-class societies. They therefore adopted and used whatever new ideas, skills, or material means they could to improve their meager social lives and their appearances to enhance their status in their own neighborhoods. These working-class women did not resent working for their African American female employers, but they envied them to the point of emulating them at any opportunity they could once back in their own communities.[82]

Besides subtle racial overtones, there were also tensions due to class differences between African American domestics and their female employers. The employee-employer relationship automatically carried with it a sense of the superordinate-subordinate, even if the relationship had existed on a personal level for decades. Like their white counterparts, African American upper- and upper-middle-class employers not only imposed their bourgeois values on their domestics but also provided them with the usual castaway clothing, household items, and tote pans.

Whether these African American domestics ever retaliated by spitting into food is not clear, but some probably did take food or other items without permission from their bosses. However, this practice was most likely more common within the white elite or middle-class households, since in these homes there was probably more food and other goods and less contact between employers and employees. Jim Crow divisions in Orangeburg created rather intimate, racially segregated neighborhoods in which African American employers and their employees were forced to live in the same parts of town. Thus the possibilities were even greater that African American employers would eventually learn about domestic servants who might have stolen or spat into food. Such discoveries would result in those particular employees losing their jobs, as well as having a blemished work reputation. This type of news or gossip in the small Orangeburg African American community would definitely narrow or destroy such employees' future chances of finding domestic employment.

The attitudes and perceptions of working-class African American women and their upper- and upper-middle-class African American boss ladies differed, reflecting the values and perspectives shared within their respective class. Their class consciousness or differences did not diminish because they belonged to the same racial group; instead, it heightened and further maintained the notion of "separateness." Most African American female employers displayed their superior class positions subtly, while a few were more pretentious and displayed superiority and social prejudice around their help. In turn, these working-class domestics displayed the usual deference to their African American female employers, as they themselves were enmeshed in a glimmer of hope that a respectful, loyal relationship with their influential employers might one day improve their own lives. To work for these families in Orangeburg's well-to-do African American community indirectly linked them to this coveted class and gave them access to significant contacts in the elite community.

With the absence of Jim Crow attitudes and stringent racial barriers traditionally found between white employers and their African American domestics, African American domestics had less reservations about seeking help from their African American employers. They confided in them regarding various social or economic problems they endured. Because of the community contacts their employers had, or even the leadership roles they held in the community, it was not unusual for these elite families to assist their servants. They procured small loans for them, helped them acquire decent housing, food, and clothing, and, at times, assisted them in providing their children with educational opportunities.[83] Whether working-class African American women worked for whites or African Americans, they still remained the lowest paid sector in the working class. They worked hard to earn meager wages that was so crucial in preventing their families from falling deeper into poverty.

Unpaid Work

Aside from their wage labor, some working-class women found time for volunteer work. Cynthia Neverdon-Morton argues that "class differences among the women diminished in importance" due to "all black women—

rich and poor, urban and rural" working together to achieve the dual goals of racial and individual betterment. This was not the case in Orangeburg, because there were no poor and well-to-do African American women working together, outside of their possibly serving on separate religious committees that might have been working together as a coalition on some project. There were rigid class lines in the African American community in Orangeburg, and even the club work "to uplift the race" was not exempted from such divisions. In some instances, working-class women might have been the participants in planned activities and definitely the beneficiaries of the clubwomen's hard work, but never the co-organizers.[84]

Exclusions from clubs due to class differences were not unique to Orangeburg, as seen with Mamie Garvin Fields of Charleston, who decided to form her own civic club, the Modern Priscilla, to include the uneducated, nonprofessional woman. In Washington, D.C., as well, Sharon Harley points out that "college-trained and socially elite reformers" were reluctant "to seek out individuals from all segments of the [African American] population." However, she adds that the "fine dress, often richly-furnished homes, social manners, and their more public lives" most likely "discouraged" these "less educated, less financially-situated women" from working with these elite organizations. Thus, they joined church-related and secular organizations that "often required less affluent lifestyles, less active public roles, and had more practical benefits for their members than did the predominantly middle-class reform associations."[85]

Upper- and upper-middle-class African American women in Orangeburg had the leisure time to do volunteer social work through various clubs. Working-class women did not have such leisure time. Nor would they have been recruited to join such organizations, as the clubs' goals were to assist the poor, and the majority of African American working-class women in Orangeburg *were* poor.

Unlike upper- and middle-class women who worked in civic clubs, working-class women usually did volunteer work through their church organizations. Continuing from slavery, poor African American women still saw the church as being the most important influence on their lives next to their families. The church, like their families, enabled these women to endure their economic problems. They served as spiritual havens away from their oppressive, back-breaking labor. The church, according to Charles Johnson, was "a forum for expression on many issues, an outlet for emotional repression, and a plan for social living." Carter G. Woodson, Eugene Genovese, W. E. B. Du Bois, and others consistently argued that the church was the most important African American organization that "affected the improvement in the [African American] race."[86]

Evelyn Brooks-Higginbotham asserted that working-class African American Baptist church women "rallied to the course of racial self-help" and "pool[ed] their scant resources for the development and support of black-owned schools" and "institutions for the elderly and the destitute." Orangeburg's working-class African American Baptist women also sang in the choir, served on the prayer bands in the church, worked for the various missionary societies that visited shut-ins and the sick, and served on fund-raising committees to raise money for the church, needy victims, or those experiencing economic emergencies due to fires, deaths, or illnesses.[87]

Some working-class women worked very hard to cook food either to sell or to serve at various functions at the church. On special occasions, such as Women's Day or Children's Day, these women spent their entire Sunday at the church, beginning with the Sunday morning school. After church services, they coordinated the program and afterward served the huge dinners they cooked earlier at home and brought to the church. How-

Working-class women's lives centered around work, family, and church. A minority volunteered to serve in choirs, prayer bands, or missionary societies. Following the path of her grandmother, Betty Jamison, in the 1930s, Dorothy Scott Mack (shown here in 1984) takes her grandchildren to St. Paul's Baptist Church, where she sings in the choir. *Left to right:* Dorothy, Nabulungi, Kafele, Yakini, and Kanika.

ever, it is important to note that while working-class women did their volunteer work through their churches, most of these already overworked women lacked the physical energy to be active in the church. According to Cynthia Neverdon-Morton, "In both [the] rural and urban South," many African American women "continued to work as domestic servants, in a system that returned many of the characteristics of slavery," spending "long hours away from their home [and] carrying out physically exhausting duties for which they received little pay."[88]

Working-class women's social life centered on attending church and some church-related functions as well as on visiting with neighbors. After working twelve to fourteen hours daily at both their regular and side jobs, most working-class women opted to attend the regular church services and pay their dues. For example, Daisy Graham remembered how she "had to work" and still "attended St. Paul Baptist Church but . . . could not do a lot of work in the church." Graham "paid . . . dues, but every day of the week, [she] had to work too much. All [her] time was spent working."[89] This routine was not unique to Graham and reflected the life-style of the average working-class African American female.

Upper-, middle-, and working-class women contributed some form of volunteer labor to their churches, but the largest class of women— the working class—appeared to have, on the whole, contributed the least amount in Orangeburg. These women had the heaviest workloads and the least amount of leisure time. In fact, most did not spend their leisure time with their children, their spouses, or frolicking with their friends like the upper- and middle-class women. Instead, they used this time to catch up with minor chores and neglected tasks around their homes or to rest. Their busy work schedules and volunteer labor interfered greatly with their child-rearing duties and family life. Working-class women's lives, indeed, centered around work, work, and even more work, particularly when their domestic roles in the home were taken into consideration.

9.

Working-Class Women's Work inside the Home

As might be expected, working-class women did their own housework. The prestige of having domestic servants was limited to upper- and middle-class households, particularly as it was the working-class white and African American women who provided domestic services for such households. White women in poor antebellum households in the South worked very hard at home; "they hoed the corn, cooked the dinner, or plied the loom." They also "took up the ax and cut the wood with which to cook the dinner." They prepared the "food, cloth, candles, . . . soap, . . . and supervised farm animals and the kitchen garden."[1]

Traditional domestic chores, such as "caring for large families, doing field work, farm work, and housework" continued to be women's work into the postbellum era among both urban and rural working white women. Even when white women were full-time wage earners, they were still responsible for the housework. Tentler argues that since their outside jobs were still seen as "temporary," even though their wages "clearly supplement[ed] the husbands,' there was no need to change the traditional domestic arrangement." Thus working-class women carried the double burden of working both outside and inside the home. Working-class white males were "not burdened with domestic chores," but their sisters were "not relieved" from "household responsibilities," even though they, too, were wage earners.[2]

Housework for African American and white working-class females included heavy physical labor, since their houses "lacked hot running water, set laundry tubs, and private indoor toilets." Because they could not afford relatively modern home appliances, working-class women were forced to shop, launder, and cook more often. After working long hours at their jobs during the day, they spent their evenings at home, usually "cooking, washing dishes, ironing, and dealing with their young children with little or no assistance."[3]

Most working-class African American women worked both outside and inside their homes. The few who did not work outside, worked at home because they had too many young children. For example, the mother of the Florida-raised writer Zora Neale Hurston stayed at home to care for her ten children while planting and reaping their crop on their farm. Working-class African American men also wanted their women to be housewives and care for the home, as was the case with Hurston's father, who took pride in boasting that "he had never allowed his wife to go out and hit a lick of work for anybody a day in her life." In fact, Carter G. Woodson pointed out that right after emancipation, many African American men "rapidly withdrew their wives and daughters from field work and restricted their efforts largely to the home" as full-time housewives. This practice ended quickly, however, since all needed to work to sustain the household. Table 12 shows that between 1880 and 1900, working-class women in Orangeburg were listed not only as washerwomen and domestic servants but also as being "at home." But they too were most likely working from their homes.[4]

The majority of upper- and upper-middle-class African American women were also listed as being "at home," but their at-home life-styles did not reflect that of women in the lower middle and working classes. Jacqueline Jones and W. E. B. Du Bois have both argued that poor, working-class women at home busily "engaged in a variety of income-producing activities throughout the year," including peddling flowers, selling "vegetables, chickens and eggs, milk and butter to neighbors, wash[ing] and iron[ing] and, sometimes, cook[ing]."[5] However, by 1910, as table 12 illustrates, the number of working-class women at home had decreased by two-thirds. In any case, working-class homemakers were generally engaged in some form of gainful employment as opposed to enjoying a life of leisure or volunteer work.

As in other households, the housework in working-class African American homes included cooking, cleaning, washing, ironing, and gardening. However, this housework was done by the women themselves along with their children. Regardless of whether they worked outside the home, the amount of housework remained the same. Working-class women were first introduced to housework when they

Table 12

Working-Class Married African American Women's Occupations in Orangeburg, 1880–1910

Occupation	1880	1900	1910
At home	28	108	74
Dress maker	0	0	4
Merchant/grocer	0	0	1
Saleswoman/dry goods	0	0	1
Sick nurse	0	1	4
Boardinghouse owner	0	1	1
Waitress	0	1	0
Restaurant keeper	0	0	2
Student	1	0	0
Saleswoman (street)	0	0	1
Cook/family	0	25	48
Domestic servant	19	4	1
Washerwoman	3	29	85
Washerwoman (hotel)	0	0	1
Washerwoman (laundry)	0	0	1
Chambermaid	0	0	1
Day laborer	0	5	6
Peddler (chickens)	0	0	1
Farm operator	0	1	2
Farm laborer	5	3	8
Total	56	178	327

Source: Bureau of the Census, Census of 1880 on Population. Orangeburg Town, Census of 1900 on Population. Orangeburg City, and Census of 1910 on Population. Orangeburg City. Note: The total number of African American households in Orangeburg for 1880 was 266; for 1900, 535; and for 1910, 708.

were children. While upper- and upper-middle-class girls performed light household chores, studied dance or piano, and were encouraged to do well in school, working-class African American girls were introduced to the work force and taught to respect work. According to Bernice Reeder, a domestic worker in Washington, D.C., originally from rural Virginia, she was working in the fields at the age four. She washed "small pieces in a tub every weekday" and brought "all the clean water for the rinsing of the clothes by six; minded the children, cooked, and washed by eight; and worked out by ten."[6]

Both working-class girls and boys had set daily chores. It appears that a strict gender division in chores was not as evident among working-class children as among upper- and upper-middle-class children. It was common for both working-class boys and girls to share in the washing of clothes, the cleaning of the house and the yard, bringing in the water or wood for the fire, and even cooking. Flossie Williams and her brother were trained to cook, clean house, and wash and iron. While she washed the clothes in the tub, he would bring fresh water, and once the clothes had dried on the line, he would take them into the house.[7] By age fourteen or fifteen, boys' household work gradually diminished as they sought paid employment and performed the more traditional male chores, such as cleaning the yard, chopping wood, and helping with repairs. Some boys held jobs where they worked as cooks.

Even children who worked outside the home still had their household chores. After leaving her domestic job each day, Emma Jane Parler still had to cook and clean the house when she returned. Aside from going to school and "taking in washing and ironing" from several white families, Pearl Green Johnson sometimes did her family's washing and cooking, but she usually kept the house clean and helped to can the vegetables during canning season.[8] As children, girls were already being trained to juggle and perform more than one task at a time.

Some girls had chores to do even before going to school or to their domestic jobs. As a little girl, Emma Whitmore had to wash dishes and sweep the floor each morning before leaving for school. Many times, since working-class mothers had to be at their jobs 6:00 or 7:00 A.M. to serve breakfast to their employers, the oldest daughter, usually a child herself, was responsible for getting herself and all the other children off to school. The oldest daughter also prepared their dinner at midday and supper in the evening.[9]

Like other poor, working-class girls in the United States, particularly among European immigrant females, completing these household chores took precedence over any leisure activities or even school attendance. After getting her younger siblings off to school by feeding and dressing them, Anna Bonaparte Shuler of Orangeburg had to wash, iron, and keep the house clean while her parents worked. Oftentimes, she stayed home from school to complete her chores, since the other children were in school and could not interfere with her work. She usually attended school for a half day, leaving at midday to prepare her siblings'

After working long hours as domestic servants for other families, women, as portrayed here by models, had their own laundry to wash, food to cook, and houses to clean. Models: Abikanile and Sibongile Mack-Williams.

dinner or to complete chores. Also in Orangeburg, Eloise Tyler Williams and her cousins had to do their chores after school, and if these
chores were not completed when their grandmother came in from work,
their grandmother "whipped" them.[10]

Even when they were young, some working-class girls had to perform the dirtiest of tasks. Although a special wagon that discarded the
waste in the "outhouses" or outdoor bathroom facilities usually made
weekly stops in neighborhoods where proper plumbing did not exist,
many working-class families were responsible for their own sanitation.
As a young girl, Annie Bonaparte Shuler had "to clean out the outdoor
toilet with a scrub mop and lye soap," taking turns with her brothers:[11]
"Usually early in the morning on Mondays, Wednesdays, and Saturdays, either me or my brothers had to clean the outhouse. When it was
heavily filled with waste, we had to cover up this hole and dig a new
one. I would wash the wooden-made toilet seat and also the inside and
outside of the toilet itself. The rent man would dig a new hole, deep
like a water well, and we would have a fresh toilet."[12]

Some of their tasks were arduous, and, at times, quite cumbersome.
Poor, working-class families usually lived in dilapidated houses with
two to three rooms without plumbing or electricity, and these disadvan-
tages created numerous and more tedious chores for the children. Besides cleaning their two room house, Eloise Tyler Williams and her six
cousins had to attend to several daily chores after school: "Outside in
the yard, there was one spigot situated between four little two-room
houses. This spigot was shared by these four houses so that each could
bring water inside when needed." Every day after school, Williams and
her cousins "had to tote water in the house, sweep the yard, and then
get a big 'crocus' sack and go down in the woods to chop wood."[13] Williams explained that after they chopped the wood, they had to "put it in
the sack and bring it back home for fire." Sometimes they "would cut
down big oak trees and bring home the big heavy logs over [their]
shoulders for firewood." She recalled how the "white people used to
curse at [them] and tried to chase [them] out of the woods by shooting
their guns at [them] as [they] hurriedly chopped wood." She points out
that the chores did not end with collecting firewood. She continues that
"at the end of each day, when [her] grandmother Ducky came home
from work, [they] had to bring in a basin of water and wash her feet.
[They] had to work or get a beating."[14]

In a few instances working-class girls in Orangeburg were not obligated to do set tasks. For example, one girl, Dorothy Scott Mack, did
not have to work and contribute money to her household like most of

Because working-class homes normally did not have lawns or manicured shrubs, they were usually kept clean of leaves and excess dirt with a broom. Here a model demonstrates. Model: Sibongile Mack-Williams.

her peers. Furthermore, she was not given any particular household chores to do at home but busied herself by sometimes joining other children in completing their tasks. At times she would assist her great-grandmother in her washing by bringing her water and, sometimes, by standing on a box to help "scrub clothes on the scrubboard."[15]

Even with their daughters and sons helping with the housework, these working-class mothers and grandmothers still had other household tasks to do. Each day after working outside the home on their jobs, they came home to complete their side jobs of washing and ironing for other families. In addition, their own families had to eat or have their clothes washed and ironed if these tasks were not already done by their children. These, along with other household chores, further lengthened the working-class woman's work day to one of twelve to fourteen hours, beginning as early as 5:00 A.M. and ending around 6:00 or 7:00 P.M.

Some working-class women had to do all of their own house chores, as they were either childless, their children were too young, or their children were already grown and had households of their own. Other working-class women chose to do their own cooking for their families or washing and ironing of the clothes, despite having children to help. After walking a long distance to and from her job, according to Dorothy Scott Mack, her grandmother, Betty Jamison, returned home to tidy up her place, bring in wood and water, and cook:[16]

> When granny came home from doing her daywork, she cooked in the chimney hatch in big, black iron pots. There was a wood stove, but she did most of her cooking in the fireplace, making "ash" cakes or "hoe" cakes in the iron frying pan. She baked potatoes in the ashes, made "hop 'n johns" [peas and rice] in the big iron pot, and she browned the cabbage in the frying pan. All these things were cooked in the big iron pots, sitting on the hot coals. There was no sink or refrigerator, but a small icebox that she would buy a block of ice for every weekend to keep it cool. She drew the water from the side of the house and would boil water on the wood stove to either wash dishes or to bathe. Granny also raised chickens for us to eat.[17]

With or without major assistance from other family members in doing household chores, these overworked women continued to do their own work at home. After going from house to house, washing clothes and cleaning up, Alice Gaines Mack came home and cooked, washed and ironed, and made clothes for the family. Addrena Cummings Tyler, a washerwoman who washed for three families, still had her own wash to do along with cooking and cleaning. When she completed these tasks, she went on to tend to her garden and "piece quilts" for her family to use in the cold months.[18]

After working all day, Daisy Salley Graham, a single parent who generally worked two jobs, would cook, clean up, and mop the floor when necessary. She also washed for her family as well as cleaned the yard. Sometimes at night, she "washed white folks' clothing and then got up early in the morning to hang them out before going to work." Anna Green, a domestic worker and a washerwoman, shared her washing, cooking, and cleaning with her daughter, but she herself "tended to the garden, prepared her vegetables for canning, and cared for the chickens in the yard."[19]

Working-class women worked from the time they rose in the morning until shortly before they retired to bed, when they performed their last minor tasks—rinsing out the garments they had worn that day or scraping leftover scraps into the "slop bucket" that hung outside their back doors. Whether they worked for African American or white families or for private homes or public businesses, these ordinary women were seldom remunerated properly for their labor. While they worked for upper- and upper-middle-class African American women, there was little or no social intimacy between working-class women and upper- and upper-middle-class women. However, there was a social bond between lower-middle and working-class women, largely as a result of their close familial ties and social relations. Relegated to the worst jobs available, these working-class economic underdogs and toiling drudges were locked into a world of tiring, strenuous, unending work.

Conclusion: A Sisterhood Denied

The agrarian-based economy of Orangeburg County in the late nine-teenth and early twentieth centuries created thousands of agricultural jobs for African Americans. As migration to the town of Orangeburg increased in the early twentieth century, many still worked as farm la-borers, going back and forth between city and county. Some depended on the seasonal agricultural jobs in the rural area to supplement the jobs they held in town. In the city, however, most African Americans gen-erally worked as domestics for either private families, mostly white, or public businesses.

Orangeburg's two African American colleges founded in the late nineteenth century further widened class cleavages in the African American community, since education became a chief determinant of class position. As more African Americans graduated from the two col-leges, the upper and middle classes increased in numbers. Higher edu-cation and greater skills allowed these African Americans to enjoy greater economic opportunities. By 1940, they were working as top ad-ministrators and faculty members at the colleges, as well as carpenters, teachers, ministers, tailors, and seamstresses in the larger community.

The work of women, in particular, changed as they shifted from one socioeconomic class to another. Upper-class women, usually well educated and from an established, propertied family, lived "pseudo-aristocratic" lives that closely resembled that of white upper-middle-class women. Most of these women owned property and had a generous inheritance and suitable income independent of their spouses. They did not have to work to make financial contributions to their households unless they chose to do so. In most cases, their class positions were determined by their family background or personal achievements. In the case of women who came from more humble economic backgrounds, higher education and/or lucrative careers placed them among the upper classes. When these women married upper-class or upper-middle-class men, their status was defined by their husbands and by their own achievements. Independent of whether they had personal wealth or not, marriage into upper-class or upper-middle-class families enabled these women to live more leisurely lives.

Upper-class women who did work between 1880 and 1940 consistently selected jobs appropriate for their class position, and their incomes were treated as pin money to be spent as they wished. During the Depression era, however, some elite homemakers sought some form of genteel employment to earn money to help sustain the family. Many employed domestic servants in their homes, while others chose to do some of their own housework. Upper-class women who were active outside of their homes and less involved in housework still remained active in the household decision-making process.

Elite women were usually active in church and club work in the community, striving to uplift the race. Conscious of their envied position within the community, some snobbish elite women proudly distanced themselves from the African American masses and treated them in a patronizing manner. While most in the upper class, did not behave in this manner, they still lived socially apart from the majority. Yet, they too had to deal with the larger problems of Jim Crowism, racism, and social and political exclusivity.

Middle-class women were generally well educated and, as proud women conscious of their class status, aspired to be as culturally enriched and economically stable as the women of the upper class. Within the middle class there was a financially secure minority of upper-middle-class women who either originated from old, established middle-class families extending back to the antebellum or Reconstruction eras or from financially secure families. While a minority of upper-middle-class women did not have to work, most did and were careful to choose the more respectable, well-regarded job.

It was not unusual for middle-class women to hire domestic help for the heavier household tasks, even though that help did not consist of a full staff of servants as often found in upper-class households. The majority of the middle-class women, particularly the lower middle class, however, performed their own housework. They hired outside help temporarily for the heavier or seasonal tasks such as heavy clothes washing or canning.

Both upper- and upper-middle-class women generally married men from similar social backgrounds, but never from the humble working class. Education was the sine qua non in their households, and attaining jobs commensurate with their training was a must. Upper- and upper-middle-class women had more leisure time than the majority of middle-class women and were able to devote more time in grooming their children in bourgeois, Euro-American culture, including dance, music, and art. Upper-middle-class women admired and emulated the life-styles of elite African American women.

The majority of middle-class women, however, were from the lower middle class. Most came from working-class backgrounds and entered the middle class as a result of attaining higher education. Others entered this class through marriage, through having lucrative incomes, or through holding prestigious jobs. While conscious of their middle-class status, which separated them from the larger working class, unlike upper- and upper-middle-class women, they did not necessarily marry men from middle-class backgrounds. These women did not have the choice of whether to work or not and had to make financial contributions to their families. If they did not work, they were still engaged in some form of income-producing activity from the home, enabling them to add to their families' income.

When upper- and upper-middle-class women worked outside the home, they usually held the gender-segmented professional or well-regarded jobs apropos to genteel culture. On the other hand, women in the lower middle class held jobs which varied from traditional genteel ones, such as teacher or dress maker, to traditional working-class menial ones, such as house servant or laundress. While some attended college or acquired a professional skill such as hairdressing or midwifery, many were semiskilled or unskilled and thus had fewer job opportunities. However, by 1940 more had entered the middle class as trained teachers, as increasing numbers of females entered the colleges. Women in the lower middle class had less leisure time to spend with their children, as compared to upper- and upper-middle-class women. Seldom were they able to afford bourgeois-cultural training in music or dance for their offspring.

Working-class African American women were the most impoverished of the working women in Orangeburg and the most conscious of their economic plight. While they desired and envied the more privileged lives of the upper classes, they remained "enclosed" in their class position as they engaged in the most demeaning labor. The poorest members of the working-class were those single-parent females who lived on their own, raising their children or their grandchildren while their mothers pursued jobs in other cities. Working-class women, along with their spouses or family members, worked very hard to help provide the basic necessities for their families.

Attaining education within the African American community in Orangeburg was definitely a class question. While education was stressed among the upper classes, within the African American working class it was secondary to working on a job and contributing financially to the household. A small minority of working-class parents did sacrifice economically to educate their sons and daughters, but they were certainly not representative of the average working-class parents in Orangeburg before 1940.

Euro-American bourgeois luxuries, such as ample leisure time or training the children in music or dance, were rarities among the working class. At times, even schooling was seen as a luxury, for most working-class families depended on the labor input of their children. Working-class girls began work in the home at a young age, performing various household chores, and many times these working class girls had to work outside the home in order to contribute financially to the family.

Aside from the active church work of a minority of working-class women, they were not usually engaged in club activities, because they were the ones civic clubs were either trying to "uplift" or, as in the case of their social clubs, "segregate" from. Like their lower-middle-class sisters who worked outside the home, they shared the "breadwinner" roles. They also remained active in their housework and continued to participate in the household decision-making process in spite of their outside work.

African American women in Orangeburg from 1880 to 1940, regardless of their class, had limited work opportunities due to their race and gender. Racism and Jim Crow segregation in the city excluded them and the entire African American community from participating in the city fully and prevented them from seeking certain political, economic, and social opportunities. They were relegated to working in the menial servile positions available in the white homes or businesses. They worked on agricultural jobs, which were seen as less prestigious than day work in the city. Others worked in the few positions available in the African American community, including those in the colleges or schools, their own businesses, or as domestics for elite African American households. For the most part, African American women worked in jobs reserved exclusively for females, although there were a few jobs, such as farmhand or teacher, that escaped gender segregation.

Although regardless of socioeconomic status, most of Orangeburg's African American women worked, their work, both inside and outside the home, varied enormously according to class. Despite class differences, however, all these women were busy, as their lives centered around either wage employment or housework and volunteer work in their churches or clubs. Lower-middle- and working-class women, however, had little or no choice in deciding whether or not to work. Their financial contributions and various perquisites, such as tote pans and castaway clothing, were indispensable to their family's survival. They worked harder than any other class of women in Orangeburg, both inside and outside the home, and earned the least amount of praise, recognition, and income. These working-class women were not only the most hard working of all African American women, but they were the true unsung heroes in the entire Orangeburg community.

My intent in this study was to provide further insight into the impact of class divisions and culture on an African American community in a small southern city. I particularly focused on the interplay among education, skin color, material resources, and family background in both class formation and social relations. While illustrating the important roles that the colleges, Claflin and State A&M, played in educating the surrounding community, I also noted the significant role they played in further stratifying it socially and economically.

A small but significant number of elite African American women in Orangeburg did not have to work. They practiced the "cult of true womanhood" and focused on the domestic sphere, serving as the social and moral uplifters in the community. Both boys and girls in upper-, middle-, and working-class households were given some form of housework to perform, but in each of the classes, husbands did little or no housework, demonstrating their cross-class, internalized Victorian views regarding men's roles in the home.

Orangeburg's African American women's class consciousness, lifestyles, and labor evolved from and reflected their specific class reality. The social and economic diversity found among these women was a reflection of their class differences, which, in turn, prevented them from becoming a united, tightly knit group. Just as race historically prevented a sisterly cohesiveness among Orangeburg's African American and white women in the United States, class prevented a cohesiveness among African American women in Orangeburg. Instead, there evolved a subtle form of intraracial Jim Crowism in Orangeburg within the African American community, a segregation based on class and skin color. Exclusivity and elitism, ranging from membership in civic and social clubs to where one should live to whom one should marry, was promoted by upper- and upper-middle-class women. There was no overall subtle or overt African American sisterhood across class lines in Orangeburg's African American female community before 1940.

While there was social bonding between upper- and upper-middle-class women, as well as between lower-middle-class and working-class women, there was little or no interclass social intimacy among all the women, except in the employer-worker social relationship. While I did not find such interclass intimacy, perhaps there was an occasional interclass alliance formed around race in Orangeburg to protest some aspect of Jim Crowism or to promote charity programs through church alliances to benefit the poor majority. Despite African American women's shared experiences of race and gender-segmented labor in Orangeburg, their obvious class differences prevented a sisterhood across class lines. Their class positions and consequential culture ultimately shaped how they worked, lived, and socialized.

Notes

Introduction

1. W. E. B. Du Bois, *The Gift of Black Folk* (reprint, Millwood, N.Y.: Kraus-Thomson, 1975), 9–10.
2. Ibid., 261.
3. Ibid., 260.
4. Asa Gordon, *Sketches of Negro Life and History in South Carolina* (reprint, Columbia: Univ. of South Carolina Press, 1971), 95–109, 174–91.
5. See Charles S. Johnson, *Growing Up in the Black Belt* (New York: Schocken, 1967); Hortense Powdermaker, *After Freedom: A Cultural Study in the Deep South* (New York: Atheneum, 1969); Michael P. Johnson and James L. Roark, *Black Masters: A Free Family of Color in the Old South* (New York: W. W. Norton, 1984); Loren Schweninger, *Black Property Owners in the South: 1790–1915* (Urbana: Univ. of Illinois Press, 1990); Willard B. Gatewood, *Aristocrats of Color: The Black Elite, 1880–1920* (Bloomington: Indiana Univ. Press, 1990); and Adele Logan Alexander, *Ambiguous Lives: Free Women of Color in Rural Georgia, 1789–1879* (Fayetteville: Univ. of Arkansas Press, 1991). E. Franklin Frazier, *The Negro Family in the United States* (Chicago: Univ. of Chicago Press, 1947) and *The Negro in the United States* (New York: Macmillan, 1957). In his study of the black family and culture, E. Franklin Frazier concluded that African Americans, as a group, had no familial cultural impact on the larger U.S. society since they had not retained any aspects of the African culture and, in fact, had no culture at all. While he has been criticized for these findings in contemporary scholarship, James B. Stewart argues that he "made important theoretical contributions . . . [on] . . . the emphasis on early patterns of class differentiation among black fami-

lies conditioned by slavery." Such a class analysis might have stemmed from Frazier's earlier membership in the Intercollegiate Socialist Society while a student at Howard University, where he, according to Stewart, "saw the emergence of an urban black proletariat as the most significant twentieth-century development pointing to possible advances for black families." See James B. Stewart, "Back to Basics: The Significance of Du Bois's and Frazier's Contributions for Contemporary Research on Black Families," in Harold E. Cheatham and James B. Stewart, eds., *Black Families: Interdisciplinary Perspectives* (New Brunswick, N.J.: Transaction, 1990), 12, 19–20. Thus Frazier's findings, along with the others listed above, will be used as a viable focal point in examining the class structure in Orangeburg, South Carolina.

6. Johnson, *Growing Up in the Black Belt*, 76; Frazier, *Negro Family in the United States*, 209–24.

7. Even though I grew up in Orangeburg between the mid-1950s and the early 1970s, significant vestiges of these earlier class distinctions still existed within the African American community in the city. Many of the people from the three major classes who lived in Orangeburg between 1910 and 1940 were senior citizens still residing in Orangeburg at the time of this research. During their interviews with me, most of these older residents still belonged to and identified strongly with the same socioeconomic class they were members of before 1940. Others, whose class positions were generally lower before 1940 but had improved either before 1940 or since that time, were frank and honest in describing their more difficult lives in their lower class status as compared to their achieved elevated ones; see Johnson, *Growing Up in the Black Belt*, 72–76. While this study does not examine South Carolina specifically, his description of the various social classes is also appropriate to rural and semirural Orangeburg.

8. Ibid.; Gordon, *Sketches of Negro Life*, 95–109.

9. See Gordon, *Sketches of Negro Life*, and I. A. Newby, *Black Carolinians: A History of Blacks in South Carolina from 1895 to 1968* (Columbia: Univ. of South Carolina Press, 1973).

10. Doris A. Derby, "Black Women Basket Makers: A Story of Domestic Economy in Charleston County, South Carolina" (Ph.D. diss., Univ. of Illinois–Urbana, 1980); Rackham Holt, *Mary McLeod Bethune: A Biography* (New York: Doubleday, 1964); Mamie Garvin Fields with Karen Fields, *Lemon Swamp and Other Places: A Carolina Memoir* (New York: Free Press, 1983); Jane Edna Harris Hunter, *A Nickel and a Prayer* (Nashville: Parthenon, 1940); Leslie A. Schwalm, *A Hard Fight for We: Women's Transition from Slavery to Freedom in South Carolina* (Urbana: Univ. of Illinois Press, 1997).

11. A. S. Salley Jr., *The History of Orangeburg County, South Carolina* (Orangeburg, S.C.: B. Lewis Berry, 1898); Marli Frances Weiner, "Plantation Mistresses and Female Slaves: Gender, Race, and South Carolina Women, 1830–1880" (Ph.D. diss., Univ. of Rochester, 1986); Jayne Morris-Crowther, "An Economic Study

of the Substantial Slaveholders of Orangeburg County, 1860–1880," *South Carolina Historical Magazine* 86 (1985): 296–314; Herbert Gutman, *The Black Family in Slavery and Freedom, 1750–1925* (New York: Pantheon, 1976); Annie M. Berry, "In the Past Fifty Years: Do You Remember?" 24 Mar. 1954, manuscript, Orangeburg County Public Library, Orangeburg, S.C.; Mrs. T. W. (Emma Mae) Bookhart, "Orangeburg County: Historical Data, Sketches, and Records," vol. 2, "Towns," manuscript, bounded by the Forewoman of the Work Project Administration Mending Room located in the basement of the Orangeburg County Courthouse, Orangeburg, S.C., 1939, Orangeburg County Public Library, Orangeburg, S.C.; Hugo Sheridan Ackerman, "Orangeburg to 1880: A Frontier Community," pamphlet written for the Caroliniana Library in Columbia, S.C. 10 Jan. 1953, Orangeburg County Public Library, and "A Brief History of Orangeburg," pamphlet, written for Home Federal Savings and Loan Association in Columbia and Orangeburg, S.C., 1974, Orangeburg County Public Library, Orangeburg, S.C.; Thomas Osmond Summers Dibble, "History of Orangeburg: 1884," manuscript, Orangeburg County Public Library, Orangeburg, S.C.; Marion Salley, *The Writings of Marion Salley. The Orangeburg Papers*, vol. 1 (Orangeburg, S.C.: R. L. Bryan, 1970). Orangeburg Historical and Genealogical Society, Orangeburg, S.C.; Willie Llew Griffin, "Orangeburg's Beginnings," *Times and Democrat*, 1970, Orangeburg County Historical Society, Orangeburg, S.C.; Ellen P. Chapling, "Facts and Legends of Orangeburg County," manuscript, Orangeburg County Public Library, Orangeburg, S.C.; J. M. Sam and W. F. Fairey Jr., "Orangeburg County: Economic and Social. A Laboratory Study in the Department of Rural Social Science of the University of South Carolina," 15 June 1923, manuscript, Orangeburg County Public Library.

12. Florrie Jones Frederick, "Wilkinson High School: A Story of Greatness," manuscript, Orangeburg County Public Library, Orangeburg, S.C., copyright 1987 by Florrie Jones Frederick; Horace E. Fitchett, "The Influence of Claflin College in Negro Family Life," *Journal of Negro History* 29, no. 4 (Oct. 1944): 429–60 and "The Role of Claflin College in Negro Life in South Carolina," *Journal of Negro Education* (Winter 1943): 42–68.

1. Upper-Class African Americans

1. Johnson, *Growing Up in the Black Belt*, 72–73.
2. See Julie Winch, *Philadelphia Black Elite*; Schweninger, *Black Property Owners in the South*; and Gatewood, *Aristocrats of Color*, 12.
3. Gatewood, *Aristocrats of Color*, 12.
4. Ibid., 12, 39–138; Roi Ottley and William J. Weatherby, *The Negro in New York: An Informal Social History* (Dobbs Ferry, N.Y.: Oceania, 1967), 134–35.
5. See Schweninger's *Black Property Owners in the South*, Gatewood's *Aristocrats of Color*, and Johnson and Roark's *Black Masters* for discussions of the antebellum

African American "aristocrats" in Charleston, South Carolina; Gatewood, *Aristocrats of Color*, 7.

6. Alrutheus Ambush Taylor, *The Negro in South Carolina During Reconstruction* (New York: Russell and Russell, 1969), 68–69.

7. Hugo Sheridan Ackerman, "1928–1929: Black Community in the Late 1920s," *Times and Democrat*, 18 June 1987.

8. Salley, *History of Orangeburg County*, 57; Sam and Fairey, *Orangeburg County*, 17; Darlene Campbell, "Minority Businesses: A Rare Species Looking at Extinction," *Times and Democrat*, 1 Feb. 1987.

9. Ibid.

10. Dibble, *History of Orangeburg*, 17; Hugo Sheridan Ackerman, "Black and the Troubled '20s," *Times and Democrat*, 26 June 1988.

11. T. K. Bythewood, interview by author, Orangeburg, S.C., 27 Mar. 1987; Campbell, "Minority Businesses."

12. See Fields and Fields, *Lemon Swamp*; Fitchett, "Influence of Claflin College," 431; Earnest McPherson Lander Jr., *A History of South Carolina: 1865–1960* (Chapel Hill: Univ. of North Carolina Press, 1960), 153, also see footnote 67.

13. Fitchett, "Influence of Claflin College," 432; Fields and Fields, *Lemon Swamp*, 84.

14. Fitchett, "Influence of Claflin College," 433; Gatewood, *Aristocrats of Color*, 39, 41, 270.

15. Fitchett, "Influence of Claflin College," 434–35.

16. Edmund L. Drago, *Initiative, Paternalism, Race Relations: Charleston's Avery Normal Institute* (Athens: Univ. of Georgia Press, 1990), 4; Lewis K. McMillan, *Negro Higher Education in the State of South Carolina* (Orangeburg, S.C.: Self-Published, 1952), 193; ibid.; Gatewood, *Aristocrats of Color*, 255.

17. Carter G. Woodson, *The Mis-Education of the Negro* (New York: AMS, 1972), 53, 56; Gatewood, *Aristocrats of Color*, 270.

18. McMillan, *Negro Higher Education*, 189.

19. Ibid., 189–92; *Palmetto Leader*, 17 Jan. 1925, p. 1.

20. Salley, *History of Orangeburg County*, 34–35; T. K. Bythewood, interview, 27 Mar. 1987.

21. T. K. Bythewood, interview, 27 Mar. 1987.

22. The Sultons, a respectable mulatto family who owned the oldest sawmill company in the South, relocated their prosperous lumber business to Orangeburg from Colleton, South Carolina, in 1916. See "The Oldest Southern Sawmill Company Is Operated by Negroes," *Southern Lumberman*, 15 Dec. 1931, 106; Maxine Sulton Crawford, interview by author, Orangeburg, S.C., 4 Mar. 1987, and Carmen Sulton Thomasson, interview by author, Orangeburg, S.C., 10 Mar. 1987.

23. Salley, *History of Orangeburg County*, 34–35; Crawford, interview; and Thomasson, interview.

24. Crawford, interview; Lula Love Wilkinson, interview by author, Orangeburg,

S.C., 9 Feb. 1987; Geraldine Pierce Zimmerman, interview by author, Orangeburg, S.C., 27 Feb. 1987; Eloise Tyler Williams, interview by author, Orangeburg, S.C., 22 Oct. 1988; and Dorothy Scott Mack, interview by author, Orangeburg, S.C., 22 Oct. 1988.

25. Gatewood, *Aristocrats of Color*, 104–5, 196–97; *Palmetto Leader*, 17 Jan. 1925, p. 8.

26. Frazier, *Negro Family in the United States*, 295–316; Marilyn Green Epps, interview by author, Orangeburg, S.C., 3 Dec. 1986; Wilkinson, interview; and Zimmerman, interview.

27. Louisa Smith Robinson, interview by author, Orangeburg, S.C., 11 Feb. 1987; Taylor, *Negro in South Carolina*, 68, 295.

28. Frazier, *Negro Family in the United States*, 257–87; Gunnar Myrdal, *An American Dilemma: The Negro Problem and Modern Democracy* (New York: Harper and Row, 1944), 700–705; Gatewood, *Aristocrats of Color*, 69–95, 141–81.

29. Johnson and Roark, *Black Masters*, 206–12; Ira Berlin, *Slaves Without Masters: The Free Negro in the Antebellum South* (New York: Pantheon, 1974), 279–83.

30. Frazier, *Negro Family in the United States*, 235, 305–8; Myrdal, *American Dilemma*, 667–705; Powdermaker, *After Freedom*, 60–65; Wilkinson, interview; Zimmerman, interview.

31. Frazier, *Negro Family in the United States*, 235, 305–8.

32. Gatewood, *Aristocrats of Color*, 80, 141–81.

33. During the interviews with women from various economic backgrounds, it was not unusual for an informant to express pride or delight over the fact that either she or someone in her family was of mixed heritage and not "all black" or "pure African." Even women with very dark skin asserted their white or Indian bloodlines with pride, denying they were "all black." E. Franklin Frazier pointed out that despite a person's mixed ancestry, if he did not have a prestigious family background, did not possess wealth, or had not achieved a certain level of higher education, he still was not accepted into upper-class society (see *Negro Family in the United States*, 408); Zimmerman, interview.

34. Amy Hill Hearth, "The American Century of Bessie and Sadie Delaney," *American Heritage* (Oct. 1993), 77; Zimmerman, interview; Susie Alexander Hubbard, interview by author, Orangeburg, S.C., 5 Dec. 1986; Wilkinson, interview; Emilie Bythewood, interview by author, Orangeburg, S.C., 16 Feb. 1987; Eloise Funchess Amaker, interview by author, Orangeburg, S.C., 18 Feb. 1987; and Thomasson, interview.

35. Hubbard, interview; E. Bythewood, interview; Amaker, interview.

36. Epps, interview; Zimmerman, interview; Amaker, interview; E. Williams, interview; Mack, interview.

37. Gatewood, *Aristocrats of Color*, 345; see *Palmetto Leader*, 8 Mar. 1930, p. 7, 24 Mar. 1930, p. 7, 19 Apr. 1930, p. 7.

38. *Palmetto Leader*, 8 Mar. 1930, p. 7.

39. Ibid., 29 Mar. 1930, p. 7, and 19 Apr. 1930, p. 7.

40. Fields and Fields, *Lemon Swamp*, 187.

41. Ibid., 187–88.

42. *Palmetto Leader*, 6 Dec. 1930, p. 7.

43. Ibid., 18 Dec. 1937, p. 3.

44. Ibid., 31 Mar. 1928, p. 5.

45. Paula Giddings, *When and Where I Enter: The Impact of Black women on Race and Sex in America* (New York: William Morrow, 1984), 115.

46. Ottley and Weatherby, *Negro in New York*, 134–35; Gatewood, *Aristocrats of Color*, 211, 221, 240–41.

47. Gatewood, *Aristocrats of Color*, 209; Ottley and Weatherby, *Negro in New York*, 216–17; see William L. Andrews, ed., *Collected Stories of Charles W. Chestnutt* (New York: Mentor, 1992), and Nella Marian Larsen Imes, *Quicksand and Passing* (New York: Collier, 1971).

48. Imes, *Quicksand and Passing*.

49. Newby, *Black Carolinians*, 124.

50. Woodson, *Mis-Education of the Negro*, 55; Gatewood, *Aristocrats of Color*, 272; *Palmetto Leader*, 17 Feb. 1925, p. 3.

51. Gatewood, *Aristocrats of Color*, 273–77.

52. Drago, *Initiative, Paternalism, Race Relations*, 102, 120–31.

53. Ibid., 102; Crawford, interview; Thomasson, interview; Zimmerman, interview; Wilkinson, interview; E. Bythewood, interview, 16 Feb. 1987; Clarence Tobin, interview by author, Orangeburg, S.C., 18 Jan. 1988.

54. E. Bythewood, interview; Tobin, interview. The majority of the women generally belonged to Trinity AME Church, which was associated with the Methodist college—Claflin University. The Episcopalian women were members of the only African American Episcopal church in Orangeburg, St. Paul's Episcopal Church, which was more closely associated with State A&M, as the church was partly founded by Robert Shaw Wilkinson—the president of the college. Both churches remained affiliates of these colleges long after their establishments.

   I am, personally, a member of St. Paul's Episcopal Church, and while growing up in the church in the early 1960s and late 1970s, vestiges of a "preferred membership" was still strongly prevalent. The rather lean-attended congregation, as compared to the other African American churches in Orangeburg, was largely constituted by professionals, usually affiliated with South Carolina State College. When I attended the church during those years, I constantly heard outside anecdotal reports of my church being "colorphobic" and prejudiced against a darker-hued African American membership. In my recollection, most people who attended the church, as members or visitors, had either very light skin or brown skin. Seldom were there dark-skinned African Americans in the church. From the early 1960s up to the early 1990s, the minister, or "Father," was usually either white (e.g., Father Taylor, Father Jenkins, or Father Snow) or a person of color from a non-African descent background (e.g., Father Ramcharan is of East Indian descent).

55. Chapling, "Facts and Legends of Orangeburg County," 128.

56. Woodson, *Mis-Education of the Negro,* 52–55.

57. Gatewood, *Aristocrats of Color,* 300–322; Schweninger, *Black Property Owners in the South,* 231–32; Drago, *Initiative, Paternalism, Race Relations,* 5.

58. Ottley and Weatherby, *Negro in New York,* 133–34.

59. Ibid.

60. Ibid.; Fields and Fields, *Lemon Swamp,* 55; Mack, interview.

61. Gatewood, *Aristocrats of Color,* 321; Drago, *Initiative, Paternalism, Race Relations,* 128–29; see the *Palmetto Leader,* vols. 1–15, 1925–40, Caroliniana Library, Columbia, S.C.

62. Examples of these newspapers include Columbia's papers, the *Southern Indicator, People's Recorder, Standard,* and *Palmetto Leader,* Charleston's paper, the *Charleston Messenger,* and Orangeburg's paper, the *Gospel Banner, Palmetto Leader,* 24 Jan. 1925, p. 5; also see the *Palmetto Leader,* vols. 1–12, 1925–37.

63. Mary P. Ryan, *Cradle of the Middle Class: The Family in Oneida County, New York, 1700–1865* (New York: Cambridge Univ. Press, 1981), 147, 192–93; *Godey's Lady Book,* July 1832; Linda Perkins, "The Impact of the 'Cult of True Womanhood' on the Education of Black Women," *Journal of Social Issues* 39, no. 3 (1983): 18.

64. Anne Firor Scott, *The Southern Lady: From Pedestal to Politics, 1830–1930* (Chicago: Univ. of Chicago Press, 1970), 4, 7, 31; Grace Kellogg, *The Two Lives of Edith Wharton: A Biography* (New York: Appleton-Century, 1965), 36, 415; Fox-Genovese, *Within the Plantation Household: Black and White Women of the Old South* (Chapel Hill: Univ. of North Carolina Press, 1988), 110, 113–14, 127; Ryan, *Cradle of the Middle Class,* 147; Chapling, "Facts and Legends of Orangeburg County," 183.

65. Nancy Woloch, *Women and the American Experience* (New York: Alfred A. Knopf, 1984), 229–30, 450.

66. Giddings, *When and Where I Enter,* 82.

67. Ibid., 109.

68. Alexander, *Ambiguous Lives,* 158.

69. E. Azalia Hackley, *The Colored Girl Beautiful* (Kansas City: Burton Publishing), 17–24; Robinson, interview.

70. Gatewood, *Aristocrats of Color,* 104–5; *Palmetto Leader,* 21 Jan. 1928, p. 2.

71. Kellogg, *Two Lives of Edith Wharton,* 45; Zimmerman, interview; Jacqueline Anne Rouse, *Lugenia Burns Hope: Black Southern Reformer* (Athens: Univ. of Georgia Press, 1989), 21–24; Beulah Williams Salley, interview by author, Orangeburg, S.C., 3 Dec. 1986.

72. B. W. Salley, interview.

73. Gatewood, *Aristocrats of Color*, 211, 240–41; Fields and Fields, *Lemon Swamp*, 23, 25; Zimmerman, interview; Crawford, interview.

74. Gatewood, *Aristocrats of Color*, 240; E. Williams, interview, and Mack, interview; see advertisements in the *Times and Democrat*, Jan. 1894 to Mar. 1935; *Palmetto Leader*, 13 Mar. 1926, p. 3.

75. Fields and Fields, *Lemon Swamp*, 2.

76. Ibid., 42–43, 47.

77. Zimmerman, interview.

78. Wilkinson, interview.

79. Zimmerman, interview; Crawford, interview.

80. See Margery Davies, "Women's Place is at the Typewriter: The Feminization of the Clerical Labor Force," *Radical America* 3, no. 4 (July–Aug. 1974): 21–42; *Sixty-Second Annual Catalogue of Claflin University, 1930*, Claflin College Archives, Orangeburg, S.C., 102–5; *Catalogue of State Agricultural and Mechanical College of South Carolina, 1928*, 6, South Carolina State College Archives, Orangeburg, S.C.

2. Upper-Class Women's Work outside the Home

1. Jacqueline Jones, *Labor of Love, Labor of Sorrow: Black Women, Work, and the Family from Slavery to the Present* (New York: Basic Books, 1985), 142–43; see Gatewood, *Aristocrats of Color*, 7–29.

2. Zimmerman, interview.

3. Epps, interview; Frazier, *Negro Family in the United States*, 325; also see Carter G. Woodson, *The Negro Professional Man and the Community* (Washington, D.C.: Associated Publishers, 1934).

4. Giddings, *When and Where I Enter*, 75–76; ibid.

5. Gatewood, *Aristocrats of Color*, 191.

6. U.S. Bureau of the Census, *Census of 1880 on Population. Orangeburg Town*; D.C. T. K. Bythewood, interview, 27 Mar. 1987.

7. *Catalogue of Claflin University and South Carolina Agricultural College, 1884–1885*.

8. Zimmerman, interview; *Catalogue of Claflin University and South Carolina Agricultural College, 1884–1885*, 7–22.

9. McMillan, *Negro Higher Education*, 189–92; based on interviews with Zimmerman, Crawford, and T. K. Bythewood (the latter on 27 Mar. 1987). To examine other authors who have addressed the elitist attitudes of the upper class and their conscious attempts to distance themselves socially, culturally, religiously, and residentially from the masses, especially those affiliated with the colleges, see works by Gatewood, *Aristocrats of Color*, 270–71; Woodson, *Mis-Education of the Negro*, 53, 56; W. E. B. Du Bois, *The Negro Family in America*, Atlanta University Study 13 (Atlanta: Atlanta Univ. Press, 1908); and Fields and Fields, *Lemon Swamp*.

10. McMillan, *Negro Higher Education*, 189–92; Gatewood, *Aristocrats of Color*, 270–71; Woodson, *Mis-Education of the Negro*, 53, 56.
11. U.S. Bureau of the Census, *Census of 1900 on Population. Orangeburg City*; T. K. Bythewood, interview, 27 Mar. 1987.
12. U.S. Bureau of the Census, *Census of 1910 on Population. Orangeburg City.*
13. See the *Annual Catalog of Claflin University*, 1911–12, and *Catalogue of the Colored Normal Industrial, Agricultural, and Mechanical College of South Carolina, 1911*; Fields and Fields, *Lemon Swamp*, 87, 89–90.
14. *Annual Catalogue of Claflin University*, 1911–12, and *Catalogue of the Colored Normal Industrial, Agricultural, and Mechanical College of South Carolina, 1911*; *Catalogue of State Agricultural and Mechanical College of South Carolina*, 1922–40.
15. Davies, "Women's Place is at the Typewriter," 232; *Catalog of State Agricultural and Mechanical College of South Carolina, 1918*, 91–97.
16. The *Annual Catalog of Claflin University*, 1908–16; *Catalogue of State Agricultural and Mechanical College of South Carolina*, 1934, 1936.
17. Ibid.
18. Fields and Fields, *Lemon Swamp*, 204; Salley, interview.
19. Zimmerman, interview.
20. Rouse, *Lugenia Burns Hope*, 34.
21. Ibid., 55.
22. See the *Annual Catalog of Claflin University, 1919*; *Sixty-Third Annual Catalogue of Claflin University, 1931*, 11–13; Linda Perkins, "The National Association of College Women: Vanguard of Black Women's Leadership in Education, 1923–1954," *Journal of Education* 72, no. 3 (1990): 65–75; see the *Catalogue of Claflin University*, 1870, 1872; *Catalogue of Claflin University and South Carolina Agricultural College*, 1877, 1879, 1881, 1882, 1883; *Annual Catalogue of Claflin University and College of Agiculture and Mechanics*, 1885–90, 1898; *Annual Catalog of Claflin University*, 1906–22, 1925, 1928; *Sixty-Second Annual Catalogue of Claflin University, 1930*; *Sixty-Third Annual Catalogue of Claflin University, 1931*; *Claflin College Catalogue*, 1934–35, 1937–40; and *Catalog of the Colored Normal Industrial, Agricultural, and Mechanical College of South Carolina*, 1911, 1919, 1920; *Catalogue of State Agricultural and Mechanical College of South Carolina*, 1918, 1920, 1922, 1924.
23. *Catalogue of State Agricultural and Mechanical College of South Carolina, 1918*, 6–12; *Catalogue of State Agricultural and Mechanical College of South Carolina, 1939*, 7–12; also see all Claflin catalogues between 1870 and 1924; and *Catalog of the Colored Normal Industrial, Agricultural, and Mechanical College of South Carolina*, 1911, 1919, 1920; *Catalogue of State Agricultural and Mechanical College of South Carolina*, 1918, 1920, 1922, 1924.
24. *Catalogue of State Agriculture and Mechanical College of South Carolina, 1918*, 6–12; *Catalogue of State Agriculture and Mechanical College of South Carolina, 1939*, 7–12;

also see all Claflin catalogues between 1870 and 1924; and *Catalog of the Colored Normal Industrial, Agricultural, and Mechanical College of South Carolina*, 1911, 1919, 1920; *Catalogue of State Agricultural and Mechanical College of South Carolina*, 1918, 1920, 1922, 1924.

25. John Hope Franklin and Alfred A. Moss Jr., *From Slavery to Freedom: A History of Negro Americans* (New York: Alfred A. Knopf, 1988), 341; Perkins, "National Association of College Women," 66; Robinson, interview; Crawford, interview.

26. Crawford, interview; Lander, *History of South Carolina*, 126–27; Jones, *Labor of Love*, 144–45.

27. Hearth, "American Century of Bessie and Sadie Delaney," 77; Wilkinson, interview; *Catalogue of State Agricultural and Mechanical College of South Carolina, 1922*.

28. Zimmerman, interview.

29. Robinson, interview; Anna deCosta Banks, "The Work of a Small Hospital and Training School in the South," in *Black Women in the Nursing Profession: A Documentary History*, ed. Darlene Clark Hine (New York: Garland, 1985), 23–28; "The Nursing Debate," in *America's Working Women*, ed. Rosalyn Baxandall, Linda Gordon, and Susan Reverby (New York: Random House, 1976), 76; Joyce Ann Elmore, "Black Nurses: Their Service and Their Struggle," in *Black Women in the Nursing Profession: A Documentary History*, ed. Darlene Clark Hine (New York: Garland, 1985), 163–64.

30. Darlene Clark Hine, ed., *Black Women in the Nursing Profession: A Documentary History* (New York: Garland, 1985), xiii, 3.

31. Robinson, interview; *Times and Democrat*, 28 Nov. 1987; Elmore, "Black Nurses," 164.

32. Zimmerman, interview; Robinson, interview.

33. Cecelia Daniels Fleming, interview by author, Orangeburg, S.C., 3 Apr. 1987.

34. Epps, interview.

35. Julia Kirk Blackwelder, *Women of the Depression: Caste and Culture in San Antonio, 1929–1939* (College Station: Texas A&M Univ. Press, 1984), 110–11; Winifred D. Wandersee, *Women's Work and Family Values, 1920–1940* (Cambridge: Harvard Univ. Press, 1981), 96; Giddings, *When and Where I Enter*, 217–18.

36. Jean E. McAllister and Dorothy M. McAllister, "Adult Education for Negroes in Rural Areas: The Work of the Jeanne Teachers and Home and Farm Demonstration Agents," *Journal of Negro Education* 14, no. 3 (Summer 1945): 331–40; Franklin and Moss, *From Slavery to Freedom*, 241; Epps, interview.

37. Franklin and Moss, *From Slavery to Freedom*, 241; Epps, interview.

38. See Linda M. Perkins, "Black Women and the Philosophy of 'Race Uplift' Prior to Emancipation," working paper, Radcliffe College, Mary Ingraham Bunting Institute, Cambridge, Mass., 1980; Gatewood, *Aristocrats of Color*, 346; also see Franklin and Moss, *From Slavery to Freedom*; Berlin, *Slaves Without Masters*; Perkins, "Impact of the Cult of True Womanhood"; Giddings, *When and Where I Enter*; Cynthia Neverdon-Morton, "Self-Help Programs as Educative Activities

of Black Women in the South, 1895–1925: Focus on Four Key Areas," *Journal of Negro Education* 51, no. 3 (1982): 207–38.

39. *Trinity Methodist Church Observes Its 100th Anniversary. January 1866 to January 1966. Orangeburg, S.C. Theme: "The First Hundred Years in Retrospect"* Trinity United Methodist Church Records and Archives, Orangeburg, S.C.; *United Methodist Women. Trinity United Methodist Church. Orangeburg, S.C. Anniversary Dinner, 1866–1984. Saturday, October 12, 1985* Trinity United Methodist Church Records and Archives, Orangeburg, S.C.; Interview with Reverend George Watson, Orangeburg, S.C., 1 Dec. 1986.

40. Reverend George Watson, 1 Dec. 1986.

41. E. Bythewood, interview, 16 Feb. 1987; T. K. Bythewood, interview, 8 Apr. 1987; Thomasson, interview.

42. Robinson, interview; Salley, interview; Reverend George Watson, 1 Dec. 1986.

43. Giddings, *When and Where I Enter,* 83; Cynthia Neverdon-Morton, *Afro-American Women of the South and the Advancement of the Race, 1895–1925* (Knoxville: Univ. of Tennessee Press, 1989), 194; See Neverdon-Morton article, "Self-Help Programs," 207, and Perkins, "Impact of Cult of True Womanhood," 25.

44. See Perkins, "National Association of College Women"; see all the Claflin catalogues between 1870 and 1924, and *Catalog of the Colored Normal Industrial, Agricultural, and Mechanical College of South Carolina,* 1911, 1919, 1920; *Catalogue of State Agricultural and Mechanical College of South Carolina,* 1918, 1920, 1922, 1924.

45. Perkins, "National Association of College Women," 71; Lander, *History of South Carolina,* 152–53.

46. In the *Catalogue of Claflin University, 1872,* see 20, and in the *Annual Catalog of Claflin University, 1922,* see 19, 21.

47. Lander, *History of South Carolina,* 152; *Catalogue of Claflin University, 1872,* 15; *Annual Catalogue of Claflin University and College of Agriculture and Mechanics, 1885,* 34; *Annual Catalogue of Claflin University and College of Agriculture and Mechanics, 1888,* 65.

48. *Catalogue of the Colored Normal Industrial, Agricultural, and Mechanical College of South Carolina, 1911,* 17–18; *Catalog of State Agricultural and Mechanical College of South Carolina, 1918,* 24.

49. *Catalogue of State Agricultural and Mechanical College of South Carolina, 1931,* 17.

50. *Catalogue of the Colored Normal Industrial, Agricultural, and Mechanical College of South Carolina, 1911,* 21; *Catalog of State Agricultural and Mechanical College of South Carolina, 1918,* 4; *Catalogue of State Agricultural and Mechanical College of South Carolina, 1926,* 5.

51. See *Catalogue of State Agricultural and Mechanical College of South Carolina, 1928,* 4; *Catalogue of State Agricultural and Mechanical College of South Carolina, 1929,* 4; *Catalogue of State Agricultural and Mechanical College of South Carolina, 1930,* 16; and *Catalogue of State Agricultural and Mechanical College of South Carolina, 1937,* 21.

52. Perkins, "National Association of College Women," 71.

53. Ibid.; Giddings, *When and Where I Enter*, 76.

54. Neverdon-Morton, "Self-Help Programs," 209.

55. Neverdon-Morton, *Afro-American Women of the South*, 6–8; Rouse, *Lugenia Burns Hope*, 91–121. *Fiftieth Anniversary. South Carolina Federation of Colored Women's Clubs, 1909–1959 (Affiliated with the National Association of Colored Women's Clubs). "Our Book of Gold,"* 1–7, Sunlight Community Center, Orangeburg, S.C.; *Fiftieth Anniversary*, 7

56. Rouse, *Lugenia Burns Hope*, 64.

57. Drago, *Initiative, Paternalism, Race Relations*, 102; Gordon, *Sketches of Negro Life*, 179–81; Wilkinson, interview; Crawford, interview.

58. *Fiftieth Anniversary*, 7; ibid.

59. Ibid.; *Palmetto Leader*, 3 Mar. 1928, p. 2, 19 Mar. 1928, p. 1.

60. *Fiftieth Anniversary*, 7.

61. Drago, *Initiative, Paternalism, Race Relations*, 102; see Adrienne Lash Jones, "Struggle Among Saints: Black Women in the YWCA, 1850–1920" (paper presented at the Annual Meeting of the Organization of American Historians, Louisville, Ky., Apr. 1991); Gordon, *Sketches of Negro Life*, 184; Crawford, interview.

62. Gordon, *Sketches of Negro Life*, 184; Crawford, interview.

63. Zimmerman, interview; Fleming, interview; Wilkinson, interview; Gordon, 184.

64. Wilkinson, interview; A. Gilbert Belles, "The College Faculty, the Negro Scholar, and the Julius Rosenwald Fund," *Journal of Negro History* 54, no. 4 (1985): 383–92; "Help Wanted," *Times and Democrat*, 1 Jan. 1929.

65. "Child Welfare in Orangeburg," *Times and Democrat*, 6 May 1938, p. 7.

66. Ibid.

67. Ibid.; Franklin and Moss, *From Slavery to Freedom*, 339–59.

68. Zimmerman, interview; Dean N. C. Nix, "Tentative History of South Carolina State College, 1872–1937," working paper, 83, South Carolina State University Library Archives, Orangeburg, S.C.

69. *Naturalis opus* is Latin for "natural work"; Gatewood, *Aristocrats of Color*, 345–46.

3. Upper-Class Women's Work inside the Home

1. Scott, *Southern Lady*, 29, 31, 34, 35–36, 39; Fox-Genovese, *Within the Plantation Household*, 110, 120; Berlin, *Slaves Without Masters*, 151–52; Alexander, *Ambiguous Lives*, 36, 38.

2. Julie A Matthaei, *An Economic History of Women in America* (New York: Schocken Books, 1982), 123.

3. Alexander, *Ambiguous Lives*, 83–84.

4. Kellogg, *Two Lives of Edith Wharton*, 17, 20.

5. Gatewood, *Aristocrats of Color*, 191, 196.

6. Wilkinson, interview; Rouse, *Lugenia Burns Hope*, 33; Mack, interview.

7. Wilkinson, interview.
8. Ibid.
9. Ibid.
10. Rouse, *Lugenia Burns Hope*, 33–34.
11. Wilkinson, interview.
12. Epps, interview.
13. Ibid.
14. Ibid.
15. Ibid.
16. Ibid.; Judy Rollins, *Between Women: Domestics and Their Employers* (Philadelphia: Temple Univ. Press, 1985), 192–94; Susan Tucker, *Telling Memories Among Southern Women: Domestic Workers and Their Employers in the Segregated South* (New York: Schocken, 1988), 50–51.
17. Crawford, interview.
18. Ibid.
19. Ibid.
20. Ibid.
21. Robinson, interview.
22. Ibid.
23. Thomasson, interview.
24. Salley, interview.
25. Fleming, interview.
26. Ibid.
27. Ibid.
28. Zimmerman, interview.
29. Ibid.

4. Middle-Class African Americans

1. Michael P. Weber and Peter N. Stearns, *The Spencers of Amberson Avenue: A Turn of the Century Memoir* (Philadelphia: Univ. of Pennsylvania Press, 1983), 9–19, 81, 89.
2. Frazier, *Negro Family in the United States*, 313–33; Fields and Fields, *Lemon Swamp*, 9; T. K. Bythewood, interview, 27 Mar. 1987; Zimmerman, interview.
3. Frazier, *Negro Family in the United States*, 313–33.
4. Ibid.
5. Fields and Fields, *Lemon Swamp*, 9.
6. Ibid., 13; Pauli Murray, *Song in a Weary Throat* (New York: Harper and Row, 1987), 64–68, 82–101.
7. Fields and Fields, *Lemon Swamp*, 94; 163–67; 171–72.
8. George B. Tindall, *South Carolina Negroes, 1877–1900* (Columbia: Univ. of South Carolina Press, 1952), 130–36; Stetson Kennedy, *Jim Crow Guide: The Way It Was*

(Boca Raton: Florida Atlantic Univ. Press, 1990), 203–77; Lander, *History of South Carolina*, 42.

9. This division of the middle class into the upper and lower middle class was based on information gathered from oral interviews, census reports, and findings from the research of E. Franklin Frazier, Gunnar Myrdal, and Hortense Powdermaker. Epps, interview; T. K. Bythewood, interview, 11, 27 Mar., 8 Apr. 1987; Tobin, interview; and Zimmerman, interview.

10. T. K. Bythewood, interview, 11 Mar. 1987.

11. Ibid.; Gatewood, *Aristocrats of Color*, 207; Frazier, *Negro Family in the United States*, 313–53.

12. See the reports from the U.S. Bureau of the Census, *Census of 1880 on Population, Census of 1900 on Population,* and *Census of 1910 on Population.*

13. Frazier, Negro Family in the United States, 313–33; T. K. Bythewood, interview, 27 Mar. 1987; Tobin, interview; and Zimmerman, interview.

14. Fields and Fields, *Lemon Swamp*, 9–13, 94, 163–67, 171–72; ibid.; T. K. Bythewood, interview, 8 Apr. 1987.

15. Janie Harrington Pearson, interview by author, Orangeburg, S.C., 13 Feb. 1987; Bernice Bryant Middleton, interview by author, Orangeburg, S.C., 23 Feb. 1987; and Edith Wilson Vaughn, interview by author, Orangeburg, S.C., 16 Apr. 1987.

16. Fifty percent of the lower-middle-class women interviewed came from agricultural backgrounds. The parents of the other 50 percent were semiskilled, working-class people who took jobs as domestics, informally trained ministers, and midwives. Marian E. Gregg, interview by author, Orangeburg, S.C., 5 Dec. 1986; T. K. Bythewood, interview, 11 Mar. 1987.

17. Hubbard, interview; Georgia Waymer Swett, interview by author, Orangeburg, S.C., 24 Feb. 1987; Leila Summers Harrison, interview by author, Orangeburg, S.C., 26 Mar. 1987; Anna Mitchell Colter, interview by author, Orangeburg, S.C., 6 Apr. 1987; and Frizell Brown Bowman, interview by author, Orangeburg, S.C., 17 Apr. 1987.

18. Swett, interview.

19. Based on interviews of the middle-class women, they usually attended the Methodist or Baptist church. Upper middle-class women were usually Methodist, not Baptist. This is not revelatory, since the African American Baptist church historically was largely attended by and identified as the church of the African American masses; Maude Haigler Lawrence, interview by author, Orangeburg, S.C., 4 Dec. 1986; Gregg, interview; Marian Gregg's father and Maude Haigler Lawrence's husband were Methodist ministers, and they were among the Methodist ministers' families living on Goff Avenue.

20. Carol Smith Rosenberg, *Disorderly Conduct: Visions of Gender in Victorian American* (New York: Oxford Univ. Press, 1986), 199; Weber and Stearns, *Spencers of Amberson Avenue*, 75–79; Woloch, *Women and the American Experience*, 276–78; ibid., 81, 83.

21. Sharon Harley, "For the Good of Family and Race: Gender, Work, and Domestic Roles in the Black Community, 1880–1930," *Signs: Journal of Women in Culture and Society* 15:2 (Winter 1990): 341–42; Fields, 28, 165–66.

22. Harley, "For the Good of Family and Race," 341–43.

23. Zimmerman, interview; Fields and Fields, *Lemon Swamp*, 27, 84, 96.

24. Fields and Fields, *Lemon Swamp*, 84–93.

25. Ibid., 93–98.

26. *Annual Catalogue of Claflin University*, 1918–22; *Catalogue of State Agricultural and Mechanical College of South Carolina*, 1918, 1920, 1922.

5. Middle-Class Women's Work outside the Home

1. Woloch, *Women and the American Experience*, 280–81, 442; Alice Kessler-Harris, *Out to Work: A History of Wage-Earning Women in the United States* (New York: Oxford Univ. Press, 1983), 15,113; Davies, "Women's Place is at the Typewriter," 233.

2. Giddings, *When and Where I Enter*, 143, 148–49.

3. Lander, *History of South Carolina*, 42; Alexander, *Ambiguous Lives*, 115, 156–57; U.S. Bureau of the Census, *Census of 1880 on Population*.

4. Jones, *Labor of Love*, 112, 142–46, 180; Giddings, *When and Where I Enter*, 101, 147.

5. U.S. Bureau of the Census, *Census of 1900 on Population*.

6. Newby, *Black Carolinians*, 133–34; Jones, *Labor of Love*, 110–231; U.S. Bureau of the Census, *Census of 1900 on Population*.

7. T. K. Bythewood, interview, 8 Apr. 1987; and Tobin, interview; Fields and Fields, *Lemon Swamp*, 204.

8. Unfortunately, specific information citing the type of jobs women held after they graduated in the early twentieth century was not available in Claflin and State A&M's catalogues.

9. Harley, "For the Good of Family and Race," 336–41, 343, 348; Fields and Fields, *Lemon Swamp*, 18–19.

10. Fields and Fields, *Lemon Swamp*, 40, 157–83, 203.

11. Ibid., 8, 10, 14–15, 25, 96, 148–56; Jones, *Labor of Love*, 142–46; Hubbard, interview.

12. Jones, *Labor of Love*, 142–46; Hubbard, interview.

13. T. K. Bythewood, interview, 6 Mar. 1987; Middleton, interview; Fields and Fields, *Lemon Swamp*, 40–41, 204.

14. Pearson, interview.

15. Ella Felder Wilson, interview by author, Orangeburg, S.C., 30 Mar. 1987; Jones, *Labor of Love*, 184–85.

16. Bowman, interview; Jones, *Labor of Love*, 41, 56, 89–90, 214; Ruth Allen, *The Labor of Women in the Production of Cotton* (New York: Arno, 1975), 178.

17. Wilson, interview.

18. Ibid.

19. Ibid.

20. Ibid.

21. Lucy Pearson Simmons, interview by author, Orangeburg, S.C., 23 Apr. 1987; U.S. Bureau of the Census, *Census of 1880 on Population* and *Census of 1910 on Population*.

22. Fields and Fields, *Lemon Swamp*, 13–14.

23. Jones, *Labor of Love*, 142–43.

24. U.S. Bureau of the Census, *Census of 1910 on Population*. See the *Catalogue of the Colored Normal, Industrial, and Agricultural and Mechanical College of South Carolina*, 1911, 1919, 1920; *Catalogue of State Agriculture and Mechanical College of South Carolina, 1929*; and the *Annual Catalog of Claflin University*, 1910–22.

25. Giddings, *When and Where I Enter*, 147–48, 244–45.

26. Fields and Fields, *Lemon Swamp*, 96; Wilson, interview; ibid.

27. Simmons, interview.

28. Gregg, interview.

29. Colter, interview; Swett, interview.

30. Ibid.

31. Vaughn, interview; Middleton, interview.

32. Pearson, interview.

33. Hubbard, interview.

34. Simmons, interview.

35. See catalogues for both Claflin and State A&M from the 1870s to the 1930s; also see Fields and Fields, *Lemon Swamp*, 96; T. K. Bythewood, interview, 6 Mar. 1987; Wilkinson, interview; *Catalogue of Claflin University, 1872*, and *Annual Catalog of Claflin University, 1922*; *Annual Catalog of Claflin University and College of Agriculture and Mechanics, 1888*; *Catalogue of the Colored Normal, Industrial, Agricultural and Mechanical College, 1911*; *Catalogue of State Agricultural and Mechanical College of South Carolina, 1918*; and *Catalogue of State Agricultural and Mechanical College of South Carolina, 1931*.

36. Colter, interview.

37. E. Williams, interview; T. K. Bythewood, interview, 8 Apr. 1987.

38. Lawrence, interview; Hubbard, interview; Swett, interview; Colter, interview. They all discussed how they returned to their homes during the summer to work on their families' farms to earn money toward their education.

39. See Fields and Fields, *Lemon Swamp* to get a sense of the type of temporary work students pursued during the summer and sometimes after graduation.

40. Ibid.

41. Gregg, interview; Simmons, interview.

42. Simmons, interview; Swett, interview.

43. Swett, interview.

44. Lawrence, interview; Clemmie Embly Webber, interview by author, Orangeburg, S.C., 10 Feb. 1987; Swett, interview; Rozela Dickson Knight, interview by author, Orangeburg, S.C., 12 Mar. 1987; Harrison, interview; Vaughn, interview; and Simmons, interview; T. K. Bythewood, interview, 8 Apr. 1987; see U.S. Bureau of the Census, *Census of 1910 on Population.*

45. Webber, interview; Gregg, interview; Beatrice Thompson, interview by author, Orangeburg, S.C., 4 Dec. 1986.

46. See all the catalogues for Claflin and State A&M between 1910 and 1940.

47. Vaughn, interview; see Perkins, "National Association of College Women," 65–75.

48. Gatewood, *Aristocrats of Color,* 196; Mamie Haigler, interview by author, Orangeburg, S.C., 9 Apr. 1987.

49. B. Thompson, interview.

50. Bowman, interview.

51. Rosenberg, *Disorderly Conduct,* 173–76; Kessler-Harris, *Out to Work,* 90–95, 113; ibid.

52. Fields and Fields, *Lemon Swamp,* 10, 55.

53. *Fiftieth Anniversary,* 20–40.

54. Fields and Fields, *Lemon Swamp,* 17–18, 23–25.

55. Ibid., 23–25, 187–200.

56. Ibid., 198.

57. Bookhardt, 122–33; *Times and Democrat,* 28 Mar. 1935, 2; *Times and Democrat,* 30 Mar. 1935, 2; *Times and Democrat,* 4 Apr. 1935, 2.

58. Knight, interview; Webber, interview; Vaughn, interview; Simmons, interview; T. K. Bythewood, interview, 8 Apr. 1987.

59. Fields and Fields, *Lemon Swamp,* 198; T. K. Bythewood, interview, 8 Apr. 1987; Zimmerman, interview.

60. Sharon Harley, "Beyond the Classroom: Organizational Lives of Black Female Educators in the District of Columbia, 1890–1930," *Journal of Negro Education* 51, no. 3 (Summer 1982): 259, 265; see the "History of the Sunlight Club," *The Sunlight Club Handbook, 1980–1981. Orangeburg, South Carolina*; Neverdon-Morton, *Afro-American Women of the South,* 6.

61. Haigler, interview.

62. Bowman, interview.

63. Haigler, interview; see Evelyn Brooks Higginbotham, *Righteous Discontent: The Women's Movement in the Black Baptist Church, 1880–1920* (Cambridge: Harvard Univ. Press, 1994); Lawrence, interview; Middleton, interview; Simmons, interview; Webber, interview.

64. Giddings, *When and Where I Enter,* 119–27.

65. Ibid.; Rouse, *Lugenia Burns Hope,* 9, 108–9; Webber, interview.

6. Middle-Class Women's Work inside the Home

1. Christine Stansell, *City of Women: Sex and Class in New York, 1789–1860* (Urbana: Univ. of Illinois Press, 1987), 156–59; Phyllis Palmer, *Domesticity and Dirt: Housewives and Domestic Servants in the United States, 1920–1945* (Philadelphia: Temple Univ. Press, 1989), 6, 10; Tucker, *Telling Memories,* 176; Weber and Stearns, *Spencers of Amberson Avenue,* 10, 23–24, 30–32.
2. See Fields and Fields, *Lemon Swamp,* 28, 159–203. Both Mamie Garvin Fields and her mother, Rebecca Garvin, were housewives at some point and worked outside the house. However, there is no mention of either one of them hiring a domestic servant at any point; Palmer, *Domesticity and Dirt,* 11.
3. Fields and Fields, *Lemon Swamp,* 5, 8–9, 28.
4. B. Thompson, interview; Webber, interview; Middleton, interview; and Wilson, interview.
5. B. Thompson, interview; Hubbard, interview; Swett, interview; Colter, interview; Webber, interview; Vaughn, interview.
6. Lawrence, interview; Middleton, interview; Simmons, interview; T. K. Bythewood, interview, 6 Mar. 1987; Knight, interview.
7. T. K. Bythewood, interview, 6 Mar. 1987; Knight, interview.
8. Knight, interview; T. K. Bythewood, interview, 11 Mar. 1987.
9. Bowman, interview.
10. Pearson, interview.
11. Wilson, interview.
12. Middleton, interview.
13. Harrison, interview.
14. See Higginbotham, *Righteous Discontent.*

7. Working-Class African Americans

1. Paul S. Boyer, Clifford E. Clark, Jr., Joseph F. Keitt, Thomas Purvis, Harvard Sitkoff, and Nancy Woloch, *The Enduring Vision: A History of the American People,* vol. 2, *From 1865* (Lexington, Mass.: D. C. Heath, 1990), 658, 683.
2. Ibid.; Sara Eisenstein, *Give Us Bread, But Give Us Roses* (Boston: Routledge and Kegan Paul, 1983), 1–11.
3. Boyer et al., *Enduring Vision,* 2:681; Mary Frances Berry and John W. Blassingame, *Long Memory: The Black Experience in America* (New York: Oxford Univ. Press, 1982), 195–96, 203; Frazier, *Negro Family in the United States,* 295–316.
4. Boyer et al., *Enduring Vision,* 2:681; Berry and Blassingame, *Long Memory,* 195–96.
5. T. K. Bythewood, interview, 6 Mar., 8 Apr. 1987; see the U.S. Bureau of the

Census, *Census of 1880 on Population, Census of 1900 on Population,* and *Census of 1910 on Population*; Jones, *Labor of Love,* 84, 92–93.

6. T. K. Bythewood, interview, 6 Mar., 8 Apr. 1987; *Census of 1880 on Population, Census of 1900 on Population,* and *Census of 1910 on Population.*

7. Harley, "For the Good of Family and Race," 348–49; Mack, interview; E. Williams, interview.

8. Newby, *Black Carolinians,* 123, 193; Giddings, *When and Where I Enter,* 146–47.

9. Jones, *Labor of Love,* 113.

10. T. K. Bythewood, interview, 27 Mar. 1987.

11. Stansell, *City of Women,* 160; Boyer et al., *Enduring Vision,* 2:641, 650, 682.

12. Leslie Woodcock Tentler, *Wage-Earning Women: Industrial Work and Family Life in the United States, 1900–1930* (New York: Oxford Univ. Press, 1982), 149

13. Du Bois, *The Negro American Family,* 55–59.

14. Gordon, *Sketches of Negro Life,* 130–33.

15. Mack, interview; E. Williams, interview; ibid., 59.

16. Mack, interview; E. Williams, interview; Hugo Sheridan Ackerman, interview by author, Orangeburg, S.C., 29 Oct. 1988; Zimmerman, interview; T. K. Bythewood, interview, 8 Apr. 1987.

17. Mack, interview; E. Williams, interview; T. K. Bythewood, interview, 8 Apr. 1987.

18. Mack, interview; E. Williams, interview.

19. E. Williams, interview.

20. Ibid.; Gordon, *Sketches of Negro Life,* 114–22; Chapling, "Facts and Legends of Orangeburg County," 63.

21. Mack, interview.

22. Carol Hymowitz and Michael Weissman, *A History of Women in America* (New York: Bantam, 1978), 127–28; Kessler-Harris, *Out to Work,* 55–56; Tentler, *Wage-Earning Women,* 93–103, 104; Eisenstein, *Give Us Bread,* 68, 80–81, 96, 101, 103–5, 109–35; Alexander, *Ambiguous Lives,* 184; see James Anderson, *The Education of Blacks in the South, 1860–1935* (Chapel Hill: Univ. of North Carolina Press, 1988) and Henry Allen Bullock, *A History of Negro Education in the South* (Cambridge: Harvard Univ. Press, 1967).

23. Kessler-Harris, *Out to Work,* 16, 97–98; Hymowitz and Weissman, *A History of Women in America,* 127; Tentler, *Wage-Earning Women,* 28, 104.

24. Jones, *Labor of Love,* 182; E. Williams, interview; Mack, interview.

25. Alexander, *Ambiguous Lives,* 167–68.

26. Ibid.

27. See Jones, *Labor of Love*; Gerda Lerner, *Black Women in White America: A Documentary History* (New York: Random House, 1972); Kessler-Harris, *Out to Work*; Giddings, *When and Where I Enter*; Sterling, *We Are Your Sisters*; Woloch, *Women*

and the American Experience; Milton Meltzer, *Mary McLeod Bethune: Voice of Black Hope* (New York: Viking, 1987), 12–14.

28. See Richard Wright, *Black Boy* (New York: Harper and Row, 1966); Mack, interview; E. Williams, interview; Giddings, *When and Where I Enter*, 72; Elizabeth Clark-Lewis, "This Work Had a' End: The Transition from Live-In to Day Work," in *To Toil the Livelong Day: American Women at Work, 1780–1980*, ed. Carol Groneman and Mary Beth Norton (Ithaca, N.Y.: Cornell Univ. Press, 1987), 6, 9; Fields and Fields, *Lemon Swamp*, 212–13.

29. Mack, interview; E. Williams, interview; Anna Bonaparte Shuler, interview by the author, Orangeburg, S.C., 6 Dec. 1986; Emma Jane Parler, interview by the author, Orangeburg, S.C., 1 Aug. 1988; See Jones, *Labor of Love*; Lerner, *Black Women in White America*; Kessler-Harris, *Out to Work*; Giddings, *When and Where I Enter*; Sterling, *We Are Your Sisters*; and Woloch, *Women and the American Experience*.

30. E. Williams, interview.

31. U.S. Bureau of the Census, *Census of 1880 on Population, Census of 1900 on Population*, and *Census of 1910 on Population*.

32. Jones, *Labor of Love*, 96–97; Jean Wheeler Smith, "Frankie Mae," in *Black-Eyed Susans*, ed. Mary Helen Washington (Garden City, N.J.: Anchor Books, 1975), 3–20; see U.S. Bureau of the Census, *Census of 1880 on Population*.

33. Fields and Fields, *Lemon Swamp*, 183–85, 212; see Giddings, *When and Where I Enter*; Lerner, *Black Women in White America*; Jones, *Labor of Love*; Woloch, *Women and the American Experience*; Sterling, *We Are Your Sisters*; and Kessler-Harris, *Out to Work*; Jones, *Labor of Love*, 83–105; Mack, interview; E. Williams, interview.

34. Hugo Sheridan Ackerman, "1898–1899: Eighteen Receive Diplomas from the Academy," *Times and Democrat*, 26 Apr. 1987; "1902–1903: School Buildings Needed," *Times and Democrat*, 21 June 1987; "1905–1906: A Museum in the Orangeburg Public School," *Times and Democrat*, 16 Aug. 1987; Chapling, "Facts and Legends of Orangeburg County," 178.

35. Chapling, "Facts and Legends of Orangeburg County," 178; Hugo Sheridan Ackerman, "Negro School Going Up," *Times and Democrat*, 30 Sept. 1988; Hugo Ackerman, "1920 Editorial: Should a Married Woman Teach?" *Times and Democrat*, 18 Sept. 1988.

36. Chapling, "Facts and Legends of Orangeburg County," 178; Hugo Sheridan Ackerman, "1907–1908: County Has 228 Schools, Only 40 Libraries," *Times and Democrat*, 13 Sept. 1987.

37. See all the catalogues for Claflin University between 1880 and 1940, and the *Catalogue of State Agricultural and Mechanical College of South Carolina*, 1920–40.

38. *Catalogue of Claflin University, 1872*, 19; *Annual Catalogue of Claflin University*

and College of Agriculture and Mechanics, 1887, 61; *Annual Catalog of Claflin University, 1913*, 61.

39. *Catalog of State Agricultural and Mechanical College of South Carolina, 1918*, 3.
40. Ibid.; *Catalogue of State Agricultural and Mechanical College of South Carolina, 1922*, 4; *Catalogue of State Agricultural and Mechanical College of South Carolina, 1920*, 4; *Catalogue of State Agricultural and Mechanical College of South Carolina, 1928*, 4.
41. Woloch, *Women and the American Experience*, 248; Harley, "Beyond the Classroom," 256.
42. Harley, "Beyond the Classroom," 256.

8. Working-Class Women's Work outside the Home

1. Tentler, *Wage-Earning Women*, 86–87, 105, 146–47; Kessler-Harris, *Out to Work*, 124, 126, 146–47; Stansell, *City of Women*, 13–15; Scott, *Southern Lady*, 35; Boyer et al., *Enduring Vision*, 2:682–83.
2. Kessler-Harris, *Out to Work*, 85, 113, 137, 152–56, 164–75, 202; Lander, *History of South Carolina*, 59, 72, 82–85.
3. See Winch, *Philadelphia Black Elite*; Gatewood, *Aristocrats of Color*; Schweninger, *Black Property Owners in the South*; Berlin, *Slaves Without Masters*; and Johnson and Roark, *Black Masters*; Kessler-Harris, *Out to Work*, 10; Stansell, *City of Women*, 13, 157.
4. Kessler-Harris, *Out to Work*, 37, 85; Giddings, *When and Where I Enter*, 77; Jones, *Labor of Love*, 135–36, 178–80, 211–12.
5. Elizabeth Clark-Lewis, "'This Work Had a' End': The Transition From Live-in to Day Work," Center for Research on Women, working paper 2, p. 6, Memphis State Univ., 1985; Woloch, *Women and the American Experience*, 228; Jones, *Labor of Love*, 160–66, 206–7; Palmer, *Domesticity and Dirt*, 74–88; see also Tera W. Hunter, *To 'Joy My Freedom: Southern Black Women's Lives and Labors After the Civil War* (Cambridge: Harvard Univ. Press, 1997).
6. Lander, *History of South Carolina*, 89, 107–8, 118; Meltzer, *Mary McCleod Bethune*, 2–11.
7. U.S. Bureau of the Census, *Census of 1880 on Population*; T. K. Bythewood, interview, 8 Apr. 1987.
8. U.S. Bureau of the Census, *Census of 1880 on Population*; Jones, *Labor of Love*, 113–14.
9. U.S. Bureau of the Census, *Census of 1880 on Population*.
10. Ibid.; Gutman, *Black Family in Slavery and Freedom*, 632; Fox-Genovese, *Within the Plantation Household*, 162–63; U.S. Bureau of the Census, *Census of 1880 on Population*.
11. Jones, *Labor of Love*, 111–13.
12. Ibid., 164–66, 206.

13. U.S. Bureau of the Census, *Census of 1900 on Population.*
14. Tindall, *South Carolina Negroes,* 121; Gordon, *Sketches of Negro Life,* 156–73; Jones, *Labor of Love,* 113, 155–56.
15. U.S. Bureau of the Census, *Census of 1910 on Population.*
16. Ibid.
17. Ibid.
18. Giddings, *When and Where I Enter,* 141–44.
19. Fannie Rufus Nix, interview by author, Orangeburg, S.C., 25 Mar. 1987; Jones, *Labor of Love,* 124; Boyer, *Enduring Vision,* 2:658–83; Eisenstein, *Give Us Bread,* 1–11.
20. U.S. Bureau of the Census, *Census of 1880 on Population, Census of 1900 on Population,* and *Census of 1910 on Population.*
21. Tucker, *Telling Memories,* 156; Emma Jane Parler, interview by author, Orangeburg, S.C., 1 Aug. 1988; see Alexander's *Ambiguous Lives* for its discussion of a similar situation with Treena Threatt Nelson and her grandparents support of her dropping out of school to work full time (167–68).
22. Parler, interview; Tentler, *Wage-Earning Women,* 86, 89; Tucker, *Telling Memories,* 113.
23. Tucker, *Telling Memories,* 113, 202; Hugo Sheridan Ackerman, "1903–1904: New School to Cost $15,000," *Times and Democrat,* 5 July 1987; Catherine Davis Livingston, interview by author, Orangeburg, S.C., 3 Mar. 1987.
24. Flossie Williams, interview by author, Orangeburg, S.C., 22 Apr. 1987; Clark-Lewis, "This Work Had A' End," 15.
25. As shown in Susan Tucker's *Telling Memories,* it was also common for young girls in Orangeburg to first get jobs working as nursemaids or babysitters to white children, sometimes only slightly younger than themselves; E. Williams, interview.
26. E. Williams, interview; Mack, interview.
27. Pearl Green Johnson, interview by author, Orangeburg, S.C., 31 Mar. 1987.
28. E. Williams, interview.
29. Mattie Mack Jeffcoat, interview by author, Orangeburg, S.C., 1 Apr. 1987.
30. Clark-Lewis, "This Work Had a' End," 10; ibid.
31. F. Williams, interview.
32. Livingston, interview.
33. Amaker, interview.
34. Florrie Jones Malichi, interview by author, Orangeburg, S.C., 25 Feb. 1987; E. Williams, interview.
35. Malichi, interview; Helen "Hallie" Reese Thompson, interview by author, Orangeburg, S.C., 23 Apr. 1987.
36. F. Williams, interview.
37. David Katzman, *Seven Days a Week: Women in Industrializing America* (New York: Oxford Univ. Press, 1978), 221, 228–29; Alana Erickson, "'I Don't Want Her in

My Home': Bias Against African American Domestic Servants, 1910–1980," *Race and Racism* 1 (1996–1997): 26, 28.

38. Carter G. Woodson, "The Negro Washerwoman: A Vanishing Figure," *Journal of Negro History* 15 (1930): 269–70; Jones, *Labor of Love*, 114; Many of Orangeburg's working-class African American women worked as laundresses (washerwomen) as well as their mothers, grandmothers, aunts, and other relatives.

39. Sadie Bodrick Fair, interview by author, Orangeburg, S.C., 3 Apr. 1987.

40. Emma Whitmore, interview by author, Orangeburg, S.C., 5 Feb. 1987; Daisy Salley Graham, interview by author, Orangeburg, S.C., 10 Apr. 1987; Mack, interview; E. Williams, interview.

41. Swett, interview.

42. Fair, interview; Jeffcoat, interview.

43. Lillie Tingsey Moody, interview by author Orangeburg, S.C., 2 Apr. 1987; Johnson, interview; Nix, interview.

44. Fair, interview; Mack, interview.

45. This information was based on interviews with Lillie Williams Thomas, Orangeburg, S.C., 22 Apr. 1987; Amaker, interview; Johnson, interview; Moody, interview; Fair, interview; T. K. Bythewood, interview, 8 Apr. 1987; Graham, interview; H. Thompson, interview; Parler, 1 Aug. 1988; Mack, interview; and E. Williams, interview; Tucker, *Telling Memories*, 92, 146–48.

46. Jones, *Labor of Love*, 130, 165; Moody, interview; Fair, interview; and Malichi, interview; Graham, interview; Tucker, *Telling Memories*, 13, 87.

47. Fair, interview.

48. Ibid.

49. Ibid.; Mack, interview.

50. Graham, interview.

51. Woloch, *Women and the American Experience*, 450–51; Kessler-Harris, *Out to Work*, 259–60.

52. Blackwelder, *Women of the Depression*, 77; see also Wandersee, *Women's Work and Family Values*, and Lois Rita Helmbold, "Making Choices, Making Do: Black and White Women During the Great Depression" (Ph.D. diss., Stanford Univ. Press, 1983); Ackerman, interview; Edwin D. Hoffman, "The Genesis of the Modern Movement for Equal Rights in South Carolina, 1930–1939," in *The Negro in Depression and War*, ed. Bernard Sternsher (Chicago: Quadrangle Books, 1969), 200; see William L. Langer, *An Encyclopedia of World History* (New York: Houghton Mifflin, 1979).

53. Ella Baker and Marvel Cooke, "The Bronx Slave Market," *Crisis* 42 (Nov. 1935): 330, 340; Jones, *Labor of Love*, 196–231.

54. Coralee Bryant Kearse, interview by author, Orangeburg, S.C., 15 Apr. 1987.

55. *Times and Democrat*, 5 Aug. 1937, p. 7, 9 June 1938, p. 9, 27 Apr. 1939, p. 9, 21 July 1939, p. 9, 25 Nov. 1939, p. 9, 5 Aug. 1937, p. 7.

56. *Times and Democrat,* 5 Aug. 1937, p. 7, 10 Oct. 1939, p. 9; Woloch, *Women and the American Experience,* 450.

57. Woloch, *Women and the American Experience,* 450; *Times and Democrat,* 1 Nov. 1939, p. 9, 21 Dec. 1937, p. 7, 30 Aug. 1938, p. 7, 7 Dec. 1938, p. 7, 7 Aug. 1940, p. 9, 26 Sept. 1940, p. 7.

58. T. K. Bythewood, interview, 8 Apr. 1987.

59. Ackerman, interview.

60. Ibid.

61. Ibid.

62. Ibid.

63. Amaker, interview; Fair, interview; Kearse, interview; Parler, interview; Jones, *Labor of Love,* 128; see also Tucker's *Telling Memories,* 25, which cites a domestic, Priscilla Butler, who worked for a lawyer and earned a relatively generous wage of ten dollars a week.

64. T. K. Bythewood, interview, 8 Apr. 1987.

65. Graham, interview.

66. E. Williams, interview; Shuler, interview; Nora Gardner Smalls, interview by author, Orangeburg, S.C., 6 Apr. 1987; Livingston, interview.

67. Woloch, *Women and the American Experience,* 450–51; Mack, interview; Smalls, interview; T. K. Bythewood, interview, 8 Apr. 1987.

68. Mack, interview.

69. Ibid.

70. George Edmund Haynes's study on African American workers in New York City around 1912 revealed that "out of a total of 2,138 females, 1,971 or 92.2 percent received less than $5.00 per week . . . [and] 0.4 percent received as much as $9.00 per week." Haynes added that "many of these wage-earners [were] furnished their meals in addition to wages; some had meals and room." While the majority of African American women worked as "general housework[ers], chambermaids, and waitresses," earning between $4.00 and $4.99 a week, the next larger group worked as "cooks and laundresses," earning between $5.00 and $5.99 a week. See George Edmund Haynes, *The Negro at Work in New York City: A Study in Economic Progress* (New York: Longman, Green, 1912), 79, 81.

David Katzman has insisted that "the active hiring market was maintained by the constant turnover in servants," resulting "from personal satisfaction rather than from low wages." He has pointed out, however, that at certain times, higher wages were used "to hire servants from the South, from the rural hinterland, or from Europe." These higher wages "served to promote urban migration to fill some of the demand." Both "live-in" and "daywork" jobs in northern cities still paid more attractive wages than the domestic jobs available in Orangeburg. See *Seven Days a Week,* 305; E. Williams, interview; F. Williams, interview; Giddings, *When and Where I Enter,* 218, 246.

71. Johnson, interview; Eisenstein, *Give Us Bread*, 118–19.

72. E. Williams, interview.

73. Smalls, interview; Jones, *Labor of Love*, 199–221; Franklin and Moss, *From Slavery to Freedom*, 352–56.

74. Graham, interview; ibid.; E. Williams, interview.

75. Graham, interview; Smalls, interview.

76. Livingston, interview.

77. Johnson, interview.

78. Mack, interview.

79. Tucker, *Telling Memories*, 152; Jones, *Labor of Love*, 127–28; Fields, 201.

80. Jones, *Labor of Love*, 129; John Rivers, interview by author, Orangeburg, S.C., 21 July 1991.

81. Newby, *Black Carolinians*, 48–49; Swett, interview; Fair, interview.

82. E. Williams, interview; Mack, interview.

83. Wilkinson, interview; Zimmerman, interview; Crawford, interview.

84. Neverdon-Morton, *Afro-American Women of the South*, 6.

85. Fields and Fields, *Lemon Swamp*, 198–99; Harley, "Beyond the Classroom," 260.

86. Clark-Lewis, "This Work Had a' End," 8; Johnson, *Growing Up in the Black Belt*, 135; Carter G. Woodson, *The Negro in Our History* (Washington, D.C.: Associated Publishers, 1924), 286; Eugene Genovese, *Roll, Jordan, Roll: The World the Slaves Made* (New York: Random House, 1974), 232–84; Du Bois, *Gift of Black Folk*, 320–40; see also Franklin and Moss, *From Slavery to Freedom*, and Berry and Blassingame, *Long Memory*, 70–113, 120.

87. See Higginbotham, *Righteous Discontent*; Mack, interview; Moody, interview; Lillie Williams Thomas, 22 Apr. 1987; E. Williams, interview.

88. Charles Johnson, 141; Neverdon-Morton, *Afro-American Women of the South*, 68–70.

89. Parler, interview; Shuler, interview; Johnson, interview; Graham, interview.

9. Working-Class Women's Work inside the Home

1. Scott, *Southern Lady*, 29; Kessler-Harris, *Out to Work*, 7; Woloch, *Women and the American Experience*, 44; Tentler, *Wage-Earning Women*, 107–8, 148.

2. Woloch, *Women and the American Experience*, 44; Tentler, *Wage-Earning Women*, 107–8, 148.

3. Tentler, *Wage-Earning Women*, 149–52; Harley, "For the Good of Family and Race," 346.

4. Zora Neale Hurston, *Dust Tracks on a Road: An Autobiography* (Urbana: Univ. of Illinois Press, 1984), 16–20; Woodson, *Negro in Our History*, 274.

5. Jones, *Labor of Love*, 113–14; W. E. B. Du Bois, *Negro American Family*, 147.

6. E. Williams, interview; Tentler, *Wage-Earning Women*, 107–8, 148; Clark-Lewis, "This Work Had a' End," 9.
7. F. Williams, interview; Livingston, interview; E. Williams, interview.
8. Parler, interview; Johnson, interview.
9. E. Whitmore, interview, and Joseph Whitmore, interview by author, Orangeburg, S.C., 5 Feb. 1987; Livingston, interview; Shuler, interview; E. Williams, interview; Mack, interview.
10. See Hasia Diner, *Erin's Daughters in America: Irish Immigrant Women in the Nineteenth Century* (Baltimore: Johns Hopkins Univ. Press, 1983); Shuler, interview; E. Williams, interview.
11. E. Williams, interview; Livingston, interview; Shuler, interview.
12. Shuler, interview.
13. E. Williams, interview.
14. Ibid.
15. Mack, interview.
16. Ibid.
17. Ibid.
18. Jeffcoat, interview; Moody, interview.
19. Graham, interview; Johnson, interview.

Bibliography

Manuscript Materials

Orangeburg County Historical Society Archives, Orangeburg, S.C.
Griffin, Willie Llew. "Orangeburg's Beginnings." *Times and Democrat.* 1970.

Orangeburg County Public Library, Orangeburg, S.C.
Ackerman, Hugo Sheridan. "A Brief History of Orangeburg." Pamphlet. Written for
    Home Federal Savings and Loan Association in Columbia and Orangeburg,
    S.C., 1974.
———. "Orangeburg to 1880: A Frontier Community." Pamphlet written for the
    Carolina Library in Columbia, S.C., 10 Jan. 1953.
Berry, Annie M. "In the Past Fifty years: Do You Remember?" 24 Mar. 1954.
Bookhardt, Mrs. T. W. (Emma Mae). "Orangeburg County: Historical Data, Sketches,
    and Records." Vol. 2, "Towns." Bounded by the Forewomen of the WPA
    Mending Room located in the Basement of the Orangeburg Courthouse,
    Orangeburg, S.C., 1939.
Chapling, Ellen P. "Facts and Legends of Orangeburg County."
Dibble, Thomas Osmond Summers. "History of Orangeburg: 1884."
Frederick, Florrie Jones. "Wilkinson High School: A Story of Greatness." Copyright
    1987 by Florrie Jones Frederick.
Sam, J. M., Jr. and W. F. Fairey, Jr. "Orangeburg County: Economic and Social. A
    Laboratory Study in the Department of Rural Social Science of the University
    of South Carolina." 15 June 1923.

College Materials

Note: The various spellings of "catalogue" and "catalog" reflect the original titles.

Claflin College Archives, Orangeburg, S.C.

Annual Catalog of Claflin University, 1905.
Annual Catalog of Claflin University, 1906.
Annual Catalog of Claflin University, 1907.
Annual Catalog of Claflin University, 1908.
Annual Catalog of Claflin University, 1909.
Annual Catalog of Claflin University, 1910.
Annual Catalog of Claflin University, 1911.
Annual Catalog of Claflin University, 1912.
Annual Catalog of Claflin University, 1913.
Annual Catalog of Claflin University, 1914.
Annual Catalog of Claflin University, 1915.
Annual Catalog of Claflin University, 1916.
Annual Catalog of Claflin University, 1917.
Annual Catalog of Claflin University, 1918.
Annual Catalog of Claflin University, 1919.
Annual Catalog of Claflin University, 1920.
Annual Catalog of Claflin University, 1921.
Annual Catalog of Claflin University, 1922.
Annual Catalog of Claflin University, 1925.
Annual Catalog of Claflin University, 1928.
Annual Catalogue of Claflin University and College of Agriculture and Mechanics, 1884.
Annual Catalog of Claflin University and College of Agriculture and Mechanics, 1885.
Annual Catalog of Claflin University and College of Agriculture and Mechanics, 1886.
Annual Catalog of Claflin University and College of Agriculture and Mechanics, 1887.
Annual Catalog of Claflin University and College of Agriculture and Mechanics, 1888.
Annual Catalog of Claflin University and College of Agriculture and Mechanics, 1889.
Annual Catalog of Claflin University and College of Agriculture and Mechanics, 1890.
Annual Catalog of Claflin University and College of Agriculture and Mechanics, 1898.
Catalogue of Claflin University, 1870.
Catalogue of Claflin University, 1872.
Catalogue of Claflin University and South Carolina Agriculture College, 1877.
Catalogue of Claflin University and South Carolina Agriculture College, 1879.
Catalogue of Claflin University and South Carolina Agriculture College, 1881.
Catalogue of Claflin University and South Carolina Agriculture College, 1882.
Catalogue of Claflin University and South Carolina Agriculture College, 1883.

Catalogue of Claflin University and South Carolina Agriculture College, 1884–1885.
Claflin College Catalogue, 1934.
Claflin College Catalogue, 1935.
Claflin College Catalogue, 1937.
Claflin College Catalogue, 1938.
Claflin College Catalogue, 1939.
Claflin College Catalogue, 1940.
Claflin University Bulletin. Vol. 8:4. December 1900.
Claflin University Bulletin. Vol. 8:7. Mar. 1901.
Claflin University Bulletin. Vol. 10:3. November 1902.
Claflin University Bulletin. Vol. 40:4. December 1903.
Sixty-Second Annual Catalogue of Claflin University, 1930.
Sixty-Third Annual Catalogue of Claflin University, 1931.

South Carolina State College Archives, Orangeburg, S.C.

Catalog of the Colored Normal Industrial, Agricultural, and Mechanical College of South Carolina, 1911.
Catalog of the Colored Normal Industrial, Agricultural, and Mechanical College of South Carolina, 1919.
Catalog of the Colored Normal Industrial, Agricultural, and Mechanical College of South Carolina, 1920.
Catalog of State Agricultural and Mechanical College of South Carolina, 1918.
Catalogue of State Agricultural and Mechanical College of South Carolina, 1920.
Catalogue of State Agricultural and Mechanical College of South Carolina, 1922.
Catalogue of State Agricultural and Mechanical College of South Carolina, 1924.
Catalogue of State Agricultural and Mechanical College of South Carolina, 1925.
Catalogue of State Agricultural and Mechanical College of South Carolina, 1926.
Catalogue of State Agricultural and Mechanical College of South Carolina, 1927.
Catalogue of State Agricultural and Mechanical College of South Carolina, 1928.
Catalogue of State Agricultural and Mechanical College of South Carolina, 1929.
Catalogue of State Agricultural and Mechanical College of South Carolina, 1930.
Catalogue of State Agricultural and Mechanical College of South Carolina, 1931.
Catalogue of State Agricultural and Mechanical College of South Carolina, 1932.
Catalogue of State Agricultural and Mechanical College of South Carolina, 1933.
Catalogue of State Agricultural and Mechanical College of South Carolina, 1934.
Catalogue of State Agricultural and Mechanical College of South Carolina, 1936.
Catalogue of State Agricultural and Mechanical College of South Carolina, 1937.
Catalogue of State Agricultural and Mechanical College of South Carolina, 1938.
Catalogue of State Agricultural and Mechanical College of South Carolina, 1939.
Catalogue of State Agricultural and Mechanical College of South Carolina, 1940.

Church Materials

First Annual of the Saint Paul Baptist Church, 1930s–1983. St. Paul Baptist Church Records and Archives. Orangeburg, S.C.

Trinity Methodist Church Observes Its 100th Anniversary. January 1866 to January 1966. Orangeburg, S.C. Theme: "The First Hundred Years in Retrospect." Trinity United Methodist Church Records and Archives. Orangeburg, S.C.

United Methodist Women. Trinity United Methodist Church. Orangeburg, S.C. Anniversary Dinner, 1866–1984. Saturday, October 12, 1985. Trinity United Methodist Church Records and Archives. Orangeburg, S.C.

Club Materials

Fiftieth Anniversary. South Carolina Federation of Colored Women's Clubs, 1909–1959 (Affiliated with the National Association of Colored Women's Clubs). "Our Book of Gold." Sunlight Community Center. Orangeburg, S.C.

The Sunlight Club Handbook, 1980–1981. A United Way Agency. Sunlight Community Center. Orangeburg, S.C.

The Sunlight Club Handbook, 1986–1987. A United Way Agency. Sunlight Community Center. Orangeburg, S.C.

U.S. Bureau of the Census, Washington, D.C.

Census of 1850 on Orangeburg Free Population.

Census of 1850 on Orangeburg Slave Population.

Census of 1860 on Orangeburg Population.

Census of 1870 on Orangeburg. Orangeburg Township Population of Orangeburg County, Southeast.

Census of 1880 on Population. Orangeburg Town.

Census of 1900 on Population. Orangeburg City.

Census of 1910 on Population. Orangeburg City.

First Census of the United States. 1790. State of South Carolina.

Interviews

Ackerman, Hugo Sheridan. Interviewed by the author. Orangeburg, S.C. 29 Oct. 1988.

Amaker, Eloise Funchess. Interviewed by the author. Orangeburg, S.C. 18 Feb. 1987.

Bowman, Frizell Brown. Interviewed by the author. Orangeburg, S.C. 17 Apr. 1987.

Bythewood, Emilie Sasportas. Interviewed by the author. Orangeburg, S.C. 16 Feb. 1987.

Bythewood, T. K. Interviewed by the author. Orangeburg, S.C. 6, 11, 27 Mar., 8 Apr. 1987.

Colter, Anna Mitchell. Interviewed by the author. Orangeburg, S.C. 6 Apr. 1987.
Crawford, Maxine Sulton. Interviewed by the author. Orangeburg, S.C. 4 Mar. 1987.
Epps, Marilyn Green. Interviewed by the author. Orangeburg, S.C. 3 Dec. 1986.
Fair, Sadie Bodrick. Interviewed by the author. Orangeburg, S.C. 3 Apr. 1987.
Fleming, Cecelia Daniels. Interviewed by the author. Orangeburg, S.C. 3 Apr. 1987.
Graham, Daisy Salley. Interviewed by the author. Orangeburg, S.C. 10 Apr. 1987.
Gregg, Marian E. Interviewed by the author. Orangeburg, S.C. 5 Dec. 1986.
Haigler, Mamie. Interviewed by the author. Orangeburg, S.C. 9 Apr. 1987.
Harrison, Leila Summers. Interviewed by the author. Orangeburg, S.C. 26 Mar. 1987.
Hubbard, Susie Alexander. Interviewed by the author. Orangeburg, S.C. 5 Dec. 1986.
Jeffcoat, Mattie Mack. Interviewed by the author. Orangeburg, S.C. 1 Apr. 1987.
Johnson, Pearl Green. Interviewed by the author. Orangeburg, S.C. 31 Mar. 1987.
Kearse, Coralee Bryant. Interviewed by the author. Orangeburg, S.C. 15 Apr. 1987.
Knight, Rozela Dickson. Interviewed by the author. Orangeburg, S.C. 12 Mar. 1987.
Lawrence, Maude Haigler. Interviewed by the author. Orangeburg, S.C. 4 Dec. 1986.
Livingston, Catherine Davis. Interviewed by the author. Orangeburg, S.C. 3 Mar. 1987.
Mack, Dorothy Scott. Interviewed by the author. Orangeburg, S.C. 22 Oct. 1988.
Malichi, Florrie Jones. Interviewed by the author. Orangeburg, S.C. 25 Feb. 1987.
Middleton, Bernice Bryant. Interviewed by the author. Orangeburg, S.C. 23 Feb. 1987.
Moody, Lillie Tingsey. Interviewed by the author. Orangeburg, S.C. 2 Apr. 1987.
Nix, Fannie Rufus. Interviewed by the author. Orangeburg, S.C. 25 Mar. 1987.
Parler, Emma Jane. Interviewed by the author. Orangeburg, S.C. 1 Aug. 1988.
Pearson, Janie Harrington. Interviewed by the author. Orangeburg, S.C. 13 Feb. 1987.
Rivers, John. Interviewed by the author. Orangeburg, S.C. New York City. 21 July 1991.
Robinson, Louisa Smith. Interviewed by the author. Orangeburg, S.C. 11 Feb. 1987.
Salley, Beulah Williams. Interviewed by the author. Orangeburg, S.C. 3 Dec. 1986.
Shuler, Anna Bonaparte. Interviewed by the author. Orangeburg, S.C. 6 Dec. 1986.
Simmons, Lucy Pearson. Interviewed by the author. Orangeburg, S.C. 23 Apr. 1987.
Smalls, Nora Gardner. Interviewed by the author. Orangeburg, S.C. 6 Apr. 1987.
Swett, Georgia Waymer. Interviewed by the author. Orangeburg, S.C. 24 Feb. 1987.
Thomas, Lillie Williams. Interviewed by the author. Orangeburg, S.C. 22 Apr. 1987.
Thomasson, Carmen Sulton. Interviewed by the author. Orangeburg, S.C. 10 Mar. 1987.
Thompson, Beatrice. Interviewed by the author. Orangeburg, S.C. 4 Dec. 1986.
Thompson, Helen "Hallie" Reese. Interviewed by the author. Orangeburg, S.C. 23 Apr. 1987.
Tobin, Clarence. Interviewed by the author. Orangeburg, S.C. 18 Jan. 1988.
Vaughn, Edith Wilson. Interviewed by the author. Orangeburg, S.C. 16 Apr. 1987.
Watson, Reverend George. Interviewed by the author. Orangeburg, S.C. 1 Dec. 1986.
Webber, Clemmie Embly. Interviewed by the author. Orangeburg, S.C. 10 Feb. 1987.

Whitmore, Emma. Interviewed by the author. Orangeburg, S.C. 5 Feb. 1987.

Whitmore, Joseph. Interviewed by the author. Orangeburg, S.C. 5 Feb. 1987.

Williams, Eloise Tyler. Interviewed by the author. Orangeburg, S.C. 22 Oct. 1988.

Williams, Flossie. Interviewed by the author. Orangeburg, S.C. 22 Apr. 1987.

Wilkinson, Lula Love. Interviewed by the author. Orangeburg, S.C. 9 Feb. 1987.

Wilson, Ella Felder. Interviewed by the author. Orangeburg, S.C. 30 Mar. 1987.

Zimmerman, Geraldine Pierce. Interviewed by the author. Orangeburg, S.C. 27 Feb. 1987.

Newspapers

Palmetto Leader. 1880–1940. Microfilm Collection, Caroliniana Library. Columbia, S.C.

Times and Democrat. 1880–1940. Microfilm Collection, Orangeburg County Free Library. Orangeburg, S.C.

Books and Articles

Ackerman, Hugo Sheridan. "1865–1867: Crisis on the Farm." *Times and Democrat*, 27 Aug. 1982.

———. "1865–1868: Crisis on the Farm." *Times and Democrat*, 4 July 1982.

———. "1868–1869: Farming Under Difficulties." *Times and Democrat*, 1 May 1983.

———. "1875–1879: Dr. Webster Writes a Letter." *Times and Democrat*, 4 Jan. 1987.

———. "1880–1881: Farming Conditions Improve." *Times and Democrat*, 2 Oct. 1983.

———. "1881–1883: Agriculture." *Times and Democrat*, 18 Dec. 1983.

———. "1884–1885: Down on the Farm 100 Years Ago." *Times and Democrat*, 22 Jan. 1984.

———. "1884–1885: Rev. Minus and the Sterling School." *Times and Democrat*, 23 June 1985.

———. "1889–1894: Five Cent Cotton." *Times and Democrat*, 29 Jan. 1984.

———. "1895: Colored People Leaving." *Times and Democrat*, 30 Jan. 1985.

———. "1898–1899: Eighteen Receive Diploma From the Academy." *Times and Democrat*, 26 Apr. 1987.

———. "1899–1900: Overcrowded Classroom Not a Novelty." *Times and Democrat*, 10 May 1987.

———. "1902–1903: School Buildings Needed." *Times and Democrat*, 21 June 1987.

———. "1903–1904: New School to Cost $15,000." *Times and Democrat*, 5 July 1987.

———. "1905–1906: A Museum in the Orangeburg Public Schools." *Times and Democrat*, 16 Aug. 1987.

———. "1907–1908: County has 228 Schools, Only 40 Libraries." *Times and Democrat*, 13 Sept. 1987.

———. "1920 Editorial: Should a Married Woman Teach?" *Times and Democrat*, 18 Sept. 1988.

———. "1928–1929: Black Community in the Late 1920s." *Times and Democrat,* 18 June 1989.

———. "Blacks and the Troubled '20s." *Times and Democrat,* 26 June 1988.

———. "Michael Gramling's Plantation Journal." *Times and Democrat,* 3 Jan. 1982.

———. "Negro School Going Up." *Times and Democrat,* 30 Sept. 1988.

Alexander, Adele Logan. *Ambiguous Lives: Free Women of Color in Rural Georgia, 1789–1879.* Fayetteville: Univ. of Arkansas Press, 1991.

Allen, Ruth Alice. *The Labor of Women in the Production of Cotton.* New York: Arno Press, 1975.

Anderson, James D. *The Education of Blacks in the South, 1860–1935.* Chapel Hill: Univ. of North Carolina Press, 1988.

Andrews, William L., ed. *Collected Stories of Charles W. Chestnutt.* New York: Mentor, 1992.

Andrews, Sidney. *The South Since the War as Shown by Fourteen Weeks of Travel and Observation in Georgia and the Carolinas.* Boston: Houghton Mifflin, 1971.

Baker, Ella, and Marvel Cooke. "The Bronx Slave Market." *Crisis* 42 (Nov. 1935): 330–31, 340.

Baxandall, Rosalyn, Linda Gordon, and Susan Reverby. *America's Working Women: A Documentary History, 1600 to Present.* New York: Random House, 1976.

Belles, A. Gilbert. "The College Faculty, the Negro Scholar, and the Julius Rosenwald Fund." *Journal of Negro History* 54, no. 4 (1985): 383–92.

Berlin, Ira. *Slaves Without Masters: The Free Negro in the Ante-bellum South.* New York: Pantheon, 1974.

Berry, Mary Frances, and John W. Blassingame. *Long Memory: The Black Experience in America.* New York: Oxford Univ. Press, 1982.

Blackwelder, Julie Kirk. *Women of the Depression: Caste and Culture in San Antonio, 1929–1939.* College Station: Texas A&M Univ. Press, 1984.

Boyer, Paul S., Clifford E. Clark, Joseph F. Keitt, Thomas Purvis, Harvard Sitkoff, and Nancy Woloch. *The Enduring Vision: A History of the American People.* Vol. 2, *From 1865.* Lexington, Mass.: D. C. Heath, 1990.

Brooks-Higginbotham, Elizabeth. *Righteous Discontent: The Women's Movement in the Black Baptist Church, 1880–1920.* Cambridge: Harvard Univ. Press, 1994.

Bullock, Henry Allen. *A History of Negro Education in the South.* Cambridge: Harvard Univ. Press, 1967.

Campbell, Darlene. "Minority Business: A Rare Species Looking at Extinction." *Times and Democrat,* 1 Feb. 1987.

Carson, Clayborne, David J. Garrow, Vincent Harding, and Darlene Clark Hine. *Eyes on the Prize: America's Civil Rights Years.* New York: Penguin, 1987.

Cheatham, Harold E., and James B. Stewart, eds. *Black Families: Interdisciplinary Perspectives.* New Brunswick, N.J.: Transaction, 1990.

"Child Welfare in Orangeburg." *Times and Democrat,* 6 May 1938.

"Colored People Leaving." *Times and Democrat,* 30 Jan. 1895.

Comer, James P. *Maggie's American Dream: The Life and Times of a Black Family*. New York: Plume, 1989.

Davies, Margery. "Women's Place is at the Typewriter: The Feminization of the Clerical Labor Force." *Radical America* 3, no. 4 (July–Aug. 1974): 21–42.

Diner, Hasia. *Erin's Daughters in America*. Baltimore: Johns Hopkins Univ. Press, 1983.

Drago, Edmund L. *Initiative, Paternalism, Race Relations: Charleston's Avery Normal Institute*. Athens: Univ. of Georgia Press, 1990.

Du Bois, W. E. B. *Black Reconstruction: An Essay Toward a Attempt to Reconstruct Democracy in America, 1860–1880*. New York: Harcourt Brace, 1935.

———. *The Gift of Black Folk*. Millwood, N.Y.: Kraus-Thomson, 1975.

———. *The Negro American Family*. Atlanta University Study 13. Atlanta: Atlanta Univ. Press, 1908.

———. *The Souls of Black Folk*. Millwood, N.Y.: Kraus-Thomson, 1985.

Eisenstein, Sara. *Give Us Bread, But Give Us Roses*. Boston: Routledge and Kegan, 1983.

Erickson, Alana. "'I Don't Want Her in My Home': Bias Against African American Domestic Servants, 1910–1980." *Race and Racism* 1 (1996–97): 26–31.

Fields, Mamie G., and Karen Fields. *Lemon Swamp and Other Places: A Carolina Memoir*. New York: Free Press, 1983.

Fitchett, Horace E. "The Influence of Claflin College in Negro Family Life." *Journal of Negro History* 29, no. 4 (Oct. 1944): 429–40.

———. "The Role of Claflin College in Negro Life in South Carolina." *Journal of Negro Education* 12, no. 2 (Winter 1943): 42–68.

Fox-Genovese, Elizabeth. *Within the Plantation Household: Black and White Women in the Old South*. Chapel Hill: Univ. of North Carolina Press, 1988.

Franklin, John Hope, and Alfred A. Moss. *From Slavery to Freedom: A History of Negro Americans*. New York: McGraw-Hill, 1994.

Franklin, Vincent P., and James D. Anderson, ed. *New Perspectives on Black Educational History*. Boston: G. K. Hall, 1978.

Frazier, E. Franklin. *Black Bourgeoisie: The Rise of a New Middle Class in the United States*. New York: Collier, 1962.

———. *The Negro Family in the United States*. Chicago: Univ. of Chicago Press, 1947.

———. *The Negro in the United States*. New York: MacMillan, 1957.

Gatewood, Willard B. *Aristocrats of Color: The Black Elite, 1880–1920*. Bloomington: Indiana Univ. Press, 1990.

Genovese, Eugene. *Roll, Jordan, Roll: The World the Slaves Made*. New York: Random House, 1974.

Giddings, Paula. *When and Where I Enter: The Impact of Black Women on Race and Sex in America*. New York: Bantam Books, 1984.

Godey's Lady Book. (Also called *Godey Magazine*.) New York: Godey, July 1832.

Gordon, Asa. *Sketches of Negro Life and History in South Carolina*. Columbia: Univ. of South Carolina Press, 1971.

Groneman, Carol, and Mary Beth Norton, ed. *To Toil the Livelong Day: American Women at Work, 1780–1980.* Ithaca, N.Y.: Cornell Univ. Press, 1987.

Gutman, Herbert G. *The Black Family in Slavery and Freedom, 1750–1925.* New York: Pantheon Books, 1976.

Hackley, E. Azalia. *The Colored Girl Beautiful.* Kansas City: Burton Publishing Co., 1916.

Harley, Sharon. "Beyond the Classroom: Organizational Lives of Black Female Educators in the District of Columbia, 1890–1930." *Journal of Negro Education* 51, no. 3 (Summer 1982): 259–65.

———. "For the Good of Family and Race: Gender, Work, and Domestic Roles in the Black Community, 1880–1930." *Signs: Journal of Women in Culture and Society* 15, no. 2 (Winter 1990): 336–49.

Harris, William H. *The Harder We Run: Black Workers Since the Civil War.* New York: Oxford Univ. Press, 1982.

Haynes, George Edmund. *The Negro at Work in New York City: A Study in Economic Progress.* New York: Longman, Green, 1912.

Hearth, Amy Hill. "The American Century of Bessie and Sadie Delaney." *American Heritage* (Oct. 1993): 70–80.

Hine, Darlene Clark, ed. *Black Women in the Nursing Profession: A Documentary History.* New York: Garland, 1985.

Holt, Rackham. *Mary McLeod Bethune: A Biography.* New York: Doubleday, 1964.

Holt, Thomas. *Black Over White: Negro Political Leadership in South Carolina During Reconstruction.* Urbana: Univ. of Illinois Press, 1977.

Hunter, Jane Edna Harris. *A Nickel and a Prayer.* Nashville: Parthenon, 1940.

Hunter, Tera W. *To 'Joy My Freedom: Southern Black Women's Lives and Labors After the Civil War.* Cambridge: Harvard Univ. Press, 1997.

Hurston, Zora Neale. *Dust Tracks on a Road: An Autobiography.* Urbana: Univ. of Illinois Press, 1984.

Hymowitz, Carol, and Michael Weissman. *A History of Women in America.* New York: Bantam Books, 1981.

Imes, Nella Marian Larsen. *Quicksand and Passing.* New York: Collier, 1971.

Janiewski, Dolores E. *Sisterhood Denied: Race, Gender, and Class in a New South Community.* Philadelphia: Temple Univ. Press, 1985.

Johnson, Charles S. *Growing Up in the Black Belt.* New York: Schocken, 1967.

Johnson, Michael P., and James L. Roark, *Black Masters: A Free Family of Color in the Old South.* New York: W. W. Norton, 1984.

Jones, Adrienne Lash. "Struggle Among Saints: Black Women in the YWCA, 1860–1920." Paper presented at the Annual Meeting of the Organization of American Historians, Louisville, Ky., Apr. 1991.

Jones, Jacqueline. *Labor of Love, Labor of Sorrow: Black Women, Work, and the Family From Slavery to the Present.* New York: Basic Books, 1985.

Jones, Lewis P. *South Carolina: A Synoptic History for the Laymen.* Orangeburg, S.C.: Sandlapper, 1978.

Katzman, David. *Seven Days a Week: Women in Industrializing America.* New York: Oxford Univ. Press, 1978.

Kellogg, Grace. *The Two Lives of Edith Wharton: A Biography.* New York: Appleton-Century, 1965.

Kennedy, Stetson. *Jim Crow Guide: The Way It Was.* Boca Raton: Florida Atlantic Univ. Press, 1990.

Kessler-Harris, Alice. *Out to Work: A History of Wage-Earning Women in the United States.* New York: Oxford Univ. Press, 1983.

Klingsberg, Frank I. *An Appraisal of Negroes in Colonial South Carolina: A Study in Americanization.* Washington, D.C.: Associated Publishers, 1972.

Lander, Earnest McPherson, Jr. *A History of South Carolina: 1865–1960.* Chapel Hill: Univ. of North Carolina Press, 1960.

Langer, William L. *An Encyclopedia of World History.* New York: Houghton Mifflin, 1980.

Leach, William. *True Love and Perfect Union: The Feminist Reform of Sex and Society.* New York: Basic Books, 1980.

Lerner, Gerda, ed. *Black Women in White America: A Documentary History.* New York: Random House, 1972.

Matthaei, Julie A. *An Economic History of Women in America: Women's Work, the Sexual Division of Labor, and the Development of Capitalism.* New York: Schocken, 1982.

McAllister, Jean E., and Dorothy M. McAllister. "Adult Education for Negroes in Rural Areas: The Work of the Jeanes Teachers and Home and Farm Demonstration Agents." *Journal of Negro Education* 14, no. 3 (June 1945): 331–40.

McCrady, Edward. *South Carolina Under the Royal Government, 1719–1776.* New York: Macmillan, 1901.

McMillan, Lewis K. *Negro Higher Education in the State of South Carolina.* Orangeburg, S.C.: Self-Published, 1952.

Meltzer, Milton. *Mary McCleod Bethune: Voice of Black Hope.* New York: Viking, 1987.

Milling, Chapman J., ed. *Colonial South Carolina: Two Contemporary Descriptions by Governor James Glen and Dr. George Milligan Johnston.* Columbia: Univ. of South Carolina Press, 1951.

Morris-Crowther, Jayne. "An Economic Study of the Substantial Slaveholders of Orangeburg County, 1860–1880." *South Carolina Historical Magazine* 86 (Oct. 1985): 296–314.

Murray, Pauli. *Song in a Weary Throat: An American Pilgrimage.* New York: Harper and Row, 1987.

Myrdal, Gunnar. *An American Dilemma: The Negro Problem and Modern Democracy.* 2 vols. New York: Harper and Row, 1944.

Neverdon-Morton, Cynthia. *Afro-American Women of the South and the Advancement of the Race, 1895–1925.* Knoxville: Univ. of Tennessee Press, 1989.

———. "Self-Help Programs as Educative Activities of Black Women in the South, 1895–1925: Focus on Four Key Areas." *Journal of Negro Education* 51, no. 3 (1982): 207–38.

Newby, I. A. *Black South Carolinians: A History of Blacks in South Carolina from 1895 to 1968.* Columbia: Univ. of South Carolina Press, 1973.

"The Oldest Sawmill Company's Operated by Negroes." *Southern Lumberman,* 15 Dec. 1931, p. 106.

Ottley, Roi, and William J. Weatherby. *The Negro in New York: An Informal Social History.* Dobbs Ferry, N.Y.: Oceania, 1967.

Palmer, Phyllis. *Domesticity and Dirt: Housewives and Domestic Servants in the United States, 1920–1945.* Philadelphia: Temple Univ. Press, 1989.

Perkins, Linda M. "Black Feminism and Black Uplift, 1890–1900." Working Paper. Radcliffe College, Mary Ingraham Bunting Institute, Cambridge, Mass., 1981.

———. "Black Women and the Philosophy of Race Uplift Prior to Emancipation." Working Paper. Radcliffe College, Mary Ingraham Bunting Institute, Cambridge, Mass., 1980.

———. "Heed Life's Demands: The Educational Philosophy of Fanny Jackson Coppin." *Journal of Negro Education* 5, no. 3 (Summer 1982): 181–90.

———. "The Impact of the Cult of True Womanhood on the Education of Black Women." *Journal of Social Issues* 39, no. 3 (1983): 17–28.

———. "The National Association of College Women: Vanguard of Black Women's Leadership and Education, 1923–1954." *Journal of Education* 173, no. 3 (1990): 65–75.

Powdermaker, Hortense. *After Freedom: A Cultural Study in the Deep South.* New York: Atheneum, 1969.

Rollins, Judith. *Between Women: Domestics and Their Employers.* Philadelphia: Temple Univ. Press, 1985.

Rosenberg, Carol Smith. *Disorderly Conduct: Visions of Gender in Victorian America.* New York: Oxford Univ. Press, 1986.

Rouse, Jacqueline Anne. *Lugenia Burns Hope: Black Southern Reformer.* Athens: Univ. of Georgia Press, 1989.

Ryan, Mary P. *Cradle of the Middle Class: The Family in Oneida County, New York, 1700–1865.* New York: Cambridge Univ. Press, 1981.

Salley, A. S. Jr. *The History of Orangeburg County, South Carolina.* Orangeburg, S.C.: B. Lewis Berry, 1898.

Salley, Marion. *The Writings of Marion Salley: The Orangeburg Papers,* vol. 1. Orangeburg: R. C. Bryan, 1970.

Sam, J. M., Jr., and W. F. Fairey Jr. *Orangeburg County: Economic and Social. A Labora-*

tory Study in the Department of Rural Social Science of the University of South Caro-lina. (Columbia: Univ. of South Carolina Press, 1923.

Schwalm, Leslie A. *A Hard Fight for We: Women's Transition from Slavery to Freedom in South Carolina*. Urbana: Univ. of Illinois Press, 1997.

Schweninger, Loren. *Black Property Owners in the South: 1790–1915*. Urbana: Univ. of Illinois Press, 1990.

Scott, Anne Firor. *The Southern Lady: From Pedestal to Politics, 1830–1930*. Chicago: Univ. of Chicago Press, 1970.

Simkins, Frances B., and Robert H. Woody. *South Carolina During Reconstruction*. Chapel Hill: Univ. of North Carolina Press, 1932.

Sirmans, M. Eugene. *Colonial South Carolina, A Political History, 1663–1763*. Chapel Hill: Univ. of North Carolina Press, 1966.

Stansell, Christine. *City of Women: Sex and Class in New York, 1789–1860*. Urbana: Univ. of Illinois Press, 1987.

Sterling, Dorothy. *We Are Your Sisters: Black Women in the Nineteenth Century*. New York: W. W. Norton, 1984.

Sternsher, Bernard, ed. *The Negro in Depression and War*. Chicago: Quadrangle Books, 1969.

Taylor, Alrutheus Ambush. *The Negro in South Carolina During Reconstruction*. New York: Russell and Russell, 1969.

Tentler, Leslie Woodcock. *Wage-Earning Women: Industrial Work and Family Life in the United States, 1900–1930*. New York: Oxford Univ. Press, 1979.

Tindall, George B. *South Carolina Negroes, 1877–1900*. Columbia: Univ. of South Carolina Press, 1952.

Toplin, Robert Brent. "Between Black and White: Attitudes Toward Southern Mulat-tos, 1830–1861." *Journal of Southern History* 45, no. 2 (May 1979): 185–200.

Tucker, Susan. *Telling Memories Among Southern Women: Domestic Workers and their Employers in the Segregated South*. Baton Rouge: Louisiana State Univ. Press, 1985.

Wallace, David Duncan. *South Carolina: A Short History, 1520–1948*. Columbia: Univ. of South Carolina Press, 1961.

Wandersee, Winifred. *Women, Work, and Family Values*. Cambridge: Harvard Univ. Press, 1981.

Washington, Mary Helen. *Black-Eyed Susans*. Garden City, N.J.: Anchor Books, 1975.

Weber, Michael P., and Peter N. Stearns. *The Spencers of Amberson Avenue: A Turn of the Century Memoir*. Philadelphia: Univ. of Pennsylvania Press, 1983.

Williams, George W. *History of the Negro Race in America: 1619–1800*, vol. 1. New York: G. P. Putnam's Sons, 1885.

Williamson, Joel. *After Slavery: The Negro in South Carolina During Reconstruction, 1861–1877*. Chapel Hill: Univ. of North Carolina Press, 1965.

Winch, Julie. *Philadelphia's Black Elite: Activism, Accommodation, and the Struggle for Autonomy, 1787–1848.* Philadelphia: Temple Univ. Press, 1988.

Wolfe, L. S. *Agriculture Unadorned: A Non-Technical Story About the Background and Evolution of Farming.* Columbia, S.C.: Cary Printing, 1956.

Woloch, Nancy. *Women and the American Experience.* New York: Knopf, 1984.

Woodson, Carter G. *The Mis-Education of the Negro.* New York: AMS, 1972.

———. *The Negro in Our History.* Washington, D.C.: Associated Publishers, 1924.

———. *The Negro Professional Man and the Community.* Washington, D.C.: Associated Publishers, 1934.

———. "The Negro Washerwoman: A Vanishing Figure." *Journal of Negro History* 15 (1930): 13–20.

Wright, Richard. *Black Boy.* New York: Harper and Row, 1966.

Unpublished Sources

Clark-Lewis, Elizabeth. "'This Work Had a' End': The Transition From Live-in to Day Work." Center for Research on Women. Working Paper 2. Memphis State Univ., 1985.

Derby, Doris A. "Black Women Basket Makers: A Study of Domestic Economy in Charleston County, South Carolina." Ph.D. diss., Univ. of Illinois–Urbana, 1980.

Frankel, Noralee. "Workers, Wives, and Mothers: Black Women in Mississippi, 1860–1870." Ph.D. diss., George Washington Univ., 1983.

Helmbold, Lois Rita. "Making Choices, Making Do: Black and White Working Class Women's Lives and Work During the Great Depression." Ph.D. diss., Stanford Univ., 1983.

Nix, Dean N. C. "Tentative History of South Carolina State College, 1872–1937. Working Paper." South Carolina State Univ. Library Archives. Orangeburg, S.C.

Weiner, Marli Frances. "Plantation Mistresses and Female Slaves: Gender, Race, and South Carolina Women, 1830–1880." Ph.D. diss., Univ. of Rochester, 1986.

Index

Parlor Ladies and Ebony Drudges was typeset on a Macintosh computer system using PageMaker software. The text is set in Caslon and uses Kollman for display. This book was designed by Kay Jursik, typeset by Kimberly Scarbrough

www.ingramcontent.com/pod-product-compliance
Lightning Source LLC
Chambersburg PA
CBHW021857020426
42334CB00013B/376